Advanced Praise for THE THREE ABRAHAMIC TESTAMENTS

"*The Three Abrahamic Testaments* is a unique contribution to interfaith understanding. Written by a committed, believing Muslim scientist and scholar, it offers a helpful and honest comparison of the Qur'an with the Hebrew Bible and New Testament that is neither polemical, apologetic nor triumphalist. It acknowledges both similarities and differences in a spirit of improving understanding and respect for the dignity of believers of other faiths. Dr. Ejaz Naqvi does not ignore differences between the Bible and the Qur'an, nor does he try to reconcile them. There are various ways to treat differences. Historically, religious thinkers have tended to assume that if there is a discrepancy between scriptures, one scripture must be right and the others are wrong. Based on this simplistic thinking, one religion must therefore hold the key to divine truth while the others are false religions and provide no benefit. Dr. Naqvi provides a deeper and much more spiritual and sophisticated analysis by demonstrating how differences need not be threatening but in fact enlightening. He shows that different versions of the same message appeal to different communities and stimulate discussion so that we can learn to know and respect one another better. From the grand perspective, all three scriptures convey the identical vital concern for ethics, compassion, and the need to respond to the divine will. This book will become a primary tool for interfaith understanding through scriptural reasoning and the comparative study of religious text."

**–Rabbi Reuven Firestone, Regenstein Professor in
Medieval Judaism and Islam, Hebrew Union College**

"At a time of perceived conflict between Muslims and Christians across the globe, Naqvi's book reminds us all of the shared mores and values—not to mention myths and stories—that bind the Qur'an and the Bible together as a single unbroken revelation. This is not just a candid and thought-pro-voking review of major topics in both the Bible and the Qur'an, but also a much-needed corrective to the negativity and conflict that have marred relations between the Abrahamic traditions."

**–Reza Aslan, author of *New York Times* bestsellers, *Zealot*
and *No god but God* and *Beyond Fundamentalism***

"Once again, Dr. Naqvi separates facts from fiction in this systematic review of the Abrahamic scriptures. As self-interested forces threaten to divide us based on faith, his book is a timely corrective. It debunks the easy accusations that would incriminate religious teachings in the spread of prejudice and hate. As in his first book, *The Quran: With or Against the Bible?*, the reader is invited to ponder rather than impose received opinion. The book's format is easy to grasp, yet it addresses complex issues, including gender and jihad. *The Three Abrahamic Testaments* makes a significant contribution to understanding among Jews, Christians and Muslims in our overly polarized world."

–Michael Wolfe, co-founder of Unity Productions Foundation and author of *The Hadj: One Thousand Roads to Mecc* and *Taking Back Islam*

"Dr. Naqvi has created another well presented overview of the Abrahamic traditions by exposing us to a greater view of the Qu'ran and the Islamic tradition. I highly recommend this resource for congregations as a way to expose their congregants to the comparative teachings of Islam, Christianity and Judaism and to ask, 'What do you believe?' and 'Why?' By starting with what we have in common, we can learn much more than taking a stance of opposition or superiority. Then, invite some Muslim families to come to your congregation to share more about what their lives are like. I know your whole congregation will be enriched."

–Rev. William McGarvey, Executive Director, Interfaith Council of Contra Costa County, California

"It is more than refreshing to probe a book that does not neutralize or sensationalize the difference found in the Abrahamic religious traditions. *The Three Abrahamic Testaments* is an important contribution to interfaith dialogue and understanding. It provides an inspiring model for how that dialogue might be engaged in a way that is both informative and healing. Dr. Naqvi celebrates the differences while challenging the reader to engage in what is no less than a transformative experience. The discussion and reflective questions found throughout this book invite the reader to become a lively part of the dialogue this book so powerfully presents. We are most grateful for the obvious energy and deep respect Dr. Naqvi displays in this fine work."

—Rev. Thomas P. Bonacci, C.P., Co-founder of The Interfaith Peace Project of Northern California

The
Three
Abrahamic
Testaments

How the Torah, Gospels, and Qur'an
Hold the Keys for Healing Our Fears

EJAZ NAQVI, M.D.

White Cloud Press
Ashland, Oregon

White Cloud Press books may be purchased for educational, business, or sales promotional use. For information, please write: Special Market Department, White Cloud Press, PO Box 3400, Ashland, OR 97520
Website: www.whitecloudpress.com

Cover and Interior Design by C Book Services

First edition: 2017
17 18 19 20 21   10 9 8 7 6 5 4 3 2 1

Printed in the United States of America

Library of Congress Cataloging-in-Publication Data

Names: Naqvi, Ejaz, author.
Title: The three Abrahamic testaments : how the Torah, Gospels, and Qur'an hold the keys for healing our fears / Ejaz Naqvi.
Description: Ashland, Oregon : White Cloud Press, 2016. | Series: Islamic encounter series
Identifiers: LCCN 2016048662 | ISBN 9781940468471 (paperback)
Subjects: LCSH: Islam--Relations--Christianity. | Christianity and other religions--Islam. | Judaism--Relations--Islam. | Islam--Relations--Judaism. | Qur'an--Criticism, interpretation ,etc. | Bible--Criticism, interpretation, etc. | BISAC: RELIGION / Islam / Koran & Sacred Writings.
Classification: LCC BP172 .N356 2016 | DDC 297.2/8--dc23
LC record available at https://lccn.loc.gov/2016048662

In the name of God, the Most Compassionate, the Most Merciful

I ask for forgiveness from the Lord of the worlds if I have unintentionally misrepresented the message contained within the Holy scriptures.

For my parents:
For guiding me.
For showing me that there is no substitute for honesty and hard work.
And for everything else …

Acknowledgments

Farhana, Alina, Mohsin, and my extended family, for filling my heart with joy, love, and tenderness that provides fuel and purpose to my life.

And above all, God Almighty, for all His blessings that I cannot even begin to enumerate.

Science without religion is lame. Religion without science is blind.
Albert Einstein

It is the perfection of God's works that they are all done with the greatest simplicity. He is the God of order and not of confusion.
Sir Isaac Newton

God, the Supreme Being, is neither circumscribed by space, nor touched by time; he cannot be found in a particular direction, and his essence cannot change.
Avicenna (Ibn Sina): A tenth-century Muslim polymath, and a foremost physician, philosopher, and theologian

Translations of the Qur'an

The English translations of the verses from the Qur'an, unless otherwise indicated, are taken from Abdullah Yousuf Ali's *The Holy Qur'an: Text, Translation and Commentary*, USA edition, 2001, published by Tahrike Tarsile Qur'an, Inc., Elmhurst, New York. I have used modern English, replacing certain words like "ye" or "thou" with "you." The other two translations of significant proportions are taken from the following three sources and are specified in parentheses at the end of the quotations.

1. M. H. Shakir. *The Qur'an: Arabic Text and English Translation.* Elmnurst, NY: Tahrike Tarsile Qur'an, 1993.
2. M. Farooq-i-Azam Malik. *English Translation of the Meaning of Al-Qur'an: The Guidance of Mankind.* Houston: Institute of Islamic Knowledge, 1997. At times, I have substituted certain English words when using this translation (e.g., "Lord" or "Sustainer" for "*Rabb*" and "apostle" or "messenger" for "*Rasul*.").
3. Michael Sells, *Approaching the Qur'an: The Early Revelations.* 2nd ed. Ashland, OR: White Cloud Press, 2007. A sensitive and fresh translation and commentary of the earliest surahs revealed to Muhammad by an American scholar of Islam. Includes audio recordings and transliterations of the Arabic text so non-Arabic speakers can better sense the oral power of the Qur'an in its original Arabic.

On a few occasions, other translations are used and are clearly indicated in parenthesis at the end of the quotations.

NOTE ON ARABIC WORDS

No attempt has been made to follow a consistent system of transliteration of Arabic words. Proper names have been spelled according to common usage. Hence: Hossein, Hussein, Husayn. Words like jihad, hijab, and fatwa, now incorporated into English dictionaries, are not italicized. However, other less used Islamic terms such as: *ahl al-kitab*, *fiqh*, and *shahada*, are italicized.

Translations of the Bible

Contents

Foreword

I can think of no time when mutual understanding and respect among the Children of Abraham is more needed. In addition to the inherent significance of Jewish, Christian, and Islamic religious faiths, the realities of globalization and international politics and their interactions in the twenty-first century make understanding of these three great faiths and the dialogue among them imperative. We live in a time of deep domestic culture wars in North America and Europe; some warn of a clash of civilizations, driven not only by competing and contesting theologies, but also by political, ideological and identity issues that affect faith and politics, domestic and foreign policies. It is a time of not only mainstream believers and theologies, but also of the theologies of religious extremists and terrorists seeking to polarize, legitimate, and recruit followers in their "war for God," who commit unspeakable acts of violence, kill and terrorize those who they see as the "other" and an enemy of God.

Relations among people of faith and no faith have changed dramatically in only a few decades. While Muslims were relatively invisible in the cognitive and demographic maps of the West prior to the Iranian revolution of 1978-79, their presence and role in the West have changed sharply. In the recent past Islam was associated primarily with foreign Muslim countries. The religious landscape of Europe and North America was seen as the home of a Judeo-Christian tradition or more precisely Protestant, Catholic, and Jew are described as Western religions. Islam was erroneously categorized with Hinduism, Buddhism, and Confucianism under the rubric of Eastern religions.

The latter half of the twentieth century witnessed a seismic change due to immigration policies that brought many professionals, students, and laborers to the West in great numbers. In a matter of decades alongside churches and synagogues, mosques and temples sprung up in cities and towns. Immigrants and their descendants populate schools, universities, the professions and service industries. Religion departments sprang up in universities and colleges; religion and theology curricula that had primarily focused on Christianity and Judaism, increasingly included research and study of other faiths. Interestingly the American Academy of Religion prior to the late twentieth century was overwhelmingly focused on Protestant and Catholic theology and eventually Jewish studies. All this would change in the late twentieth century as Islam, Hinduism, Buddhism, and other "non-Western faiths" were included.

Today the landscapes of most cities and towns include mosques and Islamic centers alongside churches and synagogues, as well as Hindu, Buddhist and Sikh temples. Moreover, Islam has emerged as the third largest religion in the US after Christianity and Judaism—in some European countries it is second only to Christianity. Thus today, consideration of Islam and the West must be accompanied by an understanding of Islam in the West or the Muslims of the West. The major Muslim communities and cities of the world of Islam are not only Cairo, Damascus, Istanbul, but also London, Bradford, Paris, Marseilles, New York, Dearborn, Los Angeles, Toronto, and Montreal. Increasingly today, scholars have come to speak of a Judeo-Christian-Islamic tradition.

Despite—some would even argue because of—close family resemblances, relations between Judaism and Christianity, Christianity and Islam, Judaism and Islam have often been characterized by tension, conflicts and persecution. The beliefs of each that it possesses the one true God's revelation and special covenant and, in the cases of Christianity and Islam, that it supersedes earlier revelations, have been stumbling blocks to religious pluralism and tolerance.

The coexistence of faiths can be seen in the early dynamic development of the Islamic world as a civilization that flourished and eclipsed Western Christendom. Under the cosmopolitan Abbasid dynasty (750–1258) seated in Baghdad, relations between Christendom and the Islamic world were marked not only by conflicts of imperial expansion but also by substantial interchange: diplomatic, intellectual, artistic, and commercial. Christian and Muslim businessmen engaged in brisk and prosperous trade.

The fruits of this learning were appropriated by the West as Europe, looking to the great learning and libraries of the East, reemerged and retrieved its philosophical and scientific roots. Europe's great philosophers, Albertus Magnus, Thomas Aquinas, Bonaventure, and Duns Scotus as well as European scientists and physicians were indebted to Arab and Muslim masters such as Avicenna, Averroes, and many others.

Understanding and appreciating their shared beliefs and values has become especially critical for the Children of Abraham post-9/11. It is a matter no longer simply of interreligious relations and religious pluralism but of international politics. In the twenty-first century, engagement in interreligious or civilizational dialogue is no longer simply the preserve of religious leaders and scholars of religion but is now pursued by policymakers and corporate leaders, a subject of national and regional foreign policy and the agendas of international organizations.

The faith and lives of the vast majority mainstream Muslims are often overshadowed by the rhetoric of a dangerous and deadly extremist minority who follow a theology of hate and engage in acts of violence and terror. The words of some Western policymakers and political commentators, media coverage, and regrettably the statements of some religious leaders perpetuate misperceptions and stereotypes and risk promoting a clash of civilizations. These conditions make Ejaz Naqvi's *The Three Abrahamic Testaments: How the Torah, Gospel and Qur'an Hold the Keys for Healing our Fears* a must read. Interfaith and inter-civilizational understanding and dialogue require a candid appreciation of differences as well as similarities, recognition not only of what divides us but also of shared beliefs and values that unite us.

Naqvi focuses on the sacred scriptures of Judaism, Christianity, and Islam; how they reveal a wealth of common beliefs, wisdom, and values that can provide the foundation for an honest, faithful, and pluralistic understanding of one's own faith as well as the common ground for mutual understanding and respect, that goes beyond older notions of tolerance, which too often simply imply minimalist understanding of coexistence. While many Christians and Jews have been raised with some appreciation of the interconnectedness of the Old (Hebrew Bible) and New Testament, few have understood and embraced that broader vision of a Judeo-Christian-Muslim Abrahamic tradition.

John L. Esposito

Author's Note

When the good folks at White Cloud Press and I first started talking about doing a second edition of my book, *The Quran: With or Against the Bible?*, my initial thoughts were that it will be an update on the prior title. As we continued to ponder on what we were attempting to accomplish, vis-à-vis, to start a much-needed healing process to smooth out the strained relationship between Jews, Christians, and Muslims in today's global village, it became clear that the work would require making significant changes to the original book. Some of the sections needed to be deleted altogether as the focus shifted to a greater emphasis on the healing process and the social elements of the similarities of the teaching. My first book's focus was on the teachings of the Quran and how they compare with similar themes in the Bible. The focus still remains on the Qur'an since its teachings remain in the limelight, perhaps even more so now than four years ago, and also because of my greater familiarity with it being a Muslim. A greater weight is now given to the social elements of the teachings in all three scriptures. We felt the additions and amendments were significant enough that the book deserved a new title.

What I present in this book is the outcome of an investigative analysis of a set of topics from the Qur'an, the Islamic holy scripture, which I conducted over the last two decades. As an investigator, I put myself in the position of a critical analyst, rather than that of a religious scholar or expert, or a devoutly religious person.

The purpose of my investigation and critical analysis was to compare the teachings of the Qur'an and the Bible; in doing so, I investigated parallel teachings wherever I could. The aim of this work is to impress upon the reader the remarkable similarities in the paths of guidance that the two scriptures have bestowed upon their followers. I also acknowledge that, at times, significant differences exist.

I have taken utmost care to be respectful to people of all faiths and especially toward the scriptures as well as the noble figures, including the prophets. I have often mentioned them by their common names only, though I have fully intended to follow in my mind the Islamic tradition of adding "Peace be upon him" (PBUH) when mentioning their names. I am aware that not all readers will agree with my discussions, my analytical techniques, or the results there from. Such disagreements are natural and even welcome as long as they are built on mutual respect and objectivity.

Ejaz Naqvi, M.D.

Before We Start …

Religion has once again taken a prominent role in our society, especially in relation to politics. Religion has been used to divide people and is blamed for violence throughout history. In more recent times, Islam and its teachings have come under the spotlight. The recent increase in violence in the Middle East and Africa by groups such as Boko Haram, the so called Islamic State (ISIS) and remaining Al-Qaida affiliates, is one of the most urgent and troubling international issues of the day.

Despite this newfound fame, the teachings of Islam and the Qur'an remain largely unknown or misunderstood by non-Muslims. This seems to be mainly a result of a lack of knowledge and a lack of communication. A bottomless informational abyss exists between those with knowledge and those who are seeking it. Unfortunately, there has been some exploitation of the situation and spread of misinformation as well, which may be worse than having no information.

Many mainstream polls in the United States have consistently shown that most Americans view Muslims, or Islam, unfavorably. Muslims scored the lowest points (40 percent favorable) in a Pew research study, compared to the Jews (63 percent) and Catholics (62 percent).[1] Zogby Associates showed a similar trend. According to their findings, favorable attitudes towards Muslims continued to decline from 43 percent in 2010 to 32 percent in 2014 for Arabs; and from 35 percent in 2010 to 27 percent in 2014 for Muslims.[2] Despite all the negative opinion, most Americans also indicate that they do not know a Muslim personally or do not know enough about Islam and Muslims, as shown by the study by Zogby Associates.

Though the western world seems to have focused on hate speeches, acts of violence and frank terrorism committed by Muslims, or in the name of Islam, a review of the current situation and history of religion would indicate that Muslims do not have a monopoly on hate, fear mongering, or religion-based violence. On July 22, 2011 Anders Brevik, a Norwegian far right terrorist, killed seventy-seven people and in his manifesto titled "2083: A European Declaration of Independence," revealed clear hatred for Muslims and expressed anti-feminist views.[3] He reportedly idolized other American right wing extremists with similar views. We are all too familiar with the bombings of abortion clinics by Christian anti-abortion activists in the past several decades. In fact there have been reports that the right wing terror threat is a bigger concern for American law enforcement. But headlines can mislead. The main terrorist threat in the United States is not from violent Muslim extremists, but from right-wing extremists. Just ask the police.[4] The authors of the article went on to cite many law enforcement agencies, studies and institutions, such as Global Terrorism Database from University of Maryland and US Military's Combating Terrorism Center. The violence involving the Irish Republican Army and Great Britain between Catholics and Protestants is well known.

As reported by Reza Aslan, the Jewish terrorism history goes back to the first century, when extreme religious groups or zealots, would use daggers or *sicae* concealed under their cloaks to kill the Romans, thereby earning the name *Sicaraii*.[6] In more recent times, many individuals and organizations, such as Rabbi Meir Kahane and his Kach organizations have been considered terrorist organizations by Israel, the European Union, and the U.S. Department of State.[7]

It is clear that religion *has* been incriminated in creating a state of fearing the other, inciting hate speeches and violence by a minority group of believers. This has lead to a perception that the religious teachings of the Abrahamic faiths and their scriptures somehow promote hatred and violence against each other, leaving one to openly wonder: do the Qur'an and the Bible promote violence and hatred or do they promote peace? Do the Qur'an and the Bible send conflicting messages to their followers?

Even though the acts of terrorism and violence committed by ISIS is often presumed to be in the name of religion, a deeper look would reveal that their actions go beyond simply a desire to establish an "Islamic" caliphate. A French captive of ISIS, Didlier Francois, in an interview with Christiane Amanpour of CNN in February 2015 illustrates that their ideology goes well beyond the religious beliefs. He went on to tell Amanpour that, "there was never really discussion about texts or—it was not a religious discussion. It was a political discussion. It was more hammering what they were believing than teaching us about the Quran. Because it has nothing to do with the Quran."[8]

Hans Küng, a Swiss catholic priest and a theologian has eloquently described the integral relationship between religion, peace and the need for interfaith dialogue and understanding.[9] *The Declaration Toward a Global Ethic*, adopted at the Council of Parliament of World's Religions in Chicago in 1993, addressed the abuse of religion in a statement "Time and again we see leaders and members of religions incite aggression, fanaticism, hate, and xenophobia—even inspire and legitimize violent and bloody conflicts. Religion often is misused for purely power political goals, including war. We are filled with disgust. We condemn these blights and declare that they need not be. An ethic already exists within the religious teachings of the world which can counter the global distress."

The *Declaration* further offered principles of global ethic as a roadmap for successful interfaith dialogue. I will address the declaration and the principles of global ethic at the end of this book in my call to action.

Other scholars have argued that blaming the religion for even the seemingly religion-based violence is an over simplification of the geopolitical and socio-economical complexities often at play. Karen Armstrong notes:

> When they discuss the reasons people go to war, military historians acknowledge that many interrelated social, material, and ideological factors are involved, one of the chief being competition for scarce resources. Experts on political violence or terrorism also insist that people commit atrocities for a complex range of reasons. Yet so indelible is the aggressive image of religious faith in the secular consciousness that we routinely load the violent sins of the twentieth century onto the back of the 'religion' and drive it out into the political wilderness.[10]

In addition to many factors noted, hate is often a result of ignorance, leading to mistrust and fear of each other. In turn, mistrust and fear of the unknown often leads to hate, leaving us in a vicious cycle of hate-fear-hate. Martin Luther King, Jr. powerfully states, "Darkness cannot drive out darkness. Only light can. Hate cannot drive out hate, only love can."[11] To his immortal words, one may add that violence cannot drive out violence, only peace can. Indeed, in the same speech, he did address violence and its impact on society: "In fact, violence merely increases hate. So it goes. Returning violence for violence multiplies violence."

Hate is a learned behavior since no one is born hating each other. It can be easily argued that we are born to love and trust each other but our upbringing and the behavior of the people around us influences our own worldview. On February 10, 2015, Craig Hill shot dead his three Muslim neighbors: Deah, his newly wed wife Yusor, and her sister Razan. This was widely reported as a hate crime. I recall the father of the two sisters was asked on CNN why he thought this was a hate crime. His response was heartfelt: "Hate cannot be seen or touched; hate is something you *feel.*" Hate is often a consequence of basic human feelings such as envy, prejudice, insecurity, suspicions, a sense of loss of control, and social, economic, and other types of threats—perceived or real. Unfortunately the hate mongers know this all too well, and often use the basic human emotions to incite or perpetuate hate and fear. The first act of violence in human history, at least for the followers of the Bible and the Qur'an, whereby Cain killed his brother Abel, is a good reminder of the negative power of envy leading to hate and violence.

The best antidote for hate is love, just as peace is the antidote for violence, and knowledge is the antidote for ignorance. This leads us to the controversial question: Are the scriptures to blame for hate? Do the scriptures divide us or unite us? The following discussion examines some of the underlying factors that contribute to fear, hate and the "othering" effect. This book in general reviews the teachings of the Qur'an and the Bible in search of finding the answer to these burning questions that would hopefully lead to healing of our fears and help us find common grounds in an effort to bring harmony and peace to our communities.

Most of us want to believe that our own religion is the right one. This in itself ought not to be an issue, unless we decide that for our religion to be "right," other religions must be "wrong." Unfortunately, "what's wrong with other religions" often takes the center stage rather than a mind-set of "what's right with our religion," leading to a neglect of practicing the "right" teachings of one's own religion. Though some scholars, like Rabbi Brad Hirschfield (*You Don't Have to be Wrong for Me to be Right*) and Dr. David Liepert (*Muslim, Christian, and Jew*) have been promoting this concept, we mostly tend to highlight our differences rather than our similarities. This is true for religion in general and the scriptures in particular.

Quite frankly, up until some twenty years ago, I was also among the ones suffering from "I am right, so you must be wrong" syndrome, though I did not consider myself deeply religious at the time. This attitude took a severe jolt after my journey to Mecca to perform *umrah*, or minor pilgrimage. One of my brothers was suffering from a condition that required a kidney-pancreas transplant. Desperately trying to do whatever I could to help, I made a pledge to God to perform *umrah* as a token of gratitude if he did receive the transplant—and he did. I still remember the first time I set my eyes on Ka'aba, the holiest site in all of Islam. It was a deeply inspirational and spiritually uplifting experience. I had never felt so peaceful in my life, and never have I felt so peaceful since. That peace was an inner feeling of calm in my heart and mind, rather than an external one. I found myself thinking *this is the closet to God I will ever come in this life*. I felt so light I thought I could fly. I was awestruck by the uniformity of people representing all continents, color, race, ethnicity and speaking different languages—all with a common goal of seeking nearness to God and that elusive inner peace. From that perspective, all of us spoke one language: the language of love, peace, and compassion.

Deeply inspired, I decided to study the Qur'an when I returned home to California. Until that time I had read the Qur'an numerous times, but in its original Arabic text without understanding much, just like most non-Arabic speaking Muslims have done over their lifetime. But this was the first time I studied it *cover to cover* in the language I understood. This opened my eyes, my mind, and my heart. I realized very quickly that Islam, as taught by the Qur'an, was much more universal in its reach. My narrow view of religion in general and Islam in particular changed dramatically.

It completely overhauled the way I looked at interfaith relations. I came across passages that changed my view on the monopoly of Muslims on the paradise and the hereafter. Following is a very tiny sample of some of the passages that completely changed my perspective on Islamic pluralism and diversity, and prompted me to engage in interfaith work.

> *And dispute ye not with the People of the Book, except with means better (than mere disputation), unless it be with those of them who inflict wrong (and injury): but say, "We believe in the revelation which has come down to us and in that which came down to you; Our Allah and your Allah is one; and it is to Him we bow (in Islam)." 29:46*
>
> *O mankind! We created you from a single (pair) of a male and a female, and made you into nations and tribes, so that you may (get to) know each other (not that you may despise each other). Verily the most honored among you in the sight of Allah is (the one) most righteous (best in conduct). 49:13*
>
> *Verily, those who have attained to faith [in this divine writ], as well as those who follow the Jewish faith, and the Christians, and the Sabian—all (anyone) who believe in God and the Last Day and do righteous deeds—shall have their reward with their Sustainer; and no fear need they have, and neither shall they grieve. 2:62*
>
> *To each among you have we prescribed a law and an open way. If Allah had so willed, He would have made you a single community, but (His plan is) to test you in what He has given you: **So vie with one another in good works.** Unto Allah you will all return, it is He that will show you the truth of the matters in which you dispute. 5:48*

Furthermore, I learned the respect the Qur'an held for the Torah and the Gospel, often referring to them as *guidance* and *light*. The study of the Qur'an actually prompted me to study the Bible—something some Muslims would frown upon. As I started to read the Torah, and later the New Testament, I often found myself saying: *hmmm, I read this in the Qur'an also.* The Ten Commandments as they appear in the books of Exodus (chapter 20) and Deuteronomy (chapter 5) starting with the proclamation that God *is* the Lord and to not share any god with Him, also form the very foundation of Islamic teachings. Giving in public for show is discouraged, along with the emphasis on humility, and not judging others—concepts very similar to the ones I learned from the study of the Qur'an.

> *But when you give to someone in need, don't let your left know what your right hand is doing.* Matthew 6:3
> *For those who exalt themselves will be humbled, and those who humble themselves will be exalted.* Luke 14:11 and Matthew 23:12
> *Do not judge others and you will not be judged.... forgive others and you will be forgiven.* Luke 6:37

It did not take me very long to appreciate the striking similarities of the core teachings of the Bible and the Qur'an, though I also recognized significant differences. The commonalities around belief in God, the angels, the hereafter, the prophetic stories and the repeated emphasis on code of conduct such as honesty, mercy, compassion, humility, helping the poor and the needy and respect for life were too obvious to ignore. After spending years of further studying and contemplation, it is now my firm belief that regardless of how deeply we are aligned to our faith traditions (or not), the scriptures can actually bring people of Abrahamic faiths close together, rather than divide us. I believe strongly that the *healing* of fears and mistrust that we may have for each other can be found right there, in our own scriptures.

Before I wrote *The Quran: With or Against the Bible?* and got actively engaged in interfaith work, I used to watch the news and often found myself talking to my television, upset that what I was watching did not represent the true teachings of the Abrahamic scriptures and Islam in particular. On one hand, I was upset that there are folks who are spreading hate and fear in the name of religion, at the violence committed, and on the other hand not happy that the main focus seems to be on the divisive aspects without equal time for all the good work that people of faith have been engaged in, such as charity, building hospitals, advancement of science and peacemaking. As a result of this stereotyping, most people can easily name five Muslim terrorist individuals or organizations quickly, but not very many people know that there are five Muslim individuals (plus one Tunisian Muslim organization) who have won the Nobel Peace Prize between 2003 and 2015. After years of talking—sometimes yelling—at my television, I had a conversation with myself: *I could continue to talk to the television or do something about it.* I chose the latter. This is when my journey into interfaith work and healing of fears started.

I am a practicing physician with a specialty in chronic pain management. Our program utilizes a comprehensive model of pain management, using a bio-psychosocial approach. We acknowledge that chronic pain leads to many psychological issues such as insomnia, anxiety and fear of losing jobs or worsening relationships and depression. Therefore we take a more holistic approach and focus on not just the physical aspects of pain but the impact it has on people's lives. Our goal is not necessarily curing the pain but giving our patients tools so they help manage their pain as they address their underlying, and often hidden, fears around pain. As I continued my work to promote interfaith understanding and harmony, I felt a need to engage in a similar program of looking at the big picture in order to heal the disease that is ailing our society: the disease of fearing others, mistrust and hate. I realized that fear makes us who we are ***not***, causing us to act in ways that we would otherwise never react. Despite the fear mongers telling us that they know Islam teaches hate and violence, Islamophobia (as well as anti-Semitism and similar fear/hate phenomena) often results from a fear of the unknown. Thus the need for us to get to know each other! (There are many published reports about Islamophobia being an industry whereby certain individuals and groups are specifically involved in spreading hate and misinformation.[12] A fuller description can be found in the three references cited below.)

As part of my interfaith work at an individual level or as a representative of my interfaith council's sponsored events, I meet people from all faiths, as well as people without any faith tradition. I share their common passion for finding peace among people of all or no faith traditions, and the desire to heal our relationships. I have also come across people who have openly shared their fears with me. For many at such gatherings, I was the first Muslim they had ever met! I entertained a question from a woman who asked, "Why do you guys want to impose your shariah on us." Instead of the knee jerk reaction to address shariah, I engaged her in a healthy conversation about "you guys" and "us" and how the fear mongers have successfully created an "othering" effect and divided Americans into "you guys" and "us." Eventually we did talk about shariah laws when she followed up with "why are 'you guys' bent on bringing shariah to America." I responded by asking her a question: Do you know a state where Muslims tried to pass a shariah law? The answer was obviously a *no*, but she knew of many states where anti-shariah laws had passed without anyone asking the question I asked her.

She was surprised to learn that shariah simply means a code of life and set of laws that a Muslim needs to abide by, just like the Jews are supposed to abide by the law of Moses. In fact, quoting the Golden Rule from Matthew 7:12: *In everything, therefore, treat people the same way you want them to treat you, for this is the Law and the Prophets.* The "law" in Arabic versions of the Bible has been translated as shariah. And just like this shariah is meant for the Jews and the Jews cannot enforce their shariah onto the non-Jews, the Muslim shariah is meant for Muslims and cannot be imposed on to non-Muslims. I could sense a big sigh of relief in the audience after the conversation. I believe the "you guys" and "us" conversation was more responsible for a better understanding than the specific explanation of shariah law. She started to finally see that I (and other Muslim Americans) was like anyone else around her except that I happened to be a Muslim, and she happened to be a Christian. We shared the same values and dreams: to live in peace without fearing the neighbors, to ensure a prosperous future for our children without endangering the planet earth.

Then there was this lady, who after a presentation on "Islam 101" approached to share with me that "I learned more about Islam in the past hour, then I have all my life." And she was about eighty-years old! In these gatherings of people from various walks of life, we often talk about the rise of Islamophobia in the United States and the real-life stories about Muslim Americans' experience as they are subject to taunts, bullying, threats, and acts of violence against their places of worship. We engage in ways to stand in solidarity to combat Islamophobia, anti-Semitism, and other forms of hateful expressions. One of the most common comments

I have received is "I did not know that," and the one that makes me want to continue this effort is, "this is much needed work in order to heal our relations and calm our mutual fears." The best way forward is to engage in a dialogue, get to know each other, and emphasize the unity in diversity. We cannot allow our fears to become who we are not.

In short, we need to humanize, not demonize each other!

The stereotyping is not limited to Christians and Jews against Muslims but also exists among Muslim Americans against Christians and Jews. Similarly, many in the predominantly Muslim countries have misconceptions about the United States and people of other Abrahamic faiths, ranging from "they are all infidels" to viewing Hollywood as representing the Christian or Judaic values. This would be tantamount to Americans looking at ISIS's theology as Islamic, which has been clearly rejected by a large majority of Muslims worldwide. In fact I think we should add a "U" in front of ISIS: "U" for un-Islamic. Many Muslim Americans still prefer to mingle with fellow Muslims and don't know a Christian or Jew firsthand, their interactions at workplace notwithstanding. Just like most non-Muslim Americans don't know a Muslim, most Muslim Americans don't know a Christian or a Jewish American personally. Therein lies the problem. As mentioned earlier, the road to healing starts with us humanizing, not demonizing each other. It is hard to demonize someone you know!

The focal point of this book is the Qur'an, since it has recently come under the spotlight with widely divergent opinions. I will review a selection of the major themes in the Qur'an and compare them with corresponding passages from the Bible. My conscious attempt to highlight the similarities of the teachings of the scriptures of the three Abrahamic faiths will hopefully serve to narrow the knowledge gap and bring people of different faiths closer together in their understanding of each other's scriptures.

There is a clear need for better understanding among people of various faiths. The Qur'an, considered by Muslims to be the literal word of God, has come under severe scrutiny. Many wonder how a book that is considered holy by 1.6 billion Muslims worldwide, and a source of inner peace and spiritual growth, could be considered the opposite by *some* non-Muslims. Though the latter may represent a small minority, a large majority of people living in the West still remain unaware of the teachings of the Qur'an. How could the same book be viewed with such divergent opinions and views? Is it blind faith versus pure bias? Is it a reflection of a lack of adequate information and education? Many questions still abound. Who wrote this book? Who is the "God" of the Qur'an? What's the Qur'anic view of the prophets, especially Moses and Jesus? What does the Qur'an teach about interfaith relations? Does the Qur'an promote peace and harmony between Muslims and the People of the Book or does it promote violence? How does the Qur'an compare to the Bible on important themes like worshipping God, the prophets, human rights, moral values, and fighting for justice and human dignity? Does the Qur'an render women as second-class citizens? This book is a humble effort to provide answers to these and many other questions.

Though many have read selected portions of the Qur'an, most people who carry negative opinions about the Qur'an have never read it in its entirety. Accordingly, my primary objective of writing this book is to provide an introduction to the key themes in the Qur'an, especially as they relate to the common values shared with Christians and Jewish scriptures. My primary intended audience, thus, are the non-Muslims, especially in the West, and those unfamiliar with the Qur'an. These include interfaith workers and leaders, students of religion and anthropology, leaders of the churches and synagogues, journalists and news media outlets searching for the perspective from "peaceful common Muslims," politicians, political and social commentators, and anyone else who may be interested in learning more about the common values shared by the scriptures of Abrahamic faiths. In doing so, this book will concentrate on the theological aspects and avoid any geo-political connotations.

A blunt truth, however, is that a significant number of Muslims around the world have some misconceptions about the Qur'an. This results from the fact that the Qur'an was revealed in the Arabic language. Most Muslims have read the Qur'an, cover to cover, many times over, but in its original Arabic text, a language they do not understand. Since they do not know Arabic, they are not reading for comprehension but simply benefiting from the sound of the Arabic, which is no small matter. Similar to other faiths where Latin (Catholic), Sanskrit (Hindu), Pali (Buddhist),

Hebrew (Jewish) may be recited but not fully comprehended. Only a tiny percentage of Muslims have actually read the entire Qur'an in *their native language,* and thus the scripture remains arcane. They believe that reciting the Qur'an is a holy act in itself, which brings God's blessings to themselves, their house, and their place of worship. As good as these intentions are, they miss out on the very *reason* that the scripture itself identifies as the divine purpose behind its bestowment: to serve as the guidance to mankind. Can people be guided if they do not understand the language of the guide? Their primary source of information remains second-hand knowledge acquired through periodic lessons, speeches, or sermons by local religious clerics. Nevertheless, the Qur'an invites people to not just read it but also make an effort to discern God's message. Then, there are those Muslims who did read the translations themselves, but *in bits and pieces,* which could lead to misinterpretation because of the risk of taking the messages out of context. Accordingly, my secondary intended audience are the Muslims of the world who have yet to read the Qur'an in their native language from cover to cover. These include Muslim interfaith workers and leaders, Muslim organizations and Muslim Student Associations, Muslim organizations working to combat Islamophobia and improve public perception and relations, mosque goers, and the "unmosqued."

Though theologians may benefit from it, I would like to emphasize that this book is written in plain English, intended mainly for all people who are intrigued by religion and have the desire and curiosity to learn about other scriptures. The topics picked are of common interest and are broad in nature. It is hoped that this book will serve as a stimulus to explore the scriptures further for a clearer and more thorough understanding, including the Qur'an.

At the risk of contradicting myself in a span of one paragraph, it must be pointed out that even though English (or any other translation) is a good way to understand the Qur'an, the best way to study and understand the Qur'an is to study it in its original text in Arabic language. This is because of the simple fact that the essence of even an ordinary book may be lost, or diluted, during a translation. According to Muslim belief, the Qur'an is the word of God, and no translation can come close to the eloquence and the stunning beauty of its original text. Since studying the Qur'an in Arabic may not be practical for non-Arabic-speaking people, the next best way to understand is to study the translation in the language one understands best. Many people mistakenly believe that the Qur'an is not subject to interpretation by Muslims. The truth is that, though the original Arabic text has remained unchanged since it was revealed to Muhammad, the translations and interpretations have varied among Muslims. (Many Muslims also point out that one needs to study the teachings of Muhammad and the guidance of his noble family to appreciate and understand its truer meanings.) The Bible, too, faces similar challenges and is subject to human errors and interpretations during translations into English and other languages.

The only version of the Qur'an that is considered *the* Qur'an by Muslims is the Qur'an in Arabic. All the translations and commentaries are considered *just that;* they introduce a human element to the divine scripture. This book is not a translation or an exegesis of the Qur'an; it is divided into a number of sections, each further subdivided into chapters. Each section discusses one key theme in the Qur'an:

- God
- The Qur'an on other scriptures, prophets, and religions
- Moral values, ethics, pillars of faith, and lessons for our daily lives

Under each section, these themes are analyzed and discussed in more detail under various chapters. Whereas it is of significant value to know the context of the revelations, various topics are reviewed mostly by quoting the verses from the Qur'an and the Bible. I will venture to let the Qur'anic verses and biblical passages convey their own message as much as possible, all the while limiting a commentary.

At the end of each chapter, I have summarized key points for a given topic under "Discussion Points for Dialogue and Healing," and presented some thoughts on how to incorporate them into building bridges and heal our fears of each other. This is followed by "Time to Ponder" for those who want to go beyond the literal and superficial meaning of the scriptures, and engage in a more thought-provoking conversation in academic and interfaith settings.

It is my hope that this book will serve as a catalyst for the reader to study and examine the Qur'an and the Bible in more detail, without prejudice and preconceptions. It is my further hope that this will result in students of religion, journalists and other people getting engaged in dialogue with fellow students, scholars, and people from faith traditions other than their own. Hopefully, such study and dialogue will help bridge the gulf between people of various faiths and help heal our fears.

Introduction to the Qur'an, the Old Testament, and the New Testament

Ironically, the first thing that appealed to me about Islam was its pluralism. The fact that the Quran praises all the great prophets of the past.
Karen Armstrong

Before discussing the key themes in the sections to follow, the Qur'an's divine source will be addressed as well as its authenticity, its compilation, and its organization. This will be compared to the composition and compilation of the Bible.

Muslims believe the Qur'an is the literal word of God, revealed to Muhammad, and that there is no doubt about its sacred nature or its content. Some of the verses are clear and explicit in nature; others have multiple meanings and are open to different understandings and interpretation. Muslims contend that the authenticity of the Qur'an can be appreciated by simply reading the Qur'an in its entirety. The Qur'an proclaims that the book itself is a miracle and that God promised to protect it from alteration and corruption. Later in this section, I will review the painstaking efforts by Muhammad himself, as well as his close companions right after his death, to compile the Qur'an in order to preserve its accuracy.

The challenges to the Qur'an existed even at the time of its revelation, and therefore there are many verses in the Qur'an addressing its own authenticity.

This Book, there is no doubt in it, is a guide to those who guard (against evil). 2:2 (Shakir)

And if you are in doubt as to what We have revealed from time to time to Our servant, then produce a Surah like thereunto; and call your witnesses or helpers (if there are any) besides Allah, if your (doubts) are true. 2:23

Those familiar with Arabic, both Muslims and non-Muslims, acknowledge the uniqueness of the poetic eloquence and believe that it is a deeply inspired work. Invariably, though, much of the literal beauty gets diluted in the process of translations from the original Arabic text. Nonetheless, God cautions that the Qur'an is not a poetry book but a guide and a message to mankind:

We have not taught him (Muhammad) poetry, nor does it behoove him. This is nothing but a reminder and a plain Qur'an. 36:69 (Malik)

There are just over six thousand verses and over seventy-nine thousand words in the Qur'an. However, there are only about two thousand unique words (or their derivatives) used in the entire Qur'an. Many see the use of so few unique words that deliver an eloquent yet very powerful message as yet another sign of the divine source of the Qur'an. Muslims contend that the message of the Qur'an touches and softens the heart if readers approach it with an open mind. Chapter 36, one of the more revered chapters in the Qur'an, named *Ya Sin*, swears by the book itself:

By the Qur'an, full of Wisdom, you [Muhammad] are indeed one of the messengers, On a Straight Way. It is a Revelation sent down by (Him), the Exalted in Might, Most Merciful. 36:2–5

And to the doubters, the Qur'an issues this challenge:

This Qur'an is not such as can be produced by other than Allah; on the contrary it is a confirmation of (revelations) that went before it, and a fuller explanation of the Book—wherein there is no doubt—from the Lord of the worlds.

Or do they say, 'He forged it'? Say: 'Bring then a Surah [chapter] like unto it, and call (to your aid) anyone you can besides Allah, if you speak the truth!' 10:37–38

History

The Qur'an was revealed through Muhammad over a period of twenty-three years, though some Muslims believe that the entire Qur'an was revealed to him at once on the night of power (*laylat al-qadr*), and under divine orders, he then revealed it to people in bits and pieces according to the circumstances. The first set of verses were revealed in the year 610 C.E., when Muhammad was forty years old and was meditating near Mecca in a cave he often used to visit. It is reported that the Archangel Gabriel appeared in a human form and asked him to recite the following verses, that later became the first five verses of chapter 96 of the Qur'an (*Al-Alaq,* or "The Clot").

Read in the name of your Lord Who created. He created man from a clot. Read and your Lord is Most Honorable, Who taught (to write) with the pen. Taught man what he knew not. 96:1–5 (Shakir)

In many ways, the Qur'an and Muhammad are inseparable. Muhammad is believed to have said nothing on his own except what was instructed by God to him through the Archangel Gabriel. The Qur'an asserts that the source of the revelations is the same as the prior scriptures revealed to the prophets that came before Muhammad, such as Prophets Abraham, Moses, David, and Jesus. Though highly revered, Muhammad is not considered the author, or the editor, of the Qur'an. Most Muslims consider Muhammad to be illiterate (*ummi*), since he did not receive worldly education.

And you [Muhammad] were not (able) to recite a Book before this (Book came), nor are you (able) to transcribe it with your right hand: In that case, indeed, would the talkers of vanities have doubted. 29:48

Composition of the Qur'an

The Qur'an has a total of 114 chapters, called *surahs*, which vary in length from three to 286 verses, called *ayahs*. The sequence of the chapters, however, does not reflect the chronological order of the verses as they were revealed to Muhammad, nor are the chapters arranged in a topical or thematic order. In addition to a number, each chapter has a name; for example, the first chapter is named *Surah al-Fatiha*, or "The Opening."

To those unfamiliar with the Qur'an and the readers of the Bible, it may seem disorganized as it seemingly moves from one topic to another frequently, often within the same chapter, and at times, even within a verse. The Qur'an is not a set of prescriptions or a detailed history of Arabs. This is in contrast to some of the very detailed accounts of Prophet Moses and the Israelites in the Torah. The Qur'an encompasses a wide variety of subjects: from historical events like the creation of Adam, to warnings and glad tidings, as well as law giving. It does so in a seemingly haphazard manner, which Muslims feel is stunningly beautiful with unparalleled poetic eloquence. Unlike the book of Genesis, one won't find long accounts of creation in one chapter. For instance, Adam's creation is mentioned in chapter 2 (*Al-Baqara*, or "The Cow").

> *Behold, your Lord said to the angels: 'I will create a vicegerent on earth.' They said: 'Will You place therein one who will make mischief therein and shed blood? While we do celebrate Your praises and glorify Your Holy (name)?' He said: 'I know what you know not.' And He taught Adam the names of all things; then He placed them before the angels, and said: 'Tell me the names of these if you are right.' They said: 'Glory to You, of knowledge We have none, save what You have taught us: In truth it is You Who are perfect in knowledge and wisdom.' He said: 'O Adam! Tell them their natures.' When he had told them, Allah said: 'Did I not tell you that I know the secrets of heaven and earth, and I know what you reveal and what you conceal?' And behold, We said to the angels: 'Bow down to Adam' and they bowed down. Not so Iblis [Satan]: he refused and was haughty (arrogant): He was of those who reject Faith. We said: 'O Adam! dwell you and your wife in the Garden;*

and eat of the bountiful things therein as (where and when) you will; but approach not this tree, or you run into harm and transgression.' Then did Satan make them slip from the (garden), and get them out of the state (of felicity) in which they had been. We said: 'Get you down, all (you people), with enmity between yourselves. On earth will be your dwelling-place and your means of livelihood—for a time.' Then learnt Adam from his Lord words of inspiration, and his Lord turned toward him; for He is Oft-Returning, Most Merciful. We said: 'Get you down all from here; and if, as is sure, there comes to you Guidance from me, whosoever follows My guidance, on them shall be no fear, nor shall they grieve. But those who reject Faith and belie Our Signs, they shall be companions of the Fire; they shall abide therein.' 2:30–39

From this account, the verses then seamlessly move on to talk about the children of Israel. The Qur'an returns to the story of Adam's creation again in chapter 7, verses 19–25, as well as many other places.

However, this method of scattering is not necessarily unique to this scripture. For example, while describing the drunks in Samaria in the Northern Kingdom of Israel, the book of Isaiah refers to the Lord's instructions piece by piece:

'Who does the LORD THInk we are?' they ask. 'Why does he speak to us like this? Are we little children, just recently weaned? He tells us everything over and over—one line at a time, one line at a time, a little here, and a little there!' Isaiah 28:9–10

The intention of this book is not to reorganize the Qur'an in a topical format, but to review various themes scattered at various places in the Qur'an.

History without specifics

The Qur'an narrates many stories, and many of them are found in the Bible as well. These include the stories of Adam, Noah, Abraham, Lot, David, Moses (and pharaoh), Jesus Christ, the Virgin Mary, Zechariah, and others. The Qur'an mentions these stories without specific dates and oftentimes refers to people without their proper names. For example, in the story of Moses, the king is called *firawn* (pharaoh), rather than by the specific pharaoh at the time of Moses. Similarly, in the story of Joseph, the son of Jacob, the woman who tried to seduce him is not named. The Qur'an's focus, when telling the stories of the past, is not on the specifics but rather the moral of the story.

Themes in the Qur'an

Many scholars have attempted to divide the Qur'anic teachings and the message into various sections based on the themes presented. For example, Amin A. Islahi (1904–1997), a South Asian Qur'anic scholar, divided the Qur'anic themes into seven sections: law (jurisprudence), Abrahamic religions, the struggle between truth and deceit, the proof of Muhammad as a messenger, the unity of God, the judgment, and warnings to non-believers. In this book, I cover various themes under different sections, by quoting verses from all over the Qur'an pertaining to a topic. This by no means is a complete list of the topics, the themes, or the verses in the Qur'an. More importantly, this is not an attempt to rearrange the order of the Qur'an, in accordance with the Muslim belief that no one has the authority to change the divine arrangement. This book should also not be considered an exegesis.

Compilation of the Qur'an

As the verses were revealed to Muhammad, he ordered his appointed scribes to store them in two forms: oral tradition (by memorization) and in written form. This was done with the clear intention of preserving the Qur'an. Arabs had a strong tradition of memorizing stories and poetry. Most of his companions memorized large portions, and many memorized the whole Qur'an. This may seem strange to some in the West, but to this date, there are many Muslims who have memorized every single word of the Qur'an and can recite it from cover to cover. They are called *Hafiz*, "one who memorizes."

After the death of Muhammad, the Muslim community was faced with a mutiny from some Arab tribes who claimed their allegiance to Islam was conditioned on Muhammad's leadership. These tribes rebelled from the leadership of Abu Bakr, the first Muslim caliph and successor to Muhammad, in what is known as the Apostasy (*ridda*) Wars. During these battles, many of Muhammad's companions who had memorized the entire Qur'an died in battle. There was concern that the integrity of the Qur'anic text could be lost.

To fully understand and appreciate how the Qur'an was organized and compiled into its current form, the methods behind how the other scriptures of the Abrahamic faith were organized and compiled should be examined.

Organization and Compilation of the Bible

The following discussion regarding the compilation of the Bible is undertaken with utmost sensitivity and respect for the scripture from God, as well as the feelings of people of all faiths.

The Qur'an frequently makes references to the "People of the Book" and previous scriptures, especially *Tawrat* (Torah), revealed to Moses; *Zabur* (Psalms), revealed to King David; and *Injil* (Gospel), revealed to Jesus Christ. These original scriptures are highly respected by Muslims, though they also believe that over a period of time, they have been modified and altered from their original content. There is a general consensus among many Muslim, Jewish, and Christian scholars that the original text of the Bible is not available anywhere and what's currently available has been edited over the centuries, along with loss of many original verses, as explained below.

Composition of the Bible

The Bible is not one scripture but rather a set of scriptures. The word "Bible" means "the books" and is derived from a Greek phrase, *ton biblion*, meaning the "scroll" or the "book." *Byblos* was an ancient city, located in the current Lebanon, famous for supplying paper and paper products to the world, and became synonymous with the word "book."

The Christian Bible is divided into two parts. The first is called the Old Testament, containing the (minimum) thirty-nine books of Hebrew scripture, and the second portion is called the New Testament, containing twenty-seven books. The first four books of the New Testament form the canonical Gospels, which recount the life and teachings of Jesus Christ and are central to the Christian faith.

The Hebrew Bible (or *Tanakh*) consists of twenty-four books (corresponding to the thirty-nine books of the Old Testament in the Christian Bible) and has three main parts:

The **Torah** ("teaching" or "law") addresses the origins of the universe, Adam, Abraham and his descendants and the Israelite nation, its laws, and its covenant with the God of Israel. There are five books in the Torah. The five books are also known as *Pentateuch*, from Greek meaning "five scrolls." Some traditions include the first book of Nevi'im (Joshua) and together are known as *Hexateuch*. The term "Torah" is also meant to refer to the written as well as the oral tradition, as well as the entire Tanakh from Genesis to the last book of the Hebrew Bible.

The *Nevi'im* ("prophets"), containing the historic account of ancient Israel and Judah as well as the work of prophecy. There are eight books in this section.

The *Ketuvim* ("writings"), poetic and philosophical works such as the Psalms and the book of Job. There are eleven books in this section.

The first five books of the Hebrew Bible, making up the Torah, are Genesis, Exodus, Leviticus, Numbers, and Deuteronomy. The Christian Bible includes the books of the Hebrew Bible, but they are arranged in a different order: the Hebrew Bible ends with the people of Israel restored to Jerusalem and the temple, and the Christian arrangement ends with the book of the Prophet Malachi. It is to be noted that the arrangement and number of books vary among various schools of thought within Judaism, though the content remains the same.

The New Testament relates to the life and teachings of Jesus (Gospels), a life of the early church (Acts of the Apostles), and the letters from the apostles of Jesus (Paul and others). The Qur'an's mention of Injeel revealed on Prophet Jesus Christ is what's known as the Gospel in the West. There are four canonical Gospels: Matthew, Mark, Luke, and John. These are not four entirely different scriptures but rather four versions of the same scripture on the life and teachings of Jesus Christ.

The word "Gospel" is derived from the Angelo-Saxon "god-spell," meaning "good news" or "good tidings." This word in turn is derived from the Greek word *Evangelion*, also meaning "good tidings."

Tradition holds that the Gospel writers were among Jesus' twelve disciples (Matthew and John) or among close traveling companions of the apostle Paul (Mark and Luke). Mark is believed to have received instructions from Peter. Current scholarship maintains that the four Gospels attributed to Matthew, Mark, Luke and John were not written by them but by others who were likely assigned by them as "ghost writers," a practice not uncommon in the first century C.E. This leads to the conclusion that we cannot know who wrote the four Gospels and focuses on the different theological goals of each Gospel, reflecting different viewpoints held among the diverse Christian communities in the early days of Christianity.[1] These four Gospel writers took different approaches to the life of Jesus and at times, differ when describing the same events or teachings. However, Matthew, Mark, and Luke share a number of similarities and are thus called "synoptic gospels," in Greek meaning "to view together."

Compilation of the Hebrew Bible

The term "canon" or canonization refers to the authoritative collection of sacred writings acknowledged by a particular religious community. The subject of canonization of the Bible is complex, to say the least, with varying views, and the following is a very brief summary of what's accepted by the majority of scholars and historians.

Currently the original writings of the Hebrew and Christian scriptures do not exist. The oldest *surviving* Christian Bibles are Greek manuscripts from the fourth century, and the oldest complete Jewish Bible is a Greek translation, also dating back to the fourth century. The original texts were written on papyrus, which deteriorated over time. The oldest complete manuscripts of the Hebrew Bible (the Masoretic text) date from the Middle Ages. However, the discovery of the Dead Sea Scrolls reveals texts dating back to 70–150 B.C.E.

The Hebrew canon took shape in stages. The first corpus to be canonized was the Torah, which is believed to have been canonized in 400 B.C.E. The canon of Nevi'im (Prophets) is less clear but is said to have occurred around 200 B.C.E. Ketuvim was put in place around 90 C.E. at the Rabbinical Council of Jamnia.

Following Moses, according to Jewish traditions, the teachings of the Torah were communicated in oral traditions and passed from one generation to another. The oral Torah is distinct from the written tradition. The oral Torah was not supposed to be written down. The intention was to maintain the sacred nature of the scripture. Jewish leadership in the centuries preceding the Common Era felt a need to capture the oral traditions in writing, as they feared the loss of this great tradition as they experienced the killings of many of Israelites.

In 586 B.C.E., the Babylonians destroyed Jerusalem, including the Jewish temple and libraries containing the sacred texts. Many scrolls survived and were taken to Babylonia. In Babylon, these documents were edited and compiled. This process involved many people; the person credited with heading up the project was Ezra, a scribe and priest. Around 450 B.C.E., he brought these scrolls back to the rebuilt Jerusalem. During this time, additional works were penned and included in a relatively complete edition of the Jewish Bible.

The Greek translation of the Hebrew Bible, *Septuagint,* was done around 250–100 B.C.E. There were checks against the translations with the Hebrew Bible as well as with oral traditions. The Masoretes Jews did not write the Masoretic text until around the tenth century C.E. It has many similarities to the text of the Septuagint but many differences and contradictions are found in the two manuscripts.

Scholarly Perspective on the Compilation of the Torah

According to the views shared by classical rabbis, Moses received the Torah in its entirety—both the oral form (with interpretations for the written Torah) and the written Torah. This view of Mosaic authorship has been challenged since the twelfth century by scholars such as Abraham ibn Ezra, in the seventeeth century C.E. by Baruch Spinoza and Thomas Hobbes, and the nineteenth century C.E. by Julius Wellhusen, pointing out various style, theological and content patterns that reflected more than one source of authorship (documentary hypothesis). According to this hypothesis, there are four sources of the Old Testament: J, E, D and P. They noted the use of passages using the letters YHWH—a word for Yahweh (Jahwe in German) for God in the book of Genesis and the first part of the book of Exodus while others used another Semitic word for the divine—Elohim. These hypothetical documents were labeled as *J* for

Yahwist (Jahwist in German) and *E* for *Elohist.* The third source is termed *D* for *Deuteronomist* and the final source was termed *P* for *Priestly.*[2] They further point out some of the "contradictions" within the text to support their view of multiple authorship, such as the creation account mentioned in genesis chapter 1:1-2:4a and the second creation story in Genesis 2:4b-3:24. In the first story, the creation of land animals occurred first followed by creation of man and woman. The second story had man created first, then the animals, then woman. For the modern scholarship, the Torah is viewed as a single text with a complex history with lack of consensus on how these various sources came together to form a single book.

The New Testament was originally written over a fifty- to seventy-five-year period. According to traditions, these works were written by Jesus Christ's disciples and early church leaders. The first writings were likely started around 50–75 C.E., and the other writings were nearly complete in various forms around 150 C.E. (but they were not in one single volume). Many scholars believe the initial texts were written before 70 C.E., since they do not refer to the destruction of the second temple in Jerusalem by the Romans. Doubts were raised shortly thereafter about their authenticity, and in the second century C.E., the canonization was ordered. The collection process was complete by the end of the second century C.E., but it was not official until 367, when St. Athanasius, a bishop of Alexandria, used the word "canonization" in his Easter letter and determined the number of books in the New Testament to what it is currently: twenty-seven. The canon includes the letters of St. Paul, canonical Gospels, the Acts of the Apostles, and the book of Revelation. The first official canon was accepted in 393 C.E. in the synod of Hippo Regius in Africa (a synod is a council established by the church to determine a doctrine or other important affairs). The acts of this council are lost. In 397 C.E., the synod of Carthage in North Africa confirmed the New Testament canon to what's accepted today. A review of the process of canonization reveals many debates and disputes among church leaders as to which books and writings to include. Many books were eventually expunged (e.g., the book of 1 Clement, The Gospels of Thomas and Mary, and the Shepherd of Hermas).[3] It is of note that Jesus and his disciples all spoke Aramaic, and God's revelations to him likely were in that language, yet there is no original Aramaic Gospel available. Traces of original Aramaic gospels can be found in the writings of the early Church Fathers. Around the year 150 C.E., Papias, bishop of Hieropolis in Asia Minor, wrote, "Matthew compiled the sayings [of the Lord] in the Aramaic language, and everyone translated them as well as he could."[4] Ireneaus of Lyons, writing around the year 180 C.E., noted:

> Matthew also issued a written Gospel among the Hebrews in their own dialect, while Peter and Paul were preaching in Rome and laying the foundation of the Church. After their departure, Mark, the disciple and interpreter of Peter, did also hand down to us in writing what had been preached by Peter. Luke, also a companion of Paul, recorded in a book the Gospel preached by him. Afterwards John, the disciple of the Lord, who also had leaned upon his breast, did himself publish a Gospel during his residence at Ephesus in Asia.[5]

The Non-Canonical Gospels: Doubts About the Accuracy of the Canon

There is a widespread belief among Muslims that the Old and the New Testaments have not retained the original revelations and have been altered over the course of many centuries. On careful review, it now appears that this is not a Muslim-only view of how the New Testament was gathered. New scholarship now holds that there was a natural process (human need for orthodoxy) where New Testament writings were altered by scribes to match more clearly with hard fought theological battles establishing Catholic and Orthodox Christologies. Professor Bart Ehrman's two books—*The Orthodox Corruption of Scripture* and *Lost Christianities*—describe the challenges faced by the early Christain groups. In *The Orthodox Corruption of Scripture,* he states: "theological disputes, specifically disputes over Christology, prompted Christian scribes to alter the words of scripture in order to make them more serviceable for the polemical task. Scribes modified their manuscripts to make them more patently 'orthodox' and less susceptible to 'abuse' by the opponents of orthodoxy."[6]

New scholarship is showing that there was great diversity of views among early Christians, that the New Testament scriptures were altered to make them better fit third- and fourth-century orthodoxy *and* that the viewpoints of those Christians who lost to the Church were preserved in groups like the Ebionites whose Christology is much more in alignment with the Qur'an.[7] Furthermore, these Christians held that they were faithful to the pure Torah and Jesus's teachings as they were practiced by Jesus's brother James, that is, those who were closest to Jesus. The non-canonical gospels in addition to those noted above include the "Q Gospel," Gospels of Judas and the Gospel of Barnabas. "Q" is from the German word *Quelle* meaning "source." New Testament scholarship now believes that the authors of Matthew and Luke used the material from the gospel attributed to Mark and a second source—the Q Gospel—referred to as the Two Document Theory or Two Sources Hypothesis. In his book *The Complete Gospels,* Robert Miller goes on to state: "Jesus appears in Q as a wise teacher and prophet. In fact, Jesus implicitly links himself to the prophets of Israel's past, who were, Q says, consistently rejected, or even killed."[8] This is a view strikingly similar to that of the Qur'an. Similarly, in his book *The Text of the New Testament,* Vincent Taylor writes that, "The manuscripts of the New Testament preserve traces of two kinds of dogmatic alterations: those which involve the elimination or alteration of what was regarded as doctrinally unacceptable or inconvenient, and those which introduce into the Scriptures proof for a favorite theological tenet or practice."[9]

Given the culture and the pressures faced by the early church of the first and second century C.E., Muslims can appreciate how Christians came to the Trinitarian perspective. However, in view of the many references noted above, the Christians can also realize that Islam's teachings around Jesus and the Gospels are not so alien and different in that they echo teachings of early Christian communties dating back to the time of Jesus and his family.

From this brief discussion, one is tempted to ask the question: If the oldest surviving texts were not written for several centuries (Old Testament) and at least many decades to about 150 years (New Testament) after their revelations, how accurate are the current versions of the Bible? Although great care has been taken to preserve oral traditions, as well as written texts over the years, there is ongoing debate among biblical scholars about the composition, compilation, translation, and its resultant accuracy. Churches of all dominions today almost universally accept the current New Testament's list of twenty-seven books. Many scholars insist that despite the challenges and some controversies early on, the current version of the Bible, having gone through a process of canonization and being looked at by religious sages, is an accurate reflection of the original texts. "The material upon which the biblical books were written (usually Papyrus made from the tall water plant of the same name) deteriorated over time … the books making up the Jewish and Christian Bibles had to be copied and recopied by hand to preserve them. Yet, the popular notion that this continued copying means that the books we now possess are hopelessly corrupted is inaccurate."[10]

We Now Return to the Compilation of the Qur'an

The history of the compilation of the Qur'an can be summarized in three phases:

1. During the lifetime of Muhammad (610–632 C.E.)
2. During the caliphate of the first caliph, Abu Bakr (632–634 C.E.)
3. During the caliphate of the third caliph, Uthman (644–656 C.E.)

DURING THE LIFETIME OF MUHAMMAD (610-632 C.E.)

The consensus among Muslims is that Muhammad himself, under divine instructions, organized the Qur'anic text in its current form and that the version we have currently available is the same as what was available at the time of Muhammad's death.

The Qur'an's compilation is made unique among all scriptures in that Muhammad appointed several scribes to write down the verses during his lifetime, and he directed its organization and placement of various chapters. The verses were written down on palm leaves, tablets of stone, leather, parchments, and other such material. The Qur'an points to the presence of a readable Qur'an on several occasions, which will be reviewed in more detail in chapter 13.

That this is indeed a Qur'an Most Honorable. In a Book well guarded, which none shall touch but those who are clean. 56:77–79

In his last sermon to a huge audience, when he was returning from the pilgrimage, about three months before he passed away, Muhammad addressed the pilgrims by stating: "I have left among you two weighty matters which if you cling to them you shall not be led into error after me. One of them is greater than the other: The Book of God which is a rope stretched from Heaven to Earth and my progeny, the people of my house."[11]

Sahih Muslim is considered by most Muslims one of the more authentic books of hadith (the sayings of Muhammad). In the statement quoted above, the use of "Book," and not "scripture" or "revelations," points to the presence of a written text at the time.

There are many passages in the Qur'an proclaiming its purity and divine source.

Other verses within the Qur'an itself also point to the writing down of the Qur'an at the time of revelation. For example:

> *By no means (should it be so)! For it is indeed a Message of instruction: Therefore let whoso will, keep it in remembrance. (It is) in Books held (greatly) in honor. Exalted (in dignity), kept pure and holy, (Written) by the hands of scribes. Honorable and pious and just.* 80:11–16

The Oral Qur'an: As the verses were revealed to Muhammad, in addition to dictating them to the appointed scribes, he would reveal them to the appointed *hafiz* (memorizers), who would repeat the verses back to him and memorize them. The following section discusses how this oral tradition became an important part of the compilation of the Qur'an into a single volume.

The Qur'an was available in a textual form during Muhammad's lifetime, and it was already named *Al-Qur'an.*

DURING THE CALIPHATE OF THE FIRST CALIPH, ABU BAKR (632–634 C.E.)
According to the most widely held view by Muslim scholars, within six months after the death of Muhammad, about seven hundred companions who had memorized the whole Qur'an were killed in the battle of Yamama. It was feared that the Qur'an's preservation would weaken. Abu Bakr then

ordered a compilation from the collections of all scribes from the time of the Prophet. This task was assigned to a well-known scribe, Zaid bin Thabit. The writings were checked against the memory of the other *hafiz* companions and all writings from other reliable scribes; it was ensured that they had met strict criteria to be included in the one, authenticated text. The final product was passed on to Hafsah, the daughter of Umar and one of the widows of Muhammad.[12]

After Muhammad's death in 632, several of his companions, including Ali ibn Abi Talib, had already collected portions of the Qur'an as a whole book. Others included Abdu'llah ibn Mas'ud in Mecca and Ubay ibn Ka'b in Medina. Ali had hand-written a copy of the Qur'an, arranged not only in its current form (as dictated by Muhammad) but "because of his close relationship to Muhammad and long companionship, didn't only collect the dispersed scrolls of the Qur'an, but he rather could accompany it with a remarkable *tafsir* (commentary, or exegesis), mentioning the occasion of each verse's descension, and this was regarded as the first tafsir of Qur'an."[13] He also had the verses arranged in chronological order. According to some scholars, Ali was the first one to collect the Qur'an and wrote the first *tafsir*.

DURING THE CALIPHATE OF THE THIRD CALIPH, UTHMAN (644–656 C.E.)

Later on, in the time of the Caliph Uthman, Islam spread fast, and many companions of Muhammad moved out of Arabia. Amongst the many countries and provinces that accepted Islam were Syria and Iraq, but their language was not Arabic. One of Muhammad's companions, Huthayfah ibn al-Yaman, during a visit to Syria and Iraq, learned that people were reciting the Qur'an in different modes, dialects, or styles. This disturbed him very much, and upon his return, he requested Uthman to reproduce and distribute copies of the Qur'an that would help Muslims read or recite the Qur'an in a single consistent manner to avoid any conflict.

Uthman appointed twelve respected Muslims, headed by Zayd bin Thabit (the same scribe used by Abu Bakr), to write the Qur'an in the mode of the tribe Quraysh, the one used by the Prophet in his recitation. The intent was to preserve the Qur'an exactly as it was revealed and organized at the time of Muhammad. Uthman relied on two sources:

the written text that had been previously ordered by Abu Bakr, and the various oral traditions of Muslims who memorized it during the lifetime of Muhammad. In Islamic history, there is no variation between these two sources, so the Uthmanic "rescension" is largely a codifying of a single version of a text. This version, the Uthmanic rescension, is the version of the Qur'an that has remained unchanged and is the one currently in use.

Of the completed official copies Uthman ordered copies sent to Syria, Iraq, and Mecca, and one was kept in Medina. The original manuscript was returned to Hafsah. Uthman then ordered that all the other Qur'anic materials, whether written in fragmentary manuscripts or whole copies, be burnt. This was a precautionary measure taken to prevent any future conflict in the mode of recitation, thus preventing the Qur'an from fabrication or corruption.[14]

Some scholars suggest that the early Uthmanic texts of the Qur'an did not contain diacritical markers for short vowels, and dots that are used to distinguish similarly written Arabic letters.[15]

Despite slight variations on the type of work and possible addition of diacritics for easier reading, it's unanimously agreed by all Muslims that the Qur'anic text and composition has been preserved, without any addition or deletions from the one that was revealed to Muhammad. The dialect present in today's texts is the same exact one since the days of Uthman, which is the same as that organized by Muhammad.

This is in contrast to large portions of the Old Testament and the New Testament, which mostly consists of writings by apostles and the church leaders. "In Christianity and Judaism, the concept of the revelation as a book developed over a period of time. For Islam, the concept of revelation as a divine book is present from the very beginning."[16]

Recitation of the Qur'an

Muslims often claim, and some non-Muslim scholars concur, that the beauty of the Qur'an is best appreciated when it is recited (and understood) in its original Arabic language. It is a common custom in Muslim countries to recite the Qur'an in Arabic on various occasions. Not uncommonly, one hears the Qur'an being recited on audiotapes and CDs in beautiful melody at mosques, as a ritual when someone dies, and at prayer gatherings.

The Oldest Surviving Copy of the Qur'an

According to the Islamic traditions, the original Uthmanic texts are preserved in Topkapi Museum, in Istanbul, Turkey. A number of ancient manuscripts of the Qur'an were discovered in Yemen in 1972. Carbon-14 dating traced these to the period between 645 and 690 C.E.[17] The calligraphic dating points to a date a little later, around 710–715. Ancient fragments of the Qur'an were recently discovered in a library in Birmingham, England that appear to be of even earlier composition, composed perhaps during the lifetime of Muhammad or shortly thereafter. David Thomas, professor of Christianity and Islam at the University of Birmingham, notes that:

> The tests carried out on the parchment of the Birmingham folios yield the strong probability that the animal from which it was taken was alive during the lifetime of the Prophet Muhammad or shortly afterwards. This means that the parts of the Qur'an that are written on this parchment can, with a degree of confidence, be dated to less than two decades after Muhammad's death. These portions must have been in a form that is very close to the form of the Qur'an read today, supporting the view that the text has undergone little or no alteration and that it can be dated to a point very close to the time it was believed to be revealed.[18]

The Secular View on the Compilation of the Qur'an

Most Western scholars basically accept the Uthmanic version of the compilation, but in addition these scholars believe that other versions continued to circulate for centuries. They point out that texts from about 800 C.E. complain about the use of another version by Ibn Mas'ud, indicating that after Uthman, at least one other version existed. Moreover, they point out that the earliest preserved Qur'an manuscript fragments date back to the end of the seventh century. The Dome of the Rock in Jerusalem was inscribed in 691–692 C.E. with verses from the Qur'an. These manuscripts, it is said, have slightly different texts of some specific passages than in the Uthmanic texts and have a different way of writing some words. Muslims would contend that these slight variations are accounted for by various dialects and special markings that were added to make the reading easier for non-Arabic-speaking Muslims and don't alter the pronunciation, meaning, and message of the Qur'an.

Recitation, Translation, and Interpretation of the Qur'an

In ways similar to the Torah, the oral tradition of the Qur'an is considered as important as, if not more important than, the written text. It is worth repeating here that the most prudent way to understand the Qur'an is to study it in its original Arabic language. The next best way is to study a translation (realizing that translations don't always convey the true meaning and spirit conveyed by the original language of the scripture).

RECITATION (TILAWAT)

The recitation of the Arabic Qur'an is a great tradition among the Muslims and is considered a source of blessings and a noble deed in itself. *Tilawat* is the word used to mean the recitation of the Qur'an. Many reciters (*qaris*) develop their own unique style, and their melodious recitations are sold around the world. These recitations are said to often leave deep impressions on even unfamiliar ears.

Tilawat comes from the root word *tala* and has a wider meaning that includes to recite, rehearse, read, and meditate.

> *When the Qur'an is recited, listen to it with complete silence so that you may be shown mercy. 7:204 (Malik).*

In this verse, listeners are instructed about the basic mannerism of listening to the Qur'an. Many Muslims do indeed stop talking when they hear the recitation:

> *When you recite the Qur'an, seek Allah's protection from the accursed Satan, surely he has no authority over those who believe and put their trust in their Lord. 16:98–99 (Shakir)*

TRANSLATION AND INTERPRETATION

It is important to remember that the scriptures under review here were revealed about 1,500-3,000 years ago and were originally revealed in Semitic languages, therefore any references to English versions should be viewed with the understanding that no translation conveys the depth of meaning found in the original language. As the Italians say, "traduttore traditore" (translator-traitor). There are two basic methods of translation: formal equivalence and dynamic equivalence. Formal equivalance method uses the linguistic equivalent of the original and represents a more literal meaning of the original. Dynamic equivalence method captures the essential underlying idea or concept behind the original text if the original language represents culture, practices, and idioms of the past that may no longer be familiar or in use today. For example, if I were to translate "he hit the jackpot"—meaning "he got lucky,"—literally into Hebrew, it may make no sense to those who are not familiar with the American lottery system.

The following verse was quoted earlier but is relevant to this discussion again:

> *He it is Who has revealed the Book to you; some of its verses are decisive, they are the basis [foundation] of the Book, and others are allegorical; then as for those in whose hearts there is perversity they follow the part of it which is allegorical, seeking to mislead and seeking to give it (their own) interpretation. But none knows its interpretation except God, and those who are firmly rooted in knowledge say: we believe in it, it is all from our Lord; and none do mind except those having understanding.* 3:7 (Shakir)

The first person to translate part of the Qur'an was Salman Farsi, a noble companion of Muhammad from Persia, who translated *Surah al-Fatiha* (the opening chapter) into Persian during the seventh century. The first translation of the Qur'an is believed to have been done in 884 in Sind (part of India at the time, now a part of Pakistan), by the orders of Abdullah bin Umar bin Abdul Aziz, at the request of the Hindu Raja, Mehruk. Robertus Ketenensis produced the first Latin translation of the Qur'an in 1143; it was titled *Lex Mahumet pseudoprophete* ("The law of Muhammad, the pseudo-prophet"). As the title suggests, it was negatively biased against the Qur'an. Many of the later European translations of the Qur'an were taken from Ketenensis's work.

The first translations into English were not undertaken by Muslims but by Christians who sought to debunk Islam and aid in the conversion of Muslims to Christianity. *The Al-coran of Mohamet* (1649) by Alexander Ross was the first English translation of the Qur'an. This translation was not from Arabic but rather based on Andre Du Ryer's French rendition, containing many distortions and misinterpretations. In 1734, George Sale produced the first English translation of the Qur'an from Arabic, *The Al Koran of Mohammed*. Sale's translation was to remain the most widely available English translation over the next two hundred years, and it is still in print today, with the release of a recent 2009 edition. According to a news brief from the Library of Congress dated January 3, 2007, Keith Ellison, the first Muslim US congressman, took the oath of office on Thomas Jefferson's personal copy of Sale's 1734 translation of the Qur'an. Since George Sale, many English translations have been made available, each with its own set of strengths, weaknesses, biases, and varying level of scholarly research. The first Muslim to translate the Qur'an into English is said to be Dr. Mirza Fazl in 1910 in India; he arranged an English translation and the Arabic text side by side.

Ponder, Reflect, and Contemplate

Contrary to the popular belief, many scientists are and have been deeply affected by religion in their pursuit of the truth in science. Many have cited religion as the basis for their interest in science, and conversely the study of science has made them reflect deeper. For example, according to the famous physicist and Nobel Prize winner, Albert Einstein (1879–1955), "Science without religion is lame. Religion without science is blind."

Sir Isaac Newton (1643–1727), a famous English physicist, mathematician, astronomer, and theologian, was inspired by his religious faith and was an ardent Bible reader; he sought to understand its deeper meaning, especially as it relates to science. He said, "It is the perfection of God's works that they are all done with the greatest simplicity. He is the God of order and not of confusion." He went on to say, "God created everything by number, weight, and measure."

Numerous Muslim scholars and scientists during the Islamic golden age (seventh to thirteenth century), like Jabir Ibn Hayyan (721–815, considered the father of chemistry), Ibn Sina (Avicenna, 980–1037, regarded as the most famous and influential Islamic polymath), and Ibn Al-Haytham (965–1040, considered father of optics and a pioneer of scientific methods), credited the Qur'an as the source of their inspiration to understand and explore nature, and many of them were deeply influenced by religion and their faith in God.

The Qur'an repeatedly draws the attention to "nature" and invites the reader to contemplate and think deeply.

> *Do you not see that Allah is He, Whom obeys whoever is in the heavens and whoever is in the earth, and the sun and the moon and the stars, and the mountains and the trees, and the animals and many of the people.* 22:18

The verse challenges the reader to ponder and reflect: *Do you not see?* It is a key concept in the Qur'an, not just for the matters related to astronomy but in all issues related to nature or otherwise.

> *Most surely in the creation of the heavens and the earth and the alternation of the night and the day there are signs for men who understand. Those who remember Allah standing and sitting and lying on their sides and reflect on the creation of the heavens and the earth: Our Lord! You have not created this in vain.* 3:190–191 (Shakir)

In the following five verses, the Qur'an emphasizes and reminds everyone that it is God who makes things happen in "nature" and informs the believers that in nature there are His signs for people of knowledge and for those who ponder and reflect:

> *Surely Allah causes the grain and the stone to germinate; He brings forth the living from the dead and He is the bringer forth of the dead from the living; that is Allah! How are you then turned away?*

He causes the dawn to break; and He has made the night for rest, and the sun and the moon for reckoning; this is an arrangement of the Mighty, the Knowing.

And He it is Who has made the stars for you that you might follow the right way thereby in the darkness of the land and the sea; truly We have made plain the communications for a people who know.

And He it is Who has brought you into being from a single soul, then there is (for you) a resting-place and a depository; indeed We have made plain the communications for a people who understand.

And He it is Who sends down water from the cloud, then We bring forth with it buds of all (plants), then We bring forth from it green (foliage) from which We produce grain piled up (in the ear); and of the palm-tree, of the sheaths of it, come forth clusters (of dates) within reach, and gardens of grapes and olives and pomegranates, alike and unlike; behold the fruit of it when it yields the fruit and the ripening of it; most surely there are signs in this for a people who believe. 6:95-99 (Shakir)

In yet another series of verses, the Qur'an spells out some of His signs and invites the readers to reflect upon creation, human relationships, diversity, and the sleep cycle [*Surah Rum* or "Rome"]:

And one of His signs is that He created mates for you from yourselves that you may find rest in them, and He put between you love and compassion; most surely there are signs in this for a people who reflect. 30:21 (Shakir)

OUR DIVERSITY AS A SIGN OF GOD:
The Qur'an invites us to not only ponder the creation of the universe but also encourages us to cherish the diversity of our colors (of the skin) and languages. In other words our diversity is to be celebrated as a sign of a common creator, rather than be used as as an excuse to discriminate, divide or dehumanize each other based on these traits.

And one of His signs is the creation of the heavens and the earth and the diversity of your tongues and colors; most surely there are signs in this for the learned.

And one of His signs is your sleeping and your seeking of His grace by night and (by) day; most surely there are signs in this for a people who would hear. 30:22-23 (Shakir)

Discussion Points for Dialogue and Healing

- The Qur'an was revealed to Muhammad over a period of twenty-three years.
- Muslims believe that Muhammad himself ordered the placement of various chapters and verses and organized the Qur'an in its current form. Oral and written accounts existed in the Prophet's life, and the Qur'an as we see it today was available during the last few months of his life.
- Only the Qur'an in Arabic is considered "the" Qur'an. All other translations are considered interpretations, since it is impossible to precisely translate the Arabic version into any other language.
- Muslims believe that the Qur'an is the literal word of God. The current Qur'an is unaltered and uncorrupted from its original revelation to Muhammad.
- The Bible is not one scripture. It consists of several scriptures. The Hebrew Bible corresponds to the Old Testament in the Christian Bible, which also includes the New Testament, containing the four Gospels and other writings of early Christians. The Torah is part of the Hebrew Bible and consists of five books: Genesis, Exodus, Numbers, Leviticus, and Deuteronomy.
- Jews and Christians believe in the divine source of their scriptures, the Torah and New Testament.
- Though we may have questions about the authenticity and accuracy given the way they were collected, it is very important to remember that the Qur'an, Torah, and the Gospels hold a special place for their perspective followers. Therefore the conversations around the scriptures should be held with utmost respect and sensitivity for each others' feelings.
- The Qur'anic scripts gathered in the days of the first caliph (Abu Bakr) and the third caliph (Uthman) were undertaken in an

attempt to preserve the Qur'an in its original form, and Muslims believe the version available today is the same as the one at the end of Muhammad's life. Secular scholars generally agree with the traditional view but believe that in addition to the Uthmanic script, there were other versions, available as late as 800 C.E.

- The Torah existed in the oral form for 500 to 1,000 years, before attempts were made to capture it in textual form to preserve the divine message. The initial writings of the New Testament were not gathered until about fifty to seventy-five years after Christ and were not authenticated (in a process called canonization) until at least the end of the fourth century.
- The Qur'an refers to itself many times as "Al-Qur'an." The Torah (*Tawrat*) and the Gospel (*Injeel*) are mentioned by name in the Qur'an repeatedly. Muslims believe in the divine nature of these scriptures.
- Feel free to ponder on the points noted below and add your own.

Time to Ponder

- After the Torah was revealed, why was another major scripture (the Gospel) needed? Similarly, after the Torah and the Gospels were revealed, was another scripture (the Qur'an) needed, and if so, why?
- Why is the Qur'an not arranged in a topical or chronological order? Would it have made a difference if it were? Whereas mere mortals can write books in a well-organized, topical, or chronological order, why did God (or Muhammad, *if* one believes he wrote the book) choose not to arrange it that way?
- Why does the Qur'an repeatedly refer to the authenticity of the Qur'an (whereas the prior scriptures didn't)?

Part One
GOD

CHAPTER 1
Allah = God

Indeed we shall find a striking similarity in Jewish,
Christian, and Muslim ideas of the divine.
Karen Armstrong

"Allah" is the Arabic word for "God." "Allah" is derived from two words: *Al* (the) and *Ilah* (deity), meaning "the deity" or simply, "God." Thus even though many people, including Muslims, may believe it is a proper name for God in Arabic, it literally means "the God," or "the only God." The etymological origins of "Allah" are also found in other languages and appear in the Hebrew Bible (*Elohim*) and the Aramaic Bible (*Elaha*). Most English translations of the Bible have translated *Elohim* as God. Some in the West believe that Allah in the Qur'an is different than the God of the Bible. However, a close analysis of the Qur'an and the Bible and an examination of various cultural practices would argue against such a belief. According to *Columbia Encyclopedia*, Arabic speakers of all Abrahamic faiths, including Christians and Jews, use the word "Allah" to mean "God." These include Mizrahi Jews, Eastern Orthodox Christians, and Eastern Catholic Christians. Many others share this view.[1] Whereas many communities in the biblical and Qur'anic stories took on many deities as their god/s, the Qur'an and the Bible emphasize, over and over, that there is no god but God (the singular deity). Allah was also used in pre-Qur'anic Mecca by pagans as a deity, but one who had associates and was not considered the sole divine power. This polytheistic view was thoroughly rejected by Muhammad and the Qur'an. Muslims believe that the Qur'an is the final word from Allah, who is the Lord of the Worlds, the Creator of the universe, All-Knowing, All-Powerful, All-Compassionate, and All-Merciful—the attributes shared by both the Qur'an and the Bible in reference to God.

Arabic translations of the Bible use *Allah* as the translation for the Hebrew *Elohim*. Thus "God," "Allah," and "Elohim" refer to the same deity.

Elohim is derived from *Eloah* (singular form), which is an expanded form of the Northwest Semitic noun *el*. It refers to the one God of Israel. The word *elohim* (with a lowercase *e*), on the other hand, is generally used in the Hebrew Bible to indicate plural pagan gods. *Elohim* is the first name for God used in the Torah: "In the beginning, God (Elohim) created heavens and the earth" (Genesis 1:1). According to Jewish scholars, Elohim is the name given to God, the Creator, and generally implies power and justice. There is some argument that the similarities of the words Allah, Elah and Elohim do not necessarily mean that these words refer to the same deity.

Another divine name used in the Hebrew Bible is *Yahweh*, a proper name for the God of Israel. It is derived from a Hebrew word that's transcribed into Roman letters as YHVH. It is the most frequently used name of God in *Tanakh*, the Jewish Bible consisting of the Torah (teaching, or law), Nevi'im (Prophets), and Ketuvim (Writings). YHVH is considered to be an unutterable name of the God of Israel and is often referred to as "tetragrammation" ("the four letters") since it's derived from four Hebrew letters: *Yod, Hay, Vav,* and *Hay*. The name YHVH implies God's mercy and one explanation of its meaning in Jewish tradition is "He Who Causes 'That Which Is' to Be." The Bible describes Yahweh as the one true God who delivered Israel from Egypt and gave the Ten Commandments. Yahweh is also translated as Jehovah in English.

> *I (am) Jehovah thy God, who hath brought thee out of the land of Egypt, out of a house of servants.* Exodus 20:2 (Darby translation)

According to biblical accounts, God appeared to Moses and Abraham with different names, but it did not change the fact that He is the same God, regardless of what name He was called.

*And God said to Moses. 'I am **Yahweh**—The Lord, I appeared to Abraham, Isaac, and Jacob as **El-Shaddai**, God Almighty, but I did not reveal my name Yahweh to them. And I reaffirmed my covenant with them.' Exodus 6:2–3*

(*El-Shaddai* is often used in the Torah and means "God, the Almighty.")

Allah, or God, is mentioned by various other attributes in the Qur'an, such as *Al-Rahman* (The Most Compassionate), *Al-Rahim* (The Most Merciful), *Al-Khaliq* (The Creator), and *Al-Nur* (The Light), among many other attributes. It is said that Allah has ninety-nine "names" in the Qur'an, although this actually refers to some of the qualities or attributes of God. Reading the attributes alone, one can conclude that the God in the Bible and the Qur'an have many of the same attributes.[2]

Indeed, Allah is the most often-repeated word used for God in the Qur'an. The following translators of the Qur'an have used the Arabic word Allah when translating the Qur'an into English, perhaps believing there is no corresponding word in English: Pickthall, Abdullah Yousuf Ali, Farooq-i-Azam Malik, Fakhry, Shakir, and Muhammad Ali.

Many other translators, especially in the modern times, have used the word "God" in translations for Allah. These include Asad, Yuksel, Pooya Yazdi, Al Ghazali, Emerick, Haleem, Sells, and Ali Unal.

The following verse is an example of the translations by the first group mentioned above:

And your Allah is One Allah. There is no god but He, Most Gracious, Most Merciful. 2:163

If Allah is indeed a proper name, this translation does not seem very clear. However, if we take Allah as the Arabic word (and not a proper name) for God, here is how the same verse would be translated, with a much more clear message.

And your God is One God. There is no god but He, Most Gracious, Most Merciful. 2:163

Therefore, when a verse is translated as "there is no god but Allah," it does not imply that "there is no god except the Arabic, or the Qur'anic, Allah." It simply means that "there is no god but God"—a more appropriate translation.

Many passages in both the Qur'an and the Bible refer to the same historical events like the creation of Adam, the floods in Noah's era, Abraham's sons Ishmael and Isaac, Moses and the Israelites and so on. This would once again indicate that the Allah mentioned in the Qur'an and the God (or Yahweh) in the Bible are the same deity.

For these reasons, I am in agreement with the latter group of translators mentioned above, who have translated "Allah" to mean "God." And since Allah and God refer to the same deity, the words "Allah" and "God" in this book are used interchangeably.

LORD, RABB, AND ADONAI

Another word used in the Qur'an for God is "Rabb," often translated as "Lord" or "Sustainer" in English. The word *Adonai* is used in the Hebrew Bible, usually side by side with Yahweh, and is often translated as "Lord" in English. Strictly speaking, "Adonai" is the plural possessive of *Adon*, meaning "my lord" and "my master," which became the replacement for YHWH, considered too holy to utter. Despite the linguistic origins, Adonai refers to a *singular* deity.

IS THE GOD OF THE QUR'AN THE SAME AS THE GOD OF THE BIBLE?

The doctrine of Trinity notwithstanding, the religious scholars of monotheistic faiths generally believe they worship the same God, the One who created the universe, the One who sent the prophets, the One who is eternal and will be the Master on the Day of Judgment.

Discussion Points for Dialogue and Healing

- "Allah" is the Arabic word used *for* God, the singular deity. Many modern Qur'an translators have used "God" rather than retain "Allah" in their translations.
- "Elohim" is the Hebrew word for God. "Yahweh" is a personal, unutterable name of God, though it is often translated as "God" or "Lord" in English translations of the Bible.

- Many non-Muslims, including Christians and Jews in the Arab world, use "Allah" to mean "God." The Arabic versions of the Bible translate "Elohim" as "Allah."
- The God mentioned in the Bible and the Qur'an refers to the same deity, whether using the words "Allah," "Elohim," or "Yahweh."
- Feel free to ponder on the points noted below and add your own.

Time to Ponder

- Does the Qur'an insist that we know Him as Allah only? Does calling Him "God" instead, somehow imply one is lowering His status?
- Conversely, did the English word "God" appear in the original Qur'an, Torah or the Gospels? If it did not, why do we want to refer to Him as "God" only?
- Is the "God of Muslims" different from the "God of Jews" and the "God of Christians"? If one believes such a dogma, what's the theological evidence to support it?

CHAPTER 2
The Nature of God

My concern is not whether God is on our side; my greatest concern is to be on God's side, for God is always right.
Abraham Lincoln

God's Existence

The question, "Is there a God?" has existed in the minds of people since ancient times, and humans have gone back and forth in their arguments. One of the fundamental beliefs among the monotheistic faiths, and for that matter most other religions, revolves around the existence of God, who created everything and to whom we shall all return. Most theologians and scholars of monotheistic faiths agree that God's nature is beyond finite human cognition. However, the signs of God are all around us. The Qur'an frequently invites us to ponder over the nature and the signs of God's existence. The Qur'an further argues that the reflection on creation should lead one to conclude that the universe and everything in it was created with an intelligent design by a supreme Creator, and that such creation was not fortuitous, for an accidental birth could not have resulted in such a complex yet orderly universe, in perfect harmony.

> *Verily in the heavens and the earth, are Signs for those who believe. And in the creation of yourselves and the fact that animals are scattered (through the earth), are Signs for those of assured Faith. And in the alternation of Night and Day, and the fact that Allah sends down Sustenance from the sky, and revives therewith the earth after its death, and in the change of the winds, are Signs for those that are wise. 45:3–5*

Say: 'It is He Who has created you (and made you grow), and made for you the faculties of hearing, seeing, feeling, and understanding.' 67:23

Similarly, Paul's invitation to study for signs of God in nature is apparent from this passage in the New Testament:

For since the creation of the world His invisible attributes, His eternal power and divine nature, have been clearly seen, being understood through what has been made, so that they are without excuse. Romans 1:20[1]

God Is One

The existence of God and the oneness of God are inseparable concepts, representing the most fundamental teaching of the Abrahamic scriptures. "There is no god, but God" is the first half of the Muslim's testimony (*shahada*) of faith. Anyone who associates other gods with Allah is considered a *mushrik*, a polytheist, or a pagan. It is considered a major sin. In the Qur'an, the oneness of God, or *wahdat*, is repeatedly emphasized. Some of the very basic teachings from the Qur'an about God are that there is no god but God, that there is only *one* God, that God has no partners, and that there is no one else worthy of worship.

The Qur'an further teaches that God is Omnipresent and Omnipotent. He is our Guardian, Helper, the Most Kind, the Most Merciful, the Most Loving, the Judge, the Most High, All-Knowing, the Hearer of all, the Seer of all, the Most Generous, All-Wise, the Majestic, the First, the Last, the Light, the Guide, and the Almighty. Scholars point out that these and other attributes of God are themselves a testimony to His oneness. The complex doctrine of Trinity notwithstanding, the Bible and the Qur'an are congruent on many of these key beliefs.

Your God is one God; there is no one worthy of worship except Him, the Compassionate, the Merciful. 2:163

And God has said: 'Do not take to worshipping two (or more) deities.' He is the One and Only God: hence, 'of Me, of Me alone stand in awe!' 16:51 (Asad)

Do not associate another deity with Allah, lest you sit back, condemned, forsaken. Your Lord has decreed to you that: You shall worship none but Him. 17:22–23 (Shakir)

That surely your God is One, the Lord of the heavens and of the earth and all that lies between them, and the Lord of the east (every point and place at the rising of the sun). 37:4–5

Say: He is Allah the One and Only; Allah is the Self-Sufficient (independent of all, while all are dependent on Him); He begets not, nor is He begotten; And there is none comparable to Him. 112:1–4 (Malik)

The Oneness of God in the Bible

The Ten Commandments of the Torah start with the declaration of the oneness of God and a prohibition of polytheism, once again highlighting the emphasis put on this fundamental belief:

I am the LORD your God, who brought you out of the land of Egypt, out of the house of slavery. You shall have no other gods before Me. You shall not make for yourself an idol, or any likeness of what is in heaven above or on the earth beneath or in the water under the earth. You shall not worship them or serve them. Exodus 20:2–5

I am the LORD your God who brought you out of the land of Egypt, out of the house of slavery. You shall have no other gods before Me. Deuteronomy 5:6–7

Hear, O Israel: The LORD is our God, the LORD is one. Deuteronomy 6:4

Jews recite a prayer known as *Shema* twice a day, and its words come from the Torah. It starts by the above-mentioned verse. In Hebrew the word *echad* ("one") is used to describe God's oneness. This word is strikingly close to the Arabic word *ahad*, used in the Qur'an in relations to God, meaning one.

Thus says the LORD, the King of Israel, and his Redeemer, the LORD of hosts: 'I am the first and I am the Last. And there is no God besides Me.' Isaiah 44:6

ONENESS OF GOD IN THE NEW TESTAMENT

The doctrine of trinity notwithstanding, the oneness of God was also emphasized by Jesus. When asked by "teachers of religious law" as to what was the most important commandment, quoting from Shema:

> Jesus replied, "The most important commandment is this: 'Listen, O Israel! The LORD our God is the one and only LORD.'" Mark 12:29

In Islam, there are three key duties of man to God:

1. Submitting to the will of God.

2. Seeking His pleasure. Engaging in activities with the intention to please God.

3. Remembering God (*dhikr Allah*) all the time so one doesn't move away from Him and thereby risk succumbing to the temptations and desires.

The concept of submission is at the core of Islamic beliefs. The word "Islam" means "submission" (to the will of God), and "Muslim" literally means "submitter." Islam is a way of life, rather than a religion consisting of a set of beliefs and rituals. According to this doctrine, one belongs to God and everything one does is for the purpose of pleasing, serving, and getting nearer to God, so much so that at the height of this state God's will becomes your will.

> Nay, whoever submits his whole self to Allah and is a doer of good, he will get his reward with his Lord; on such shall be no fear, nor shall they grieve. 2:112
>
> We shall surely test your steadfastness with fear and famine, with loss of property, life, and produce. Give good news to those who endure with patience; who, when afflicted with calamity, say: 'We belong to Allah and to Him we shall return.' 2:155–156 (Malik)
>
> Serve Allah, and join not any partners with Him. 4:36
>
> When Isa [Jesus] found out that they had no faith, he asked: 'Who will help me in the cause of Allah?' The Disciples replied: 'We will help

you in the cause of Allah. We believe in Allah. Be our witness that we are Muslims.' 3:52 (Malik)

Farooq-i-Azam and Yousuf Ali have translated the Arabic word *muslimun* at the end of the verse as "Muslims." Other translators have used the word *submitters*, the literal meaning of the word "Muslim." For example, Asad translates the same verse as follows:

And when Jesus became aware of their refusal to acknowledge the truth, he asked: 'Who will be my helpers in God's cause?' The white-garbed ones replied: 'We shall be (thy) helpers (in the cause) of God! We believe in God: and bear thou witness that we have surrendered (submitted) ourselves unto Him!'

REMEMBER GOD OFTEN

The Qur'an not only commands followers to submit to His will but emphasizes that God must be remembered often, and His remembrance must be part of our daily lives.

For sure, in the creation of the heavens and the earth and the alternation of the night and the day there are signs for men of understanding. **Those who remember Allah while standing, sitting, and lying on their sides,** *and meditate on the creation of the heavens and the earth, then cry out: 'Our Rabb [Lord]! You have not created this in vain. Glory to You.' 3:190–191 (Malik)*

Another verse is often cited about the remembrance of God:

Therefore, remember Me, and, I will remember you, be grateful to Me and never deny Me. 2:152 (Malik)

The Arabic word for remembrance of God is *dhikr*. This can be in the form of repeating His name, keeping His name in the heart and mind, remembering His commands (doing good deeds and avoiding bad ones), as well as elevating and glorifying His name. Many consider this verse a bargain and sign of God's mercy. This verse seeks to elevate the spirituality and love for God by remembering Him and urges us to be grateful to Him in good times and bad times. In his commentary of the verse, Pooya Yazdi writes: "To be grateful (*shukr*) is the key to the fulfillment and application of remembrance which neutralizes desires and generates joy of inner contentment—deep and peaceful. The opposite of this condition is *kufr*—the falling over hurdles on the road of disobedience."

SUBMISSION TO GOD IN THE TORAH

The concept of submission is not unique to Muslims. It is similar to the concept of *d'veykut,* meaning "clinging" in Jewish tradition. *D'veykut* means one is clinging to God with such faith and devotion that his will and God's will merge into one will. The following is a passage from the Torah (Moses is addressing his people):

> *Now, Israel, what does the LORD your God require from you, but to fear the LORD your God, to walk in all His ways and love Him, and to serve the LORD your God with all your heart and with all your soul and to keep the LORD'S commandments and His statutes which I am commanding you today for your good.* Deuteronomy 10:12–13

And in the oldest prayer in Judaism, the *Shema:*

> *Hear, O Israel! The LORD is our God, the LORD is one! You shall love the LORD your God with all your heart and with all your soul and with all your might. These words, which I am commanding you today, shall be on your heart. You shall teach them diligently to your sons and shall talk of them* **when you sit in your house and when you walk by the way and when you lie down and when you rise up.** *You shall bind them as a sign on your hand and they shall be as frontals on your forehead. You shall write them on the doorposts of your house and on your gates.* Deuteronomy 6:4–9

The similarity of Qur'an verses 3:190–191, quoted above, and Deuteronomy 6:4–9 is striking. Both command the followers to remember God in all phases: sitting, standing, and lying. In addition to submitting to Him, the constant remembrance throughout the day is meant to encourage one to do good deeds and eschew bad deeds as ordained by God.

SUBMISSION IN THE NEW TESTAMENT

Friendship with the world is discouraged, as friendship with the world makes one an enemy of God; therefore, one must submit to Him and seek nearness to Him. Even though the passage quoted below is being addressed to adulterers, it can be easily applied to everyone, adulterer or not.

> *Submit therefore to God. Resist the devil and he will flee from you. Draw near to God and He will draw near to you.* James 4:7–8

God Is Light

The Qur'an, the Hebrew Bible, and the New Testament have all embraced the concept of the light (*nur*) of God. God is characterized as light, and all the light in the universe is a reflection of His light. This light is the source of guidance, and without this light, everything will be in total darkness, or ignorance. The divine light is knowledge, from which all forms of knowledge flow. The following verse in the Qur'an points to this luminous Glory of God in a verse that Muslims and many non-Muslim Islamic scholars quote often to praise its immense poetic and literal beauty. This is from a chapter that itself is named *Al-Nur*, or "The Light":

> *God is the light of the heavens and the earth. The example of His light is like a niche wherein is a lamp: the lamp is in a crystal, and the crystal shining as if a pearl-like radiant star, lit from the oil of a blessed olive tree that is neither of the east nor of the west. The oil almost gives light of itself though no fire touches it. Light upon light. God guides to His light whom He wills. God strikes parables for people. God has full knowledge of all things.* 24:35 (Unal)

When promising future glory for Jerusalem, the book of Isaiah foretells that the brightness from God's light will shine upon Jerusalem:

No longer will you have the sun for light by day, Nor for brightness will the moon give you light; But you will have the LORD for an everlasting light. Isaiah 60:19

Similar characterization is apparent in the book of Revelation, when God gives Jesus the vision of events to come. John also shares that vision. John then reports all that he saw during his trip to heaven:

And the city has no need of the sun or of the moon to shine on it, for the glory of God has illumined it. Revelation 21:23

Discussion Points for Dialogue and Healing

- The oneness of God is fundamental to the Qur'anic teachings and forms the cornerstone of the Islamic faith. Worshipping anyone other than God is the biggest sin. The oneness of God is an essential part of the Ten Commandments in the Old and New Testaments as well.
- Trinitarian Christians believe in oneness of God too, except that according to this doctrine, God appeared in three persons: the Father, the Son, and the Holy Spirit. This view is not shared by some Christian churches, as well as by Muslims, Jews, and other non-monotheistic religions. During Christian-Muslim dialogue, an important point to remember is that the doctrine of trinity is not just a point of differentiation between Christians and Muslims but rather between (trinitarian) Christians and people of all other faiths.
- "Islam" means submission. However, the concept of submission to the will of God is shared by all three monotheistic religions. "Muslim" means submitter. However in a global sense, Jews, Christians and Muslims are "Muslims" since they all submit to one God. Please realize that not everyone would agree or appreciate this logic.
- There is consensus among the Jews, Christians and Muslims that it is beyond the cognitive capacity of humans to imagine God. "God's light" is a shared though complex concept. All the light in the uni-

verse is a reflection of His light and He is the source of guidance. Without this light, one remains in the darkness (of ignorance).

- Feel free to ponder on the points noted below and add your own.

Time to Ponder

- Does remembering God at all times mean one needs to wear religion on one's sleeve? If not, how can one remember God without ostentatious shows of public piety?
- Can one align one's will with God's will without submitting to Him? How do we know what God's will is?

CHAPTER 3
God Is Kind and Loving

Where mercy, love, and pity dwell, there God is dwelling too.
William Blake

A not uncommon misgiving that abounds is that the "God of the Qur'an" and the "God of the Torah" is always angry, full of vengeance, and that these scriptures have used fear to subjugate followers. In this chapter, I will review this claim and compare relevant attributes of God mentioned in the Qur'an and the Bible.

This misconception is not unique to non-Muslims. Some Muslim clerics dogmatically focus on God's vengeance and the Day of Judgment. Instead of describing how God will reward people for good deeds, they focus more on how He will punish them for bad deeds; they remind followers to always be on the right path, or else! Muslims often talk about the "99 names of Allah" with great reverence. Those who preach God's vengeance seem to forget that by far the most often-repeated attributes of God in the Qur'an are *al-Rahman* (the Most Compassionate) and *al-Rahim* (all chapters of the Qur'an, except chapter 9 start with the verse, *bismillah al-Rahman al-Rahim*, "In the name of God, the Most Compassionate, the Most Merciful." Various scholars have translated the word *al-Rahman* into "the Most Kind," "the Most Compassionate," "the Most Gracious," or "the Most Beneficent." As Michael Sells has noted, the root for these words of compassion and mercy is *rahm* or the "mother's womb."[1] So all but one chapter of the Qur'an begins with this powerful feminine sense of God's mercy and compassion for all his children and all of creation.It is worth pointing out here that the verses proclaim God as the Lord (Sustainer) of all the worlds and that He is the Most Kind and the Most Merciful—period. Not just for Muslims, not just for people of faith or for only humans, but for the entire universe (and everything in it). Muslims are encouraged to recite the verse "In the name of God, the Most Compassionate, the Most Merciful," whenever they begin a task—when leaving home for work, upon starting a journey, or during take-off when flying. The message is not just that Muslims are to remember God in their everyday life but to serve as a reminder that God wants them to remember Him as *the Most Kind* and *the Most Merciful*. God could have chosen many of His other attributes, for example, "In the name of God, the Almighty," or "In the name of God, the All-Knowing," or "In the name of God, the Creator," and so on. None of His attributes related to His Might and Justice are the chosen attributes for this oft-repeated verse. Here are some other names (attributes) often mentioned in the Qur'an that reflect God's kindness:

- *Al-Wadud:* The Loving One
- *Al-Ghaffar:* The Forgiving
- *Al-Ghafur:* The Forgiver and the Hider of Faults
- *Al-Karim:* The Most Generous
- *Al-Wali:* The Protecting Friend
- *Al-Afu:* The Forgiver, as in "The Eraser (of sins)"
- *Al-Rau'f:* The Clement (Lenient)/Kind
- *Al-Salam:* The Source of Peace
- *Al-Mujib:* The Responder to Prayers

It is true that the Qur'an and the Bible repeatedly warn people who do evil of the negative consequences of their actions, often in graphic details; however, these verses in the Qur'an are often followed (or preceded) by verses alluding to the reward for good deeds and His mercy and forgiveness.

The following verses serve as a very small sample alluding to the love, kindness, and mercy of God:

> *And He is the Oft-Forgiving, Full of Loving-Kindness.* 85:14
> *And there is the type of man who gives his life to earn the pleasure of Allah. And Allah is full of kindness to (His) devotees.* 2:207

Our Lord! You are indeed full of Kindness, Most Merciful. 59:10

What is the matter with you, that you place not your hope for kindness and long-suffering in Allah? 71:13 [Noah asking his people to seek forgiveness from God and warning them of the great flood.]

But ask forgiveness of your Lord, and turn unto Him (in repentance): For my Lord is indeed full of mercy and loving-kindness. 11:90

The concept of accountability is pervasive in the Islamic doctrine. The Qur'an indicates that everyone is responsible for their actions—good and bad—and will have to answer to God on the Day of Judgment. However, most Muslims also believe that individuals will enter heaven on account of God's mercy, and not merely on their good deeds—a belief often shared by Christians and Jews.

The Kind and Loving God in the Bible

The Old Testament too has been a target of the same type of criticism: "The God of the Old Testament is harsh and full of vengeance, and the God of New Testament is loving and kind." Once again, reading the scripture, it becomes clear that the God of these scriptures indeed has the same attributes, for He is the same God. These few quotes cannot do justice to the immense subject of God's love and do not substitute a complete review of the texts:

Nevertheless in Your great Mercy, You did not utterly consume them nor forsake them; For You are God, Gracious and Merciful. Nehemiah 9:31

How precious is Your loving Kindness, O God! Therefore the children of men put their trust under the shadow of Your wings. Psalm 36:7

I will mention the loving kindnesses of the LORD And the praises of the LORD, According to all that the LORD has bestowed on us, And the great goodness toward the house of Israel, Which He has bestowed on them according to His Mercies, according to the multitude of His loving kindnesses. Isaiah 63:7

And we have known and believed the love that God has for us. God is love, and he who abides in love abides in God, and God in him. 1 John 4:16

> *Don't tear your clothing in your grief, but tear your hearts instead. Return to the LORD YOUR GOD, for He is Merciful and Compassionate, slow to get angry and filled with unfailing love. He is eager to relent and not punish.* Joel 2:13

Should We "Fear" God?

Perhaps one of the reasons to believe that God should be "feared" is the word *Taqwa*, which is often translated as "to fear God." The person who practices *Taqwa* is known as *Muttaqi*, often translated as "God fearing." However, many others have more appropriately translated it as "God-conscious," "pious," "righteous," or "in awe of God." A similar parable is perhaps found in Hebrew. "The Hebrew word *Yir'at HaShem* is sometimes translated as 'fear of God' but is better understood as 'in awe of God.'"[2]

In some ways, "fearing God" is similar to a loving parent-child relationship, whereby children do not want to do anything against the wishes of their parents, not because they are afraid of their parents, but out of love and respect for them. This is indeed the essence of the teachings of the scriptures. As we get to know God, we will then get close to Him, worship Him out of love, and be in awe of Him, not because of fear of Him or a fear of going to hell. For the ones "in awe of God," fear of hell is replaced by fear of disobeying Him, a fear of making Him unhappy. In fact in Jewish traditions, hell is despised since that means one will be not in the company of God, as the ultimate goal is to seek nearness to God.

Discussion Points for Dialogue and Healing

- The most frequent attributes of God mentioned in the Qur'an are *al-Rahman* and *al-Rahim*, meaning "the Most Kind" and "the Most Merciful."
- The Old Testament often refers to God's wrath (against wrongdoers for abominable acts) but also declares His mercy for the righteous. The Gospel repeatedly proclaims God's mercy and forgiveness. The teachings of Jesus Christ center on God's love, kindness, and forgiveness.

- As we will note in the next chapter, humans were created as vicegerents (*khalifa*) of God and in the image of God, and are therefore His representative on this planet. Thus, we should therefore strive to show kindness and mercy to each other.
- Feel free to ponder on the points noted below and add your own.

Time to Ponder

- If one believes that God is going to judge people based on their deeds alone, how is His mercy and kindness going to play out?
- Conversely, how is His clemency and kindness going to help if people continue to disobey His laws, without repentance, or if they reject His signs? If He forgives everyone out of His mercy, who will be the subjects of His judgment?

CHAPTER 4

God, the Creator

God will never reject you. Whether you accept Him is your decision.
Charles Stanley

Both the Qur'an and the Bible have put tremendous emphasis on God as the Creator of the universe—a belief central to the monotheistic faiths. According to the Qur'an and the Bible, He existed before any thing existed or was created. Moreover, He is eternal, whereas everyone else and everything else is mortal. Thus, He is the First (*al-Awwal*) and the Last (*al-Akhir*). The Qur'an asserts that God created the heavens and the earth and everything in between in perfect balance, proportion, and harmony. Every creation has a design and a plan, and each creation has a fixed term of existence. This chapter will review some of the verses in the Qur'an and the Bible on the subject of creation and its various aspects.

GOD, THE CREATOR OF EVERYTHING

God is the Creator of everything living and non-living; some can be seen and perceived by our special senses, others cannot.

> *Allah is Creator of all things, and He is the Guardian and Disposer of all affairs.* 39:62
> *Glory to Allah, Who created in pairs all things that the earth produces, as well as their own (human) kind and (other) things of which they have no knowledge.* 36:36

All praise is due to Allah, Who created the heavens and the earth and made the darkness and the light; yet those who disbelieve set up equals with their Lord. 6:1 (Shakir)

Where Does God "Live"?

Where is God's throne? In what part of the universe is heaven located? To be perfectly honest, no one knows the real answer.

People of the Abrahamic faiths believe God existed before the universe was created, therefore He must have been *outside* of the universe we know. So is there a universe outside of the universe we know? God is also omnipresent. The Qur'an addresses that by stating that God is nearer to us than our jugular vein: *And certainly We created man, and We know what his mind suggests to him, and We are nearer to him than his life-vein. 50:16 (Shakir)*, and He is with us all the time: *He is with you wherever you are; and Allah sees what you do. 57:4 (Shakir).* The metaphoric reference "so far away yet so near" seems applicable in this regard. It must be pointed out that trying to define where God lives as if He were a "person" is a fallacy, since all religious scholars concur that His nature is beyond the human imagination.

God creates with ease; the "Be verses"

As complex and, at times, incomprehensible the universe around us seems, the Qur'an states that not only has God created everything but also that the creation of the universe was very easy for Him:

> *Rather, to Him belongs all that is in the heavens and in the earth; all are obedient to Him. He is the Creator of the heavens and the earth! When He decrees a thing, He needs only to say, 'Be,' and there it becomes. 2:116–117 (Malik)*
>
> *Verily, when He intends a thing, His Command is, 'Be,' and it is! 36:82*
>
> *She said: My Lord! when shall there be a son (born) to me, and man has not touched me? He said: Even so, Allah creates what He pleases; when He has decreed a matter, He only says to it, 'Be,' and it is. 3:47* [This verse is about the Virgin Mary when the Angel Gabriel gave her the news that she will have a son named Jesus.]

However easy it is for God to create, it does not imply that the process of creation does not follow certain rules. According to the Qur'an, the process of creation is set in motion by the divine orders, and every living and nonliving creation then follows His commands to behave in a certain fashion (laws of science). Nothing in nature is without logic; the laws of physics, chemistry, and biology are set forth by divine orders. In other words, God's act of creation does not negate the laws of science but merely indicates that these laws were not spontaneous but were rather established by the Creator Himself.

God Created the Earth for Mankind's Benefit

According to the Qur'an, God is especially merciful to mankind, and everything on the earth was created for the benefit of man. He has made all that is between the heavens and the earth for man's service and made them subservient. This includes animals as well as what's "in the earth."

> *How can you deny Allah? Did He not give you life when you were lifeless; and will He not cause you to die and again bring you to life; and will you not ultimately return to Him?* **It is He Who has created for you all that there is in the earth.** *2:28–29 (Malik)*

As noted earlier, some portions of the verses are bolded in this book for emphasis. The bold fonts are not part of the original translation.

> *Do you not see that Allah has made subservient to you whatsoever is in the earth and the ships running in the sea by His command? And He withholds heaven from falling on the earth except with His permission; most surely Allah is Compassionate, Merciful to men.* 22:65 (Shakir)
>
> *Do you not see that Allah has made what is in the heavens and what is in the earth subservient to you, and made complete to you His favors outwardly and inwardly?* 31:20 (Shakir)
>
> *And surely We have honored the children of Adam, and We carry them in the land and the sea, and We have given them of the good things, and We have made them to excel by an appropriate excellence over most of those whom We have created.* 17:70 (Shakir)

God, the Creator, in the Bible

In contrast to the Qur'an, the Old Testament gives a detailed account of the creation in one long sequence in chapters 1 and 2 of Genesis. The very first verse of the first chapter of the first book of the Bible speaks about the creation of heavens and the earth, underlining that the belief in God, as the Creator of the universe, is of utmost importance.

> *In the beginning God created the heavens and the earth.* Genesis 1:1

And it goes on to describe the creation in more detail, explaining that God created celestial bodies, animals, and plants in successive days, interpreted by many Bible scholars as stages, though some argue that the sequence mentioned in Genesis is not consistent with current scientific knowledge regarding the creation of the solar system, as they point out that the sun ("the light") was formed before the planet earth. The passages start with the creation of earth first, which may be why the early Christian churches believed in a geocentric view of our solar system until Copernicus and Galileo's description of the heliocentric solar system.

> *The earth was formless and void, and darkness was over the surface of the deep, and the Spirit of God was moving over the surface of the waters. Then God said, 'Let there be light'; and there was light. God saw that the light was good; and God separated the light from the darkness.* Genesis 1:2–4

In the next day, or stage, the oceans on earth and then the vegetation were produced. The next phase of creation was described:

> *Then God said, 'Let there be lights in the expanse of the heavens to separate the day from the night, and let them be for signs and for seasons and for days and years; and let them be for lights in the expanse of the heavens to give light on the earth'; and it was so. God made the two great lights, the greater light to govern the day, and the lesser light to govern the night; He made the stars also. God placed them*

in the expanse of the heavens to give light on the earth, and to govern the day and the night, and to separate the light from the darkness; and God saw that it was good. Genesis 1:14–18

Man's creation is mentioned later in the same chapter:

God created man in His own image, in the image of God He created him; male and female He created them. Genesis 1:27

What's in and on earth is made for the benefit of man. Plants were created for the benefit of mankind. Compare this with some of the verses from the Qur'an, quoted in the preceding segment.

Then God said, 'Behold, I have given you every plant yielding seed that is on the surface of all the earth, and every tree which has fruit yielding seed; it shall be food for you.' Genesis 1:29

ALL CREATIONS PRAISE AND PROSTRATE TO GOD

According to the Bible and the Qur'an, humans are not the only creation praising and worshipping God. All creations, living or nonliving, worship and praise God but in their own unique ways.

The Old Testament's Account (the Biblical Version of the "Be Verse")

Though not as explicit as the "Be verses" in the Qur'an, the Bible also proclaims that God created the heavens and the earth with ease with a simple command.

Praise Him, all the angels. Praise Him, all the armies of the heavens! Praise Him, sun and moon! Praise Him, all you twinkling stars! Praise Him, skies above! Praise Him, vapors above the clouds! Let created thing give praise to the Lord, for He issued his command and they came into being. Psalm 148:2–5 (NLT)

The Qur'an's View

> *To Allah prostrate all the creatures of the heavens and the earth, including the angels; and they are not arrogant.* 16:49 (Malik)
>
> *Whatever is in the heavens and the earth do prostrate before Allah alone willingly or unwillingly, and so do their shadows in the mornings and evenings.* 13:15 (Malik)

This prostration is not necessarily physical, like humans do. The prostration is described as submitting to, or obeying, the laws God has set forth. A related concept mentioned many times in the Qur'an is that all creatures glorify God but in their own unique ways:

> *The seven heavens, the earth and all beings therein declare His glory. There is not a single thing but glorifies Him with His praise, but you do not understand their hymns of His glory. The fact is that He is very Forbearing, Forgiving.* 17:44 (Malik)
>
> *Do you not see that everything in the heavens and the earth glorify Allah, including the birds in flight? He knows the prayer of each one and its glorification, and Allah is Cognizant of what they do.* 24:41 (Shakir)

The Purpose of Human Life

Why are we here? Why were we created? These questions often arise within pondering minds. The answer from the evolutionary perspective is rather simple: we fortuitously evolved into human form; therefore, there cannot be a defined purpose of our existence.

The Qur'an and the Bible are very clear as to where we came from and where we are going—we came from God and to Him we shall return. A detailed discussion of the purpose of life is beyond the scope of this book, but it would be prudent to mention that the Qur'an spells out three primary purposes of human creation in various places:

> *I created the jinn and humankind only that they might worship Me.* 51:56 (Pickthall)

(The *jinns* or genies are often mentioned the Qur'an as one of the three sentient creations of God: angels, jinns, and humans. The jinns are made from smokeless fire. Both the jinns and the humans have free will, whereas angels do not.)

However, in the next verse, the Qur'an goes on to clarify that God is free of all *need,* implying that to worship Him is in the human's own interest:

> *I do not desire from them any sustenance and I do not desire that they should feed Me.* 51:57 (Shakir)

To act as His viceroy or vicegerent: *Behold, your Lord said to the angels: 'I will create a vicegerent on earth.'* 2:30

This role makes humans responsible to represent God and His attributes, including compassion, mercy, and justice.

To test and try:

> *He Who created death and life, that He may try which of you is best in deed: and He is the Exalted in Might, Oft-Forgiving.* 67:2 (Shakir)
> *Verily We created Man from a drop of mingled sperm, in order to try him: So We gave him (the gifts), of Hearing and Sight. Surely We have shown him the way: he may be thankful or unthankful.* 76:2–3

Mankind is given the knowledge, the intellect, and all other necessary faculties to know God and the power to self-control, and yet have the free will to choose the right way or the wrong way. Only after giving them the knowledge, the guidance, and the faculties to make the right choices, will He judge mankind.

The Hebrew Bible on the Purpose of Life

Though not mentioned explicitly in the Bible as the reasons for the creation of mankind, the concepts of worship, submission, and trial are fundamentally no different in Jewish and Christian traditions, maintaining that God puts men through various tests and trials for our own benefit though we may often not see it that way. The subject of submission to God was also discussed in chapter 2. The Hebrew Bible does not directly talk about man being God's viceroy. However, the book Genesis declares man's creation was in God's image:

> *Then God said, 'Let Us make man in Our image, according to Our likeness; and let them rule over the fish of the sea and over the birds of the sky and over the cattle and over all the earth, and over every creeping thing that creeps on the earth.' God created man in His own image, in the image of God He created him; male and female He created them.* Genesis 1:26–27

However, one should not stretch the likeness to God and "created in His image" too far, to mean that men are "like God," as is explained elsewhere in the Bible:

> *Remember the former things long past, For I am God, and there is no other; I am God, and there is no one like Me.* Isaiah 46:9
> *That there is no one like Me in all the earth.* Exodus 9:14

Discussion Points for Dialogue and Healing

- Jews, Christians, and Muslims agree that God is the Creator of everything. They further agree that God existed before anything existed. He will exist after everything ceases to exist (the *Awwal* and the *Akhir*—or the First and the Last, the Eternal). The creation is an ongoing process, according to the Qur'an. God created everything with a designed plan, reflecting His tremendous wisdom.
- Even though Jews, Christians, and Muslims often refer to God as "He" or "Him," it is widely understood that this is not a reference to God's masculinity and that God's nature is beyond human cognition.
- According to the Qur'an, the purpose of the creation of humans is to act as God's viceroy and to worship Him. Additionally, God created humans to be tested and tried. Since we were created as vicegerents (*khalifa*) of God and in the image of God, we are therefore His representatives on this planet. This will be a good reminder that we should

therefore show kindness, forgiveness and mercy to each other.

- Both the Qur'an and the Bible make mention of humans as not the only creatures who worship and praise God. Other creations do too, but in their own unique way, and they follow the laws of God.
- Feel free to ponder on the points noted below and add your own.

Time to Ponder

- Did we evolve or were we created? The scriptures unanimously and very clearly state that Adam was created and humans are descendants of Adam. Are the creation doctrine and evolution theories mutually exclusive? Is evolution part of God's intelligent design in creation?

CHAPTER 5

Praise the Lord

Coincidence is God's way of remaining anonymous.
Albert Einstein

A central theme of the Qur'an and the Bible is that all praise belongs to God, the Lord of the heavens and the earth. Submission to God, glorifying and praising Him, goes hand in hand. One cannot submit to God without glorifying Him. Conversely, one cannot glorify the Lord without fully submitting to Him. He alone is deserving of all the praise and the worship. As mentioned at the end of the last chapter, *all* creations of God praise and glorify Him, in one form or another.

The very first chapter of the Qur'an, named *Al-Fatiha,* or "The Opening," is considered by the Muslims to be the heart and soul of the Qur'an. It has been called "the Mother of the Book," its essence and its foundation. It is recited in all five daily, mandatory prayers, seventeen times a day.

> *In the name of Allah, the Compassionate, the Merciful.*
> *All praise is for Allah, the Lord of all worlds.*
> *The Compassionate, the Merciful.*
> *Master of the Day of Judgment.*
> *You alone we worship and You alone we call on for help.*
> *Guide us to the right way.*
> *The way of those whom You have favored;*
> *not of those who have earned Your wrath,*
> *or of those who have lost the way.* 1:1–7

Many commentators have written chapter after chapter on the exegesis of this Surah. Some key elements of the Surah are pointed out here by examining the sequence of verses alone, in a rather simplistic manner. The sequence is perhaps an indication how the Lord wants to be remembered. *In the name of God, the Compassionate, the Merciful* is followed by the declaration *All praise is for God, the Lord of all worlds.* He is the Lord of the worlds (plural) because God created everything and thus existed before everything. The word "Lord" does not truly translate the essence of the Arabic word *Rabb* used here, which signifies the sustainer, someone who is the supreme caretaker. The verse calls for the *Rabb* to be the sustainer for all the worlds and not just the *Rabb* of the Muslims or the people of faith. He oversees and takes responsibility to take care of everything and everyone in all the worlds, and He provides sustenance and bounties for everyone (and everything), regardless of their faith in Him (or lack of it). This is followed by what may explain the prior verse further: *The Compassionate, the Merciful,* indicating He is the sustainer for all regardless of their beliefs *because* He is their Creator and the Most Compassionate and the Most Merciful. He then reminds us that He will be the *Master of the Day of Judgment.* Everything will perish, and just as He existed before anything was created, He will exist after everything vanishes. His Compassion and Mercy are mentioned *before* the Day of Judgment. This is then followed by a fundamental commandment: *You alone we worship and You alone we call on for help.*

The Qur'an is very clear on its displeasure and prohibition of seeking help from or worshipping idols, other deities, or people besides God. This is a key concept of monotheism. Also note that worshippers address God in this verse by "You" and not in the third person, "God" or "Lord," putting worshippers in direct, one-on-one communication with God after affirming their faith in Him. A prayer then follows: *Guide us to the right way.* This puts in perspective asking Him for help in the previous verse. Seeking His help is not for worldly matters (a beautiful house, a beautiful spouse, job, money, etc.) but to be guided to the right path, as ordained by and leading to Him. It then goes on to further describe what the right path is: *The way of those whom You have favored (or bestowed grace); not of those who have earned Your wrath, or of those who have lost the way.*

Many Muslim scholars believe that the opening chapter is the prayer of the worshipper and the rest of the entire Qur'an is an answer to that prayer. Right after the end of this short Surah, which ends in a prayer "guide us to the right path," chapter 2 (*Surah al-Baqarah*) opens with this declaration:

> *This is the scripture whereof there is no doubt,* **a guidance** *unto those who ward off (evil).* 2:1–2 (Pickthall)

Also translated by Yahiya Emerick as follows: *This is the Book, in which there is no doubt. It is* **a guide** *to those who are mindful (of their duty to God).*

Many other verses in the Qur'an refer to God being the only one worthy of all praise:

> *Those who believe, and work righteousness, their Lord will guide them because of their faith: beneath them will flow rivers in gardens of bliss. (This will be) their cry therein: 'Glory to You, O Allah.' And 'Peace' will be their greeting therein! And the close of their cry (prayer) will be:* **'Praise be to Allah, the Lord of the worlds!'** 10:9–10

The Qur'an makes numerous references to the prayers of many prophets praising the Lord.

ABRAHAM PRAISING GOD

> *'All praise is due to God, who has bestowed upon me, in my old age, Ishmael and Isaac! Behold, my Sustainer hears indeed all prayer.'* 14:39 (Asad)
>
> *And say: 'All praise is due to God, who begets no offspring, and has no partner in His dominion, and has no weakness, and therefore no need of any aid and (thus) extol His limitless greatness.'* 17:111 (Asad)

NOAH PRAISING GOD

> *Then when you have embarked on the ark with your companions, say: 'Praise be to Allah Who has delivered us from the nation of wrongdoers.'* 23:28 (Malik)

MOSES PRAISING GOD

> *And Moses said: 'If you show ingratitude, you and all on earth togeth-er, yet is Allah free of all wants, worthy of all praise.'* 14:8

DAVID AND SOLOMON PRAISING GOD

> *We gave (in the past) knowledge to David and Solomon: And they both said: 'Praise be to Allah, Who has favored us above many of his servants who believe!'* 27:15

Praise the Lord in the Hebrew Bible

You alone we worship in the Bible:

> *He alone is your God, the only One who is worthy of your praise, the One who has done these mighty miracles that you have seen with your own eyes.* Deuteronomy 10:21

Praising the Lord is a central theme emphasized frequently in various books of the Bible. All the prophets have been given the commands to praise Him and taught how to praise Him. Subservience to God, praising and glorifying Him, forms the essence of the biblical teachings about God:

> *'Praise the Lord,' Jethro said, 'for he has rescued you from the Egyptians and from Pharaoh.'* Exodus 18:10
> *When you have eaten your fill, be sure to praise the Lord your God for the good land he has given you.* Deuteronomy 8:10
> *David replied to Abigail, 'Praise the Lord, the God of Israel, who has sent you to meet me today!'* 1 Samuel 25:3

The Lord's Prayer

Considered a basic prayer among Christians, the Lord's Prayer is memo-rized by heart by many; Jesus taught it to his disciples. It is derived from the two passages from the New Testament: Matthew 6:9–13 and Luke 11:2–4. Compare it side by side with *Surah al-Fatiha*, quoted at the beginning of this chapter, to appreciate resemblance of the two prayers considered central to Christianity and Islam:

Our Father in Heaven,
Hallowed be your name.
Your Kingdom come,
Your will be done,
on earth as in heaven.
Give us today our daily bread.
Forgive us our sins,
as we forgive those who sin against us.
Lead us not into temptation,
but deliver us from evil.
For the kingdom, the power, and the glory are yours.
Now and forever. Amen.

Discussion Points for Dialogue and Healing

- Praising the Lord is an essential part of prayer for Jews, Christians and Muslims alike. Most prayers start with "praise the Lord." All prophets used the same phrase to honor God. Praising the Lord and worshipping Him go hand in hand.
- The opening chapter in the Qur'an, called *Surah Al-Fatiha*, or "The Opening," is in the form of a prayer. Some view the rest of the Qur'an as the guidance or the answer to that prayer of the worshipers. It bears resemblance to the Lord's Prayer. It will be prudent to compare them side by side during Christian-Muslim dialogue.
- Feel free to ponder on the points noted below and add your own.

Time to Ponder

- Can we worship God without praising Him? Can we praise Him without worshipping Him?
- Can we praise holy figures without worshipping them? Where do we draw the line between praising the prophets, apostles, and other holy figures, and worshipping them? What differentiates the two acts?
- If Jews, Christians, and Muslims praise and worship the same God, why can't we do this together?

CHAPTER 6
Attributes of God

*I believe in God, but not as one thing, not as an old man in the sky.
I believe that what people call God is something in all of us. I believe
that what Jesus and Mohammed and Buddha and all the rest said
was right. It's just that the translations have gone wrong.*
John Lennon

"Ninety-Nine Names of God"

Muslims often refer to the "ninety-nine names of God" mentioned in the Qur'an. Table 1 lists these names, which are essentially His attributes; they shed light into His nature. However, it must be emphasized, again, that God is limitless and thus limiting His attributes to a certain number is assigning bounds for Him. A more appropriate way to put this in perspective might be to state, "There are ninety-nine names or attributes mentioned in the Qur'an," rather than, "God has ninety-nine names." These attributes relate to God's nature, His power, oneness, will, kindness, and so on. God has no comparable being. He is infinite, and the attributes mentioned in the Qur'an, and the Bible, are to help us humans understand Him with our finite ability.

> *The most beautiful names belong to Allah; so call on Him by them.*
> 7:180
>
> *Say: 'Call upon Allah, or call upon the Most Gracious: by whatever name you call upon Him (it is well): To Him belong the Most Beautiful Names.'* 17:110

According to the teachings of the scriptures, God is not limited by time or space (or by anything, for that matter). He is self-sufficient and has no partners and no equals. He has no form or figure. He has no needs. The various names can be grouped into categories referring to His various attributes. The following is a small sample from the Qur'an:

All-Knowing: Some of the names expressing this attribute are *al-Khabir* (the Aware), *al-Hakim* (All Wise), *al-Raqib* (the Watcher), *al-Hadi* (the Guide), and *al-Alim* (All-Knowing).

Most Merciful, Most Kind: *al-Rahman* (the Most Kind), *al-Rahim* (the Most Merciful), *al-Wadud* (the Loving One), *al-Ghaffar* (the Forgiving), *al-Ghafur* (the Forgiver and the Hider of Faults), and *al-Karim* (the Most Generous).

Almighty: He is Almighty, all-powerful, and to Him belongs everything in the universe, and everyone and everything is subservient to His will. Attributes related to His might and supreme nature include *al-Malik* (the King), *al-Qa'dir* (the Powerful), *al-Azeem* (the Grand), *al-Qawi* (the Strong and the Powerful), *al-Aziz* (the Mighty), *al-Kabir* (the Most Great), *al-Jalil* (the Mighty), and *al-Muta'ali* (the Supreme One).

> *It is He Who begins (the process of) creation; then repeats it; and for Him it is most easy. To Him belongs the loftiest similitude (we can think of) in the heavens and the earth: for He is Exalted in Might, full of wisdom. 30:27 (Malik)*

And many of the attributes are mentioned in the following, oft-quoted set of verses:

> *Allah is He, besides Whom there is no god, the Knower of the unseen and the seen. He is the Compassionate, the Merciful. Allah is He, besides Whom there is no god, the King, the Holy, the Giver of peace, the Granter of security, the Guardian, the Almighty, the Irresistible, the Supreme: Glory be to Allah! He is far above the 'shirk' they commit (by associating other gods with Him). He is Allah, the Creator, the Evolver, the Fashioner. His are the most beautiful names. All that is in*

the heavens and the earth declares His glory, and He is the All Mighty, the All Wise. 59:22–24 (Malik)

GOD: THE GUARDIAN AND HELPER

Do you not know that to Allah belongs the dominion of the heavens and the earth, and that besides Allah, you have no protector [wali] or helper [nasir]! 2:107 (Malik)

The literal meaning of *wali* is variously translated as "protecting friend" (Pickthall, Mir Ali), "protector" (Malik, Asad, Mir Ali, Fakhry, Emerick, and Yousuf Ali), "guardian" (Ali Unal), and "supporter" (Yuksel). *Nasir* is translated as "helper" by most translators with the exception of Yuksel translating it as "victor". These two words are often used together to highlight that the believers should not make anyone else their guardian and helper.

Surely Allah is the kingdom of the heavens and the earth; He brings to life and causes to die; and there is not for you besides Allah any Guardian or Helper. 9:116 (Shakir)

Surely your Lord is Allah Who created the heavens and the earth in six periods, and He is firm in power, regulating the affair, there is no intercessor except after His permission; this is Allah, your Lord, therefore serve Him. 10:3

And Allah best knows your enemies; and Allah suffices as a Guardian, and Allah suffices as a Helper. 4:45 (Shakir)

Verily, my protector is God, who has bestowed this divine writ [scripture] from on high: for it is He who protects the righteous. 7:196 (Asad)

So establish regular Prayer, give regular Charity, and hold fast to Allah. He is your Protector—the Best to protect and the Best to help. 22:78

[The word for "protector" used in Arabic in this verse is *mawla*. Mir Ali translates *mawla* as "Master."]

The "ninety-nine names" only give a glimpse of God's attributes. The following verse puts it all in perspective:

*(He is) the Creator of the heavens and the earth: He has made for you pairs from among yourselves, and pairs among cattle: by this means does He multiply you: **there is nothing whatever like unto Him** and He is the One that hears and sees (all things). 42:11*

Simply put, God is way above our imagination, without similitude, a concept universally accepted by all people of faith.

Many of his attributes are eloquently expressed in the following verse (known by Muslims as *ayatul kursi*, or "the verse of the throne"):

Allah! There is no god but Him: the Living, the Eternal. He neither slumbers nor sleeps. To Him belongs all that is in the heavens and the earth. Who can intercede with Him without His permission? He knows what is before them and what is behind them. They cannot gain access to any thing out of His knowledge except what He pleases. His throne is more vast than the heavens and the earth, and guarding of these both does not fatigue Him. He is the Exalted, the Supreme. 2:255 (Malik)

NINETY-NINE NAMES (ATTRIBUTES) OF GOD MENTIONED IN THE QUR'AN

al-Rahim	1	The Compassionate
al-Raham	2	The Merciful
al-Malik	3	The Absolute Ruler
al-Quddus	4	The Pure One
al-Salam	5	The Source of Peace
al-Mu'min	6	The Inspirer of Faith
al-Muhaymin	7	The Guardian
al-'Aziz	8	The Victorious
al-Jabbar	9	The Compeller
al-Mutakabbir	10	The Greatest
al-Khaliq	11	The Creator
al-Bari'	12	The Maker of Order
al-Musawwir	13	The Shaper of Beauty

al-Ghaffar	14	The Forgiving
al-Qahhar	15	The Subduer
al-Wahhab	16	The Giver of All
al-Razzaq	17	The Sustainer
al-Fattah	18	The Opener
al-'Alim	19	The Knower of All
al-Qabid	20	The Constrictor
al-Basit	21	The Reliever
al-Khafid	22	The Abaser
al-Rafi'	23	The Exalter
al-Mu'izz	24	The Bestower of Honors
al-Mudhill	25	The Humiliator
al-Sami	26	The Hearer of All
al-Basir	27	The Seer of All
al-Hakam	28	The Judge
al-'Adl	29	The Just
al-Latif	30	The Subtle One
al-Khabir	31	The All-Aware
al-Halim	32	The Forebearing
al-'Azim	33	The Magnificent
al-Ghafur	34	The Forgiver and Hider of Faults
al-Shakur	35	The Rewarder of Thankfulness
al-'Ali	36	The Highest
al-Kabir	37	The Greatest
al-Hafiz	38	The Preserver
al-Muqit	39	The Nourisher
al-Hasib	40	The Accounter
al-Jalil	41	The Mighty
al-Karim	42	The Generous
al-Raqib	43	The Watchful One
al-Mujib	44	The Responder to Prayer

al-Wasi'	45	The All-Comprehending
al-Hakim	46	The Perfectly Wise
al-Wadud	47	The Loving One
al-Majíd	48	The Majestic One
al-Ba'ith	49	The Resurrector
al-Shahid	50	The Witness
al-Haqq	51	The Truth
al-Wakil	52	The Trustee
al-Qawi	53	The Possessor of All Strength
al-Matin	54	The Forceful One
al-Wáli	55	The Governor
al-Hamid	56	The Praised One
al-Muhsi	57	The Appraiser
al-Mubdi	58	The Originator
al-Mu'id	59	The Restorer
al-Muhyi	60	The Giver of Life
al-Mumit	61	The Taker of Life
al-Hayy	62	The Ever Living One
al-Qayyum	63	The Self-Existing One
al-Wajid	64	The Finder
al-Wahid	65	The Only One
al-Ahad	66	The One
al-Samad	67	The Satisfier of All Needs
al-Qadir	68	The All Powerful
al-Muqtadir	69	The Creator of All Power
al-Muqaddim	70	The Expediter
al-Mu'akhkhir	71	The Delayer
al-'Awwal	72	The First
al-Akhir	73	The Last
al-Zahir	74	The Manifest One
al-Batin	75	The Hidden One
al-Walí	76	The Protecting Friend

al-Muta'ali	77	The Supreme One
al-Barr	78	The Doer of Good
al-Tawwab	79	The Guide to Repentance
al-Muntaqim	80	The Avenger
al-'Afuw	81	The Forgiver
al-Ra'uf	82	The Clement
al-Malik al-Mulk	83	The Owner of All
al-Dhul-Jalali wa'l-Ikram	84	The Lord of Majesty and Bounty
al-Muqsit	85	The Equitable One
al-Jami'	86	The Gatherer
al-Ghani	87	The Rich One
al-Mughni	88	The Enricher
al-Mani'	89	The Preventer of Harm
al-Mu'ti	90	The Giver
al-Darr	91	The Creator of the Harmful
al-Nafi'	92	The Creator of Good
al-Nur	93	The Light
al-Hadi	94	The Guide
al-Badi'	95	The Originator
al-Baqi	96	The Everlasting One
al-Warith	97	The Inheritor of All
al-Rashid	98	The Righteous Teacher
al-Sabur	99	The Patient One

Attributes of God in the Hebrew and Christian Bible
GOD'S ONENESS

God's oneness is at the core of the teachings of the Bible, and is indeed the foundation for the three monotheistic religions. The Jewish daily prayer, Shema, starts with the declaration:

Hear, O Israel: The LORD our God, the LORD is One. Deuteronomy 6:4

GOD IS GRACIOUS AND MERCIFUL

*But in your great mercy, you did not destroy them completely or abandon them forever. What a **Gracious and Merciful** God you are!* Nehemiah 9:31

For the LORD your God is a Merciful God; he will not abandon or destroy you or forget the covenant with your ancestors, which he confirmed to them by oath. Deuteronomy 4:31

Consider therefore the kindness and sternness of God: sternness to those who fell, but kindness to you, provided that you continue in his kindness. Otherwise, you also will be cut off. Romans 11:22

GOD IS ALMIGHTY

The Lord, the Mighty One, is God! The Lord, the Mighty One, is God! He knows the truth, and may Israel know it, too! Joshua 22:22

Look, God is all-powerful. Who is a teacher like him? Job 36:32

'I am the Alpha and the Omega—the beginning and the end,' says the Lord God. 'I am the one who is, who always was, and who is still to come—the Almighty One.' Revelation 1:8

GOD IS THE JUDGE

God is an honest judge. He is angry with the wicked every day. Psalm 7:11

God alone, who gave the law, is the Judge. He alone has the power to save or to destroy. So what right do you have to judge your neighbor? James 4:12

GOD IS FORGIVING

But the Lord our God is merciful and forgiving, even though we have rebelled against him. Daniel 9:9

The LORD is slow to anger, abounding in love and forgiving sin and rebellion. Yet he does not leave the guilty unpunished. Numbers 14:18

O Lord our God, you answered them. You were a forgiving God to them, but you punished them when they went wrong. Psalm 99:8

GOD IS THE FIRST (AL-AWWAL) AND THE LAST (AL-AKHIR)

This is what the LORD says, Israel's King and Redeemer, the LORD Almighty: I am the first and I am the last; apart from me there is no God. Isaiah 44:6

'I am the Alpha and the Omega, the beginning and the end,' says the Lord God. 'I am the one who is, who always was, and who is still to come—the Almighty One.' Revelation 1:8

The question whether Jews, Christians and Muslims worship the same God has been asked often. A full discussion is avoided here to maintain the brevity of this book but I would like to end by quoting from Neusner's book around this theme:

> From a logical point of view it would seem relatively easy for Muslims to say that Jews, Christians and Muslims worship the same God. Muslims can afford to be theologically open-minded because Islam is the latest of the three Abrahamic religions historically and recognizes Christianity and Judaism as its predecessors.[1]

Discussion Points for Dialogue and Healing

- The Qur'an refers to the "names" of God, which are essentially His attributes.
- Similar attributes of God are mentioned in the Bible as well, though not all of them.
- The Jews, Christians, and Muslims acknowledge that He is limitless, cannot be comprehended by humans' finite cognition, and cannot be bound by numbers. All of the attributes have one thing in common:

they emphasize His Oneness. His oneness has to do with Him being unique, and does not reflect a numerical value since God is limitless.

- The Qur'an and the Bible teach that God is the creator of all, and He was not created. He is the first and the last (the alpha and the omega).

- The most frequently mentioned attributes in the Qur'an are *al-Rahman* and *al-Rahim,* meaning "the Most Kind" and "the Most Merciful," rather than those attributes reflecting His power and might.

- Feel free to ponder on the points noted below and add your own.

Time to Ponder

- The descriptions of various attributes of God in the Qur'an and the Bible are strikingly similar. Are the "God of the Qur'an," the "God of the Old Testament," and the "God of the New testament" different Gods? If so, what's the basis for such a belief? How does one explain the similarity of the attributes? Do we believe in different Gods who happen to possess the same attributes?

Part Two
The Qur'an on Prophets, Scriptures, & People of the Book

CHAPTER 7
The Prophets

Ironically, the first thing that appealed to me about Islam
was its pluralism. The fact that the Koran praises
all the great prophets of the past.
Karen Armstrong

According to the Qur'an, Adam was the first prophet and Muhammad was the last prophet. The Qur'an recognizes (and commands believers to respect) all the prophets that came before Muhammad—from Adam, to Noah, to Abraham, to Moses, and Jesus, among others. The Qur'an mentions twenty-five prophets by name, twenty-one of which also appear in the Bible. Although the total number of all the prophets sent down by God is not mentioned in the Qur'an, the Muslims believe, through hadith, that God sent down 124,000 prophets in all.

> *Of some messengers We have already told you the story; of others We have not; And to Moses Allah spoke direct. 4:164*
>
> *We did aforetime send messengers before you [Muhammad]: of them there are some whose story We have related to you, and some whose story We have not related to you. It was not (possible) for any messenger to bring a sign except by the leave of Allah. 40:78*

There are various words for prophets, which are often used interchangeably, but they have different connotations.

Nabi or Prophet: In both Arabic and Hebrew, the word *nabi* means "a prophet" (pronounced in Hebrew as *navi*). A prophet is chosen by God and receives divine inspirations from Him about theological and other teachings and then relays it to his nation. The noun *nabi*, in its various forms, occurs seventy-five times in the Qur'an. The second subdivision of the Hebrew Bible, Tanakh (which stands for "Torah, Nevi'im, Ketuvim"), is devoted to the Hebrew prophets. *Navi* is derived from the term *niv sefatayim*, meaning fruit of the lips, indicating the emphasis on speaking (on God's behalf).

Rasul is often translated as "apostle" by some Qur'an translators; it literally means "messenger." A *rasul* is a prophet who brings a set of divine law or jurisprudence (*Sharia*) and is also given a scripture (e.g., the Torah, the Psalms, the Gospel, or the Qur'an). The word **rasul** occurs more than three hundred times in the Qur'an. The term "apostle" in Christianity, however, is not used for prophets but rather for the original disciples of Jesus Christ sent out to various lands to convey his teachings. Abraham, Moses, David, Jesus Christ, and Mohammad are all considered God's messengers.

It is therefore important to understand that according to Islamic traditions, all apostles/messengers (*rasuls*) were prophets but not all prophets were apostles/messengers.

All monotheistic faiths concur that only God can choose the prophets. According to the Qur'an, the basic message and teachings as well as the warnings of *all* the prophets were the same: there is only one God, and He is the only one worthy of worship. Moreover, most Islamic traditions hold the view that all prophets were *masum*, meaning innocent, pure, and without sins. Still others believe the prophets had some flaws and may have committed minor mistakes but nonetheless lived without committing major sins.

PROPHETS IN THE CHRISTIAN BIBLE

In Christianity, the prophets are inspired by God through the Holy Spirit to deliver specific messages. They delivered the truth about God and also warned their people of God's wrath for disobedience. Prophets are recognized to be human and fallible; they may make wrong decisions, have incorrect personal beliefs or opinions, or sin from time to time. Their hearing of God's revelation does not remove all their humanity or perfect them, nor did they always want to deliver the messages they had received. Though various prophets are mentioned in many books of the Bible (Judges, Samuel, Job, Psalms, etc.), the Christian Bible has a set of books on prophets, termed Major Prophets (Isaiah, Jeremiah, Lamentations of Jeremiah, Ezekiel, and Daniel) and Minor Prophets (twelve of them, from Hosea to Malachi). The terms "major" and "minor" are based on the length of the books, not the importance of the prophet. They are all part of the Old Testament portion of the Christian Bible.

PROPHETS IN THE HEBREW BIBLE

The Hebrew Bible ends before the Gospel of Matthew in the New Testament, as arranged in the Christian Bible. Like the Christian Bible, the prophets are mentioned in many places in the Old Testament, though there are books dedicated to the prophets and their stories. The Books of Prophets include "The Former Prophets" (Joshua, Judges, Samuel, and Kings), the "Latter Prophets" (Isaiah, Jeremiah, and Ezekiel), and "The Twelve" (which are the same as the Christian Minor Prophets).

There are fifty-five prophets of Israel named in the Hebrew Bible, or Tanakh (not recognizing Jesus and Muhammad as prophets). Nevi'im (Prophets) is a major section that tells the stories of prophets in the Hebrew Bible; it falls between the Torah (Law) and the Ketuvim (Writings). However, many other books of the Hebrew Bible narrate stories of other prophets (Abraham, Isaac, Jacob, and Moses in the Torah, for example; the book of Daniel is considered part of the Ketuvim). A Jewish tradition suggests that there were twice as many prophets as the number of Israelites that left Egypt, which would make 1.2 million prophets, far more than the traditional Islamic belief. The Talmud is a central text of mainstream Judaism, from a record of rabbinic discussions pertaining to Jewish law, ethics, and customs. It recognizes the existence of forty-eight male prophets, who gave permanent messages to mankind. According to the Talmud, there were also seven women prophets, whose message bears relevance for all generations: Sarah (wife of Abraham), Miriam (sister of Moses and Aaron), Deborah (wife of Lapidoth), Hannah (mother of the Prophet Samuel), Abigail (a wife of King David), Huldah (from the time of Jeremiah), and Esther (a queen of Persia, raised by her cousin, Mordecai).

NAMED PROPHETS IN THE QUR'AN

The following is a list of the twenty-five prophets named in the Qur'an. The Qur'anic names are used here, with the English names in parenthesis. The names that do not appear in the Bible are mentioned by their Qur'anic names only:

- Adam (Adam)
- Idris (Enoch)
- Nuh (Noah)
- Houd
- Saalih
- Ibrahim (Abraham)
- Isma'il (Ishmael)
- Ishaq (Issac)
- Lut (Lot)
- Yaqub, or Israel (Jacob)
- Yousuf (Joseph)
- Shu'aib (Jethro)
- Ayub (Job)

- Musa (Moses)
- Haroon (Aaron)
- Dhul-Kifl (Ezekiel)
- Dawood (David)
- Sulaiman (Solomon)
- Ilyas (Elijah or Elyas)
- Al-Yasa (Elisha)
- Younus (Jonah)
- Zakariyya (Zachariah)
- Yahya (John the Baptist)
- Isa (Jesus)
- Muhammad

The following verses alone mention seventeen prophets by name, and Muhammad is addressed without naming him at the end.

> That was the reasoning about Us, which We gave to Abraham (to use) against his people: We raise whom We will, degree after degree: for your Lord is full of wisdom and knowledge. We gave him Isaac and Jacob: all (three) guided: and before him, We guided Noah, and among his [meaning Abraham's] progeny, David, Solomon, Job, Joseph, Moses, and Aaron: thus do We reward those who do good: And Zechariah and John, and Jesus and Elias: all in the ranks of the righteous: And Ishmael and Elisha, and Jonas, and Lot: and to all We gave favor above the nations: (To them) and to their fathers, and progeny and brethren: We chose them, and we guided them to a straight way. This is the guidance of Allah: He gives that guidance to whom He pleases, of His

worshippers. If they were to join other gods with Him, all that they did would be vain for them. These were the men to whom We gave the Book, and authority, and prophethood: if these (their descendants) reject them, Behold! We shall entrust their charge to a new people who reject them not. Those were the (prophets) who received Allah's guidance: Copy [follow] the guidance they received; Say [addressing Muhammad]: No reward for this do I ask of you. This is no less than a message for the nations. 6:83–90

THE EXALTED PROPHETS (ULU'L AZM ANBIYA)

Even though Muslims are asked to respect and recognize all prophets, some are given preferences over the others. There are five messengers, traditionally considered *ulu'l azm*, or exalted prophets. They are Noah, Abraham, Moses, Jesus, and Muhammad.

Allah did choose Adam and Noah, the family of Abraham, and the family of Imran above all people. 3:33

Imran is considered the father of Mary and *Ahl al-Imran*, or the "family of Imran," include Mary and Jesus. In another family tree, and commentary by Pooya, Imran is shown as the father of Moses and Aaron.

And it is your Lord that knows best all beings that are in the heavens and on earth: We did bestow on some prophets more (and other) gifts than on others: and We gave to David (the gift of) the Psalms. 17:55
  These are the Signs [revelations] of Allah: we rehearse them to you [Muhammad] in truth: verily you are one of the messengers. Those (some) messengers We endowed with gifts, some above others: To one of them Allah spoke; others He raised to degrees (of honor); to Jesus, the son of Mary We gave clear (signs), and strengthened him with the holy spirit. 2:252–253

Though David is not mentioned by Muslim scholars as one of the *ulu'l azm*, or exalted prophets, his name is mentioned among the "preferred prophets" in verse 17:55 quoted above.

The Belief in Prophets

In addition to belief in One God, the Qur'an demands belief in all prophets. The Qur'an recognizes all "Hebrew" prophets, as well as prophets who came before and after, and of course Muhammad, who the Qur'an often refers to as the "seal of the prophets," meaning the last of the prophets.

> *Say: We believe in God, and in that which has been bestowed from on high upon us, and that which has been bestowed upon Abraham and Ishmael and Isaac and Jacob and, their descendants, and that which has been vouchsafed (given) to Moses and Jesus; and that which has been vouchsafed to all the (other) prophets by their Sustainer: we make no distinction between any of them. And it is unto Him that we surrender [submit] ourselves.* 2:136 (Asad)

Pooya Yazdi writes in his commentary of this verse:

> The religion of Islam is universal, for all people, in every age. Therefore, it is necessary for every follower of Islam to believe in all the prophets and messengers of Allah and in what was revealed to them. No other religion besides Islam demands from its followers to believe equally in the sinless purity of the conduct and character of other prophets of Allah, and in the truthfulness of other sacred scriptures as the revealed words of Allah.

The Purpose of Sending the Prophets

The purpose of sending all prophets according to the Qur'an was the same: to teach their people that there is one God, and no one else is worthy of worship. The prophets served two basic purposes. They were warners and bearers of glad tidings.

> *Not a messenger did We send before you without this inspiration sent by Us to him: that there is no god but I; therefore worship and serve Me.* 21:25
> *(We sent) messengers who gave good news as well as warning, that mankind, after (the coming) of the messengers, should have no plea against Allah: For Allah is Exalted in Power, Wise.* 4:165

God chose the prophets from within the same communities, who spoke their own language. The purpose was to make it easy on the people to understand the clear message.

> *We sent not a messenger except (to teach) in the language of his (own) people, in order to make (things) clear to them.* 14:4

The Qur'an also mentions that the messengers were sent to guide every nation or community.

> *To every people (was sent) a messenger: when their messenger comes (before them), the matter will be judged between them with justice, and they will not be wronged.* 10:47
>
> *Verily We have sent you in truth, as a bearer of glad tidings, and as a warner: and there never was a people, without a warner having lived among them (in the past).* 35:24
>
> *For We assuredly sent amongst every People a messenger, (with the Command), 'Serve Allah, and eschew [shun] evil.'* 16:36 (Pickthall translated "evil" as "false gods.")

GOD TOOK COVENANT FROM ALL PROPHETS:
The Old Testament (as well as the Qur'an) refers to the well-chronicled covenant from Abraham and the Israelites. Additionally, the Qur'an makes several references to the covenants from all prophets to carry out their mission of proclaiming the truth and passing along the message from God to their people.

> *And remember We took from the prophets their covenant: As (We did) from you [Muhammad]: from Noah, Abraham, Moses, and Jesus the son of Mary: We took from them a solemn covenant.* 33:7

Because the messengers simply were passing on the commandments from God, obeying them is tantamount to obeying God.

> *He who obeys the Messenger [Muhammad], obeys Allah.* 4:80
> *Obey Allah, and obey the Messenger, and beware (of evil).* 5:92

Some of the messengers and the prophets will be discussed in more detail in the chapters that follow.

Discussion Points for Dialogue and Healing

- The Qur'an instructs its followers to recognize and respect all prophets. Therefore Muslims recognize and respect Adam, Noah, Abraham, Isaac, Ishmael, Jacob, Jospeh, David, Soloman, Moses, Jesus, and Muhammad (among others) as prophets sent by the same God. Among the prophets, in Islam, five are considred exalted ones (*ulu'l azm*): Noah, Abraham, Moses, Jesus Christ, and Muhammad.
- The Qur'an mentions twenty-five prophets by name. The Hebrew Bible names fifty-five prophets.
- The basic purpose of all the prophets, from Adam to Muhammad, was the same: to give the singular message about one God and to worship Him only, to warn people of the consequences for nonbelief and bad deeds, and to give glad tidings to those who believe and do good deeds. In short, the essential message from all the prophets was the same: worship one God, do good and avoid evil.
- Feel free to ponder on the points noted below and add your own.

Time to Ponder

- Why did God have to send 124,000 prophets (according to Muslim belief), or over a million prophets (according to Jewish traditions)? What if He had stopped after sending a few? Conversely, why did He stop sending prophets after Muhammad (according to Muslims), Jesus (according to Christians, though Jesus is not viewed as a prophet in Christianity—at least by the Trinitarian church), and Malachi (believed to be the last of the Hebrew prophets)?
- Did the prophets give conflicting messages (or religions) to their communities? If one believes that, then how can one reconcile varying religions coming from the same God? Did Jesus bring a different religion from that of Moses before him? Did Muhammad bring a different religion from that of Jesus, and Moses before him?

CHAPTER 8
Adam and Noah

How lucky was Adam. He knew when he said a good thing,
nobody had said it before.
Mark Twain

Allah did choose Adam and Noah, the family of Abraham, and the family of
'Imran above all people. 3:33

Adam was the first human God created, according to the Qur'an and the
Bible. He was also the first prophet. The basic story of the creation of Adam
is fairly similar in the Qur'an and the Bible, though there are some differences, as outlined later in this chapter. The story of Adam is mentioned in
four different chapters of the Qur'an. The Qur'an speaks of the creation of
Adam from clay and that God then inspired the body of Adam with "holy
spirit" to give him life. He then created Eve. Both lived in heaven and were
forbidden to eat from "that tree." God gathered all the angels and the jinns,
including Satan (*Shaytan* or *Iblis*, as he is called in the Qur'an), and then
God asked everyone to prostrate to Adam. Jinns are known by Muslims
to be one of the creations of God, believed to be created from "the fire
of scorching wind, or intensely hot fire." (15:27) Jinns, like humans, have
free will but are invisible to humans. The assembly of the angels and the
jinns obeyed God's order except Satan, as he became arrogant and cited his
superiority for being made from fire, rather than from clay. The early part
of chapter 2 of the Qur'an refers to the creation of Adam, and his eventual
expulsion from paradise, which is mentioned in a fairly long set of verses
(2:30–39), quoted earlier in the introduction of this book.

In another verse, God addresses mankind as "children of Adam" and warns them of the seductive powers of Satan:

O you Children of Adam! Let not Satan seduce you, in the same manner as He got your parents out of the Garden, stripping them of their raiment, to expose their shame: for he and his tribe watch you from a position where you cannot see them. 7:27

Though not mentioned in the Qur'an, Muslims believe that Adam and Eve came forth on the earth, at a place currently known as Mecca, Saudi Arabia: Adam on the mountain Safa, and Eve arrived on mountain Marwa. These are two most famous hills in Mecca, near the Ka'aba, the holiest Islamic shrine. Adam and Eve are said to have wept for forty years in repentance for their disobedience, until their repentance was accepted by God, at which time God sent them the Black Stone, which is considered by Muslims to be a piece of rock from heaven. It is a part of one of the corners of Ka'aba. It is believed that at this time, God taught Adam the initial rituals of Hajj around Ka'aba, which is covered in more detail in chapter 14, "Pillars of Islam."

VARIATIONS IN QUR'ANIC AND TORAH'S ACCOUNTS[1]
Most of the story of Adam and Eve, from the creation from clay, to the temptation and deceit of Satan, to their expulsion from heaven and Satan being cursed eternally, are similar in both the Bible and the Qur'an. There are, however, some differences in the two accounts, and though the focus of this book is to highlight the similarities, it would be counterintuitive to completely ignore the differences; a few of them are listed below.

- In the Torah, Eve was created from Adam's ribs.

The LORD God fashioned into a woman the rib which He had taken from the man, and brought her to the man. The man said, 'This is now bone of my bones, And flesh of my flesh; She shall be called Woman, because she was taken out of Man.' Genesis 2:22–23
Some biblical scholars feel this was metaphoric and meant Eve was cre-

ated side by side with Adam. The Qur'an does not specifically contradict the biblical account of Eve's creation from Adam's ribs but refers to the creation of "its mate of the same" in verse 4:1.

O people! Be careful of (your duty to) your Lord, Who created you from a single being and created its mate of the same (kind) and spread from these two, many men and women. (Shakir)

- The Qur'an states Satan deceived both Adam and Eve and seems to put the blame equally on both of them for disobeying. The Bible states that the serpent (who was Satan in the form of a serpent) tempted Eve into eating the forbidden fruit, and she in turn asked Adam to eat it.

But from the fruit of the tree which is in the middle of the garden, God has said, 'You shall not eat from it or touch it, or you will die.' The serpent said to the woman, 'You surely will not die! For God knows that in the day you eat from it your eyes will be opened, and you will be like God, knowing good and evil.' When the woman saw that the tree was good for food, and that it was a delight to the eyes, and that the tree was desirable to make one wise, she took from its fruit and ate; and she gave also to her husband with her, and he ate.' Genesis 3:3–6

This made God angry at the serpent, Eve, and Adam; the serpent for deceiving Eve, Eve for getting deceived and disobeying God, and Adam for listening to Eve and disobeying God.

Then the LORD God said to the woman, 'What is this you have done?' And the woman said, 'The serpent deceived me, and I ate.' The LORD God said to the serpent, 'Because you have done this, Cursed are you more than all cattle, And more than every beast of the field; On your belly you will go, And dust you will eat all the days of your life; And I will put enmity between you and the woman, And between your seed and her seed; He shall bruise you on the head, And you shall bruise him on the heel.' To the woman He said, 'I will greatly multiply your pain in childbirth, In pain you will bring forth children; Yet your desire will be for your husband, And he will rule over you.' Then to Adam He said, 'Because you have listened to the voice of your wife, and have eaten from the tree about which I commanded you, saying, 'You shall not eat from it'; Cursed is the ground because of you; In toil you will eat of it All the days of your life.' Genesis 3:13–17

- As noted above, in the Qur'an, God informed the angels and the jinns that he is creating a vicegerent on earth and asked the angels and the jinns to prostrate to Adam. Satan refused. The Bible makes no such references.

The Lessons in Adam's Story

Many Qur'anic and biblical scholars have drawn their take-home message from Adam's story as told in the Qur'an and the Bible, which can be summarized as follows:

Man is a viceroy of God on earth. God created Adam and Eve, told them to live in the beautiful gardens in heaven, where they were spiritually pure and innocent, until they sinned and disobeyed God as they succumb to the temptations by Satan. The humans, too, are pure, when they are born. They can stay pure or succumb to the temptations. Just like Adam and Eve had to face the consequences of their actions, so will the rest of mankind. Satan was one of God's most ardent worshippers until he refused to prostrate to Adam out of his arrogance, and he became a subject of God's wrath and anger. The Qur'an and the Bible repeatedly instruct man to avoid arrogance and teach humility.

Noah (Nuh, Noach)

The Qur'an does not specify the lineage of Prophet Noah like the Old Testament does. As mentioned earlier, Noah is considered one of the exalted prophets in the Qur'an, who received inspirations from God and preached to his people, who remained sinful and extreme in transgression and remained unrepentant, which eventually led God to punish them with the famous deluge.

The Qur'an mentions Noah and his story many times, and chapter 71 is named after him (*Surah al-Nuh*), which contains twenty-eight verses and is entirely dedicated to the story of Noah, a rarity in the Qur'an. The chapter refers to the sinful nature of the people of Noah and names the idols they used to worship (*Wadd, Suwa, Yaghut, Yaüq,* and *Nasr*). According to the commentary by Pooya Yazdi, these five false gods represented the following:

Name	Shape	Quality represented
Wadd	Man	Manly powers
Suwa	Woman	Beauty
Yaghut	Lion (or Bull)	Brute strength
Yaüq	Horse	Swiftness
Nasr	Eagle (or Falcon)	Insight

Noah's story is not limited to chapter 71; it is spread throughout the Qur'an. The story is well summarized in the following six verses of chapter 7, *Al-A'raaf* ("The Heights").

We sent Noah to his people. He said: 'O my people! Worship Allah! you have no other god but Him. I fear for you the punishment of a dreadful day!' The leaders of his people said: 'Ah! we see you evidently wandering (in mind).' He said: 'O my people! No wandering is there in my (mind): on the contrary I am a messenger from the Lord and Cherisher of the worlds! I but fulfill toward you the duties of my Lord's mission: Sincere is my advice to you, and I know from Allah something that you know not. Do you wonder that there has come to you a message from your Lord, through a man of your own people, to warn you, so that you may fear Allah and haply receive His Mercy?' But they rejected him, and We delivered him, and those with him, in the Ark: but We overwhelmed in the flood those who rejected Our signs. They were indeed a blind people!' 7:59–64

NOAH BUILDS THE ARK

And it was revealed to Noah: 'None of your people will believe now, other than those who have already believed. So do not grieve at their evil deeds. Build an ark under Our supervision in accordance with Our revelation, and beware not to plead with Me on behalf of those who are wrongdoers: for they are all to be drowned in the flood.' So he started to build the ark; and whenever the chiefs of his people passed by him they laughed at him. He said: 'Laugh at us now if you will, soon the time is going to come when we too will laugh at you as you are laughing at us. Soon you will come to know who will be seized by a humiliating scourge, and who is afflicted with everlasting punishment.' Finally when Our Command came and the water from Al-Tannur (the fountains of the earth) gushed forth! We said to Noah: 'Take into the Ark a pair from every species, your family—except those against whom the Word has already gone forth—and the believers and those who believed with him were only a few.' Thus he said: 'Embark in it, in the name of Allah in whose hands is its sailing and its stopping; surely my Lord is Forgiving, Merciful.' 11:36–41 (Malik)

And on one of the rare occasions, the Qur'an does give specific information about a prophet's time or age, and according to this verse, Noah lived for 950 years:

We sent Noah to his people and he lived among them a thousand years less fifty. 29:14

VARIATIONS IN THE QUR'ANIC AND TORAH'S ACCOUNTS

While the story of Noah by and large is similar in both the Qur'an and the Torah, there are some differences. Both talk about Noah being a righteous person and a messenger of God.

These are the records of the generations of Noah. Noah was a righteous man, blameless in his time; Noah walked with God. Genesis 6:9

Both talk about his people ridiculing him when he was building the ark, God's ordering Noah to include all animals in pairs (one male and one female from each species), and the deluge.

- The Bible names three sons of Noah. The Qur'an does not.
- The Qur'an mentions the son of Noah who did not take heed and was among those left behind and died in the floods. The Torah states the three sons and their wives accompanied him on the boat.

As the ark floated with them on board over the mountainous waves and Noah called out to his son, who stood apart: 'O my son! Embark with us and be not with the unbelievers! He replied: 'I will take refuge on some mountain, which will save me from the flood.' Noah said: 'None shall be secure today from the judgment of God, except the one on whom He has mercy!' And thereupon a wave came between them and he (Noah's son) became among one of those who drowned. 11:42–43

But I will establish My covenant with you; and you shall enter the ark—you and your sons and your wife, and your sons' wives with you. Genesis 6:18

- The Qur'an states Noah's wife was also among the ones left behind, and was not among the righteous:

For those who are bent on denying the truth God has propounded a parable in (the stories of) Noah's wife and Lot's wife: they were wedded to two of Our righteous servants, and each one betrayed her husband; and neither of the two (husbands) will be of any avail to these two women when they are told (on Judgment Day), 'Enter the fire with all those (other sinners) who enter it!' 66:10 (Malik)

- According to the Qur'an, the ark came to rest on Mount Judi. The Torah states it came to rest on Mount Ararat. Al-Joudi (Judaea) is a mount in the biblical range of Ararat. The Qur'an cites a particular mount in the Ararat Range, and the Torah mentions the Ararat Range. Judaea is still present in the Ararat Range in Turkey, so perhaps they are both talking about the same area. Moreover, the Torah gave a specific time the ark was afloat for (the duration of the flood), as noted below:

Then the word went forth: 'O earth! Swallow up thy water, and O sky! Withhold (your rain)!' and the water abated, and the matter was ended. The Ark rested on Mount Judi, and the word went forth: 'Away with those who do wrong!' 11:44

In the seventh month, on the seventeenth day of the month, the ark rested upon the mountains of Ararat. Genesis 8:4

(Some translations have put this number at "exactly one hundred fifty days" or five months: New Living Translation and New Century Version.)

- The Torah gives very detailed instructions about the ark, as well as about the duration and timings of the great flood. The Qur'an does not mention the dimensions.

This is how you shall make it: the length of the ark three hundred cubits, its breadth fifty cubits, and its height thirty cubits. You shall make a window for the ark, and finish it to a cubit from the top; and set the door of the ark in the side of it; you shall make it with lower, second, and third decks. Genesis 6:15–16

One cubit is 1.5 feet, and many translations have used the measurements in feet. This would come out to be about one and a half the length of a U.S. football field and about five stories tall.

- Noah getting drunk: According to the Torah, Noah started to drink and lay naked. The Qur'an (as well as the Bible) considers drunkenness a sin and regards the prophets, especially an exalted prophet like Noah, as sinless:

Then Noah began farming and planted a vineyard. He drank of the wine and became drunk, and uncovered himself inside his tent. Ham, the father of Canaan, saw the nakedness of his father, and told his two brothers outside. But Shem and Japheth took a garment and laid it upon both their shoulders and walked backward and covered the nakedness of their father; and their faces were turned away, so that they did not see their father's nakedness. Genesis 9:20–23

Despite these differences, the moral of Noah's story is essentially the same in both Genesis and the Qur'an. They both outline Noah's righteous character and prophetic teachings. Only those who were on the ark survived, including animal species, and the rest of the people drowned and were killed for their transgressions. Noah carried on humankind upon his return to dry land. Noah is thus referred to in Islamic traditions as *Adam al-Thaani*, or "Second Adam," as he was literally the father of mankind that survived the great flood.

Discussion Points for Dialogue and Healing

- The basic story of Adam and Eve is similar in the Qur'an and the Bible. Adam was the first human created. Eve was the first woman created. They were tempted by Satan and were expelled from paradise for disobeying God, though God accepted their repentance.
- Satan is cursed in the Qur'an and the Bible. The Qur'an sheds some light as to what events took place earning him the cursed status, whereas that aspect is not chronicled in the Bible.
- The basic story of Noah is also fairly similar in the Qur'an and the Bible. He was a righteous person and one of the exalted and sinless prophets in the Qur'an. The Bible also calls him righteous and "blameless," but subsequently also talks about his drunkenness.
- Evolutionary theory notwithstanding, the monotheists believe that the humans are descendants of Adam and Eve. As simplistic and naïve as it may sound, the story of Adam and Eve is a constant reminder of our common ancestry.
- Feel free to ponder on the points noted below and add your own.

Time to Ponder

- Satan (*Iblis*) was a believer (in God, paradise, angels, etc.) and was one of the most devout worshippers of God until he disobeyed God's orders after the creation of Adam. As a result, he was expelled from paradise and cursed forever. Why did he disobey, and what lessons can one draw from the story? Does believing in God alone make one "righteous"?

CHAPTER 9
Abraham: The Father of Monotheistic Religions

We belong to the camp of peace. We believe in peace. We believe that our one God wishes us to live in peace and wishes peace upon us, for these are His teachings to all the followers of the three great monotheistic religions, the Children of Abraham.

King Hussein I of Jordan

This chapter pertains to the stories of the patriarchs of the monotheistic religions: Abraham, Isaac, and Jacob, as well as Ishmael and Joseph, as told in the Qur'an and the Bible. The story of Abraham is reviewed first.

Abraham, (Avraham or Avaram in Hebrew, or *Ibrahim*, as he is known in the Qur'an), is highly revered and an exalted prophet according to the Qur'an and is the second most-mentioned prophet (sixty-nine times) after Moses. Chapter 14 is named "Ibrahim" after him. Abraham is considered the father of the monotheistic religions: Judaism, Christianity, and Islam. However, both Qur'anic and biblical commentators point out that he was not the "pioneer" of the concept of monotheism, which had preceded Abraham. The Qur'an does not relate Abraham's genealogy, but according to biblical accounts, he was the tenth generation from Noah. The Qur'an talks about God's covenant with Abraham with a promise to exalt his descendants. Abraham and his first son, Ishmael (*Ismail*), built the Ka'aba, the cubical structure in Mecca, considered the holiest shrine in Islam. The Qur'an also narrates the sacrifice of his son as a test, which Abraham passed, and God promised him an exalted status, as well as to exalt his descendants. The sacrifice alone was of course not the only reason for his exalted status.

> *Abraham was indeed a model, devoutly obedient to Allah, (and) true in faith, and he joined not gods with Allah: He showed his gratitude for the favors of Allah, who chose him, and guided him to a straight way. And We gave him good in this world, and he will be, in the hereafter, in the ranks of the righteous.* 16:120–122

God gives Abraham one of the highest honors a human can have by calling him a friend, hence his nickname in Arabic, *Khaleelal Allah*, meaning "the friend of God."

> *Who can be better in religion than one who submits his whole self to Allah, does good, and follows the way of Abraham—the true in faith? For Allah did take Abraham for a friend.* 4:125

Abraham's Life Story According to Tradition

Most biblical commentators agree that Abraham was born in a city called Ur, in the present country of Iraq. Abraham's first wife Sarah had borne him no children. She had a handmaid whose name was Hagar (*Hajira*). In their old age, having no hope for children from herself, Sarah gave permission to Abraham to take Hagar as a wife, in order to have children and maintain his progeny. From this marriage, they had a son named Ishmael, who became a source of friction between Hagar and Sarah. The peace and harmony of the family was disturbed. Sarah asked Abraham to send them away. Abraham sought God's help and was directed to send away Hagar and Ishmael to a place currently known as Mecca. They stopped at a place where the Ka'aba now stands. As Abraham was leaving them on his way back to his native land, he said a prayer:

> *O our Lord! I have made some of my offspring to dwell in a valley without cultivation, by Your Sacred House; in order, O our Lord, that they may establish regular Prayer: so fill the hearts of some among men with love toward them, and feed them with fruits: so that they may give thanks.* 14:37

Soon Hagar and the very young Ishmael ran out of water and lay on the desert sand, crying in thirst while Hagar ran back and forth between the mountains of Safa and Marwa. When she was at Safa, she saw water in the direction of Marwa—a mirage. Upon reaching Marwa, she looked back and once again saw the same in the direction of Safa. She ran back and forth seven times in search of water. God showed mercy on them, and a spring of fresh and sweet water gushed forth from the earth under the feet of Ishmael, from a well that came to be known as Zamzam. The word is derived from the word *zumé*, meaning *stop*, named after Hagar telling the gushing water to stop when she saw water that kept gushing forth. This well is still present in the Grand Mosque of Ka'aba and is considered holy water by Muslims around the world. Moreover, the pilgrims performing the hajj are required to walk between Safa and Marwa seven times to honor the memory of Hagar and Ishmael.

Though a common belief among Muslims, the Zamzam well is not mentioned, or even referred to, in the Qur'an. Interestingly, though, it is recorded in the Old Testament, in the book of Genesis chapter 21. This will be reviewed in more detail later in this chapter, under "Ishmael in the Bible."

The flow of water increased day by day, and the surrounding land became fertile. People began to come and settle there. Soon it became a flourishing town. When Abraham returned, he found the wasteland in the desert a busy trade center.

ABRAHAM'S ATTEMPTED SACRIFICE OF HIS SON, ISHMAEL (AND PASSING THE TEST)

Though the name Ishmael is not mentioned in the verse, Muslims commonly believe the son Abraham attempted to sacrifice was Ishmael, and not Isaac as mentioned in Genesis. They point out the verse after the sacrifice, where God gives him the good news about another righteous son, Isaac.

> *(Abraham) said: 'I am going to take refuge with my Lord, He will surely guide me. O Lord! Grant me a righteous son.' So We gave him the good news of a gentle son. When he reached the age to work with*

him, (Abraham) said to him: 'O my son! I have seen a vision that I should offer you as a sacrifice, now tell me what is your view.' He replied: 'O my father! Do as you are commanded: you will find me, if Allah so wills, of the patient.' And when they both submitted to Allah and (Abraham) laid down his son prostrate upon his forehead for sacrifice; We called out to him: 'O Abraham stop! You have fulfilled your vision.' Thus do We reward the righteous. That was indeed a manifest test. We ransomed his son for a great sacrifice and We left his good name among the later generations. Salutation (and peace) to Abraham. Thus We reward the righteous. Surely he was one of Our believing devotees. We gave him the good news of Isaac —a prophet— one of the righteous. 37:99–112

ABRAHAM AND ISHMAEL BUILD THE KA'ABA WITH A PRAYER

Upon his return to Mecca, when Ishmael had grown older, the father and the son built the Ka'aba at the ancient site, where many Muslim scholars believe Adam built the original house of worship.

And remember Abraham and Ishmael raised the foundations of the House (with this prayer): Our Lord! Accept (this service) from us: For You are the all-hearing, the all-knowing. 2:127

In another set of verses, the Qur'an mentions Abraham's prayers:

Remember Abraham said: 'O my Lord! Make this city one of peace and security: and preserve me and my sons from worshipping idols.'

'O our Lord! I have made some of my offspring to dwell in a valley without cultivation, by Your Sacred House; in order, O our Lord, that they may establish regular Prayer: so fill the hearts of some among men with love toward them, and feed them with fruits: so that they may give thanks.'

'O our Lord! truly You do know what we conceal and what we reveal: for nothing whatever is hidden from Allah, whether on earth or in heaven. Praise be to Allah, Who hath granted unto me in old age Ishmael and Isaac: for truly my Lord is He, the Hearer of Prayer!'

'O my Lord! make me one who establishes regular Prayer, and also (raise such) among my offspring O our Lord! and accept You my Prayer.'

'O our Lord! cover (us) with Your forgiveness—me, my parents, and (all) Believers, on the Day that the Reckoning will be established!'
14:35–41

ABRAHAM NOT A JEW OR A CHRISTIAN

The Qur'an addresses the dispute among people about whether Abraham was a "Jew," a "Christian," or a "Muslim."

People of the Book! Why dispute you about Abraham, when the Law [Torah] and the Gospel were not revealed till after him? 3:65

It further goes on to say:

Abraham was not a Jew nor a Christian but he was an upright man, a Muslim [submitter], and he was not one of the polytheists. Most surely the nearest of people to Abraham are those who followed him and this Prophet [Muhammad] and those who believe. And Allah is the guardian of the believers. 3:67–68 (Shakir)

GOD SHOWS ABRAHAM A MIRACLE FROM DEAD BIRDS

The Qur'an narrates a story when Abraham asked God to show how he will bring life to the dead:

When Abraham said: 'Show me, Lord, how You will raise the dead,' He replied: 'Have you no faith?' He said, 'Yes, but just to reassure my heart.' Allah said, 'Take four birds, draw them to you, and cut their bodies to pieces. Scatter them over the mountaintops, then call them back. They will come swiftly to you. Know that Allah is Mighty, Wise.' 2:260

A similar story is told in Genesis, except there are multiple animals, rather than four birds; and it is not in reference to God's giving life to the dead. It ends somewhat abruptly as Abraham falls asleep.

And Abram (Abraham's birth name) believed the LORD, *and the* LORD *counted him as righteous because of his faith. Then the* LORD *told him, 'I am the* LORD *who brought you out of Ur of the Chaldeans to give you this land as your possession.' But Abram replied, 'O Sovereign* LORD, *how can I be sure that I will actually possess it?' The* LORD *told him, 'Bring me a three-year-old heifer, a three-year-old female goat, a three-year-old ram, a turtledove, and a young pigeon.' So Abram presented all these to him and killed them. Then he cut each animal down the middle and laid the halves side by side; he did not, however, cut the birds in half. Some vultures swooped down to eat the carcasses, but Abram chased them away. As the sun was going down, Abram fell into a deep sleep, and a terrifying darkness came down over him.* Genesis 15:6–12[1]

Abraham in the Torah

As in the Qur'an, the Bible holds Abraham in high esteem. He has an exalted status among the followers of the Old Testament, as well as the New Testament. He is considered the father of the Jewish and Christian faiths. According to Genesis, his birth name was Abram (*Av Aram*), meaning "father of Aram," or "exalted father," which was changed by God to Abraham (*Avraham*), meaning "father of many (nations)," as God promised him that he would be the father of many nations. (Genesis 17:5) At the same time, God also changed the name of his first wife, *Sarai* (meaning "my princess") to *Sarah* (meaning "princess to all nations of the world").

God's first call to Abram is mentioned in Genesis chapter 12. God called on Abram to leave for the Promised Land. This journey took Abram from Ur to Haran (near the Turkey-Syria border today), to Schechem (West Bank of Israel today), to Bethel (West Bank), to Egypt, and eventually to Hebron (West Bank of Israel today).

Now the LORD said to Abram, 'Go forth from your country, And from your relatives And from your father's house, To the land which I will show you; And I will make you a great nation, And I will bless you, And make your name great; And so you shall be a blessing; And I will bless those who bless you, And the one who curses you I will curse. And in you all the families of the earth will be blessed.' Genesis 12:1–3

ISHMAEL'S BIRTH: SARAH AND HAGAR DON'T GET ALONG

God once again talks to Abraham in Genesis 15 and promises great descendants. Abraham replies that he does not even have a son and worries that his servant will be the heir, whereupon God gives him the good news of a son as well as having as many descendants as stars in the sky:

> *Then behold, the word of the LORD came to him, saying, 'This man will not be your heir; but one who will come forth from your own body, he shall be your heir.' And He took him outside and said, 'Now look toward the heavens, and count the stars, if you are able to count them.' And He said to him, 'So shall your descendants be.' Then he believed in the LORD; and He reckoned it to him as righteousness.* Genesis 15:4–6

Chapter 16 of Genesis goes on to tell the story of Ishmael's birth. Sarah had attained old age; she was in her sixties and was barren, so she gave permission for Abraham to take her Egyptian maid as his wife:

> *After Abram had lived ten years in the land of Canaan, Abram's wife Sarai took Hagar the Egyptian, her maid, and gave her to her husband Abram as his wife.* Genesis 16:3

The chapter describes how the relationship between the two wives sours. Chapter 17 of Genesis deals with God's covenant again and explains that in return, Abraham and his progeny must be circumcised (Genesis 17:5).

ISAAC IS BORN, INFORMED BY THE ANGELS ON THE WAY TO SODOM AND GOMORRAH

In the meantime, angels visit Abraham on the way to the twin cities of Sodom and Gomorrah. They tell Abraham that they are on the way to where Lot (a prophet and a nephew of Abraham) lives and that God is going to bring about destruction of the two towns. This happens despite Abraham's plea to spare them. This story is also told in the Qur'an. The angels also gave the glad tidings of the birth of Isaac:

He [one of the angels] said, 'I will surely return to you at this time next year; and behold, Sarah your wife will have a son.' And Sarah was listening at the tent door, which was behind him. Now Abraham and Sarah were old, advanced in age; Sarah was past childbearing. Sarah laughed to herself, saying, 'After I have become old, shall I have pleasure, my lord being old also?' And the LORD said to Abraham, 'Why did Sarah laugh, saying, 'Shall I indeed bear a child, when I am so old?' Is anything too difficult for the LORD'? At the appointed time I will return to you, at this time next year, and Sarah will have a son.' Sarah denied it however, saying, 'I did not laugh'; for she was afraid. And He said, 'No, but you did laugh.' Genesis 18:10–15

This story of the angel's visit to Abraham on the way to Sodom, and giving the glad tidings about Isaac, is also told in the Qur'an in various places: verses 11:69–74, 15:51–58, and 51:24–37.

ABRAHAM AND THE SACRIFICE OF HIS SON, ISAAC; ABRAHAM IS BLESSED

The story, told in many places in the Qur'an about Abraham sacrificing (actually attempting to sacrifice) his son, is also told in the Bible, except Genesis mentions Isaac by name as the son being sacrificed. The biblical account is noted in the following set of verses:

*Now it came about after these things, that God tested Abraham, and said to him, 'Abraham!' And he said, 'Here I am.' He said, '**Take now your son, your only son,** whom you love, Isaac, and go to the land of Moriah, and offer him there as a burnt offering on one of the mountains of which I will tell you.'* Genesis 22:1–2

One may see a contradiction in this passage, in that though the name of the son mentioned is Isaac, he is also referred to as "your only son." The Bible already had told the story of Ishmael, as Abraham's first son, and so one would wonder why Isaac was referred to as the only son. The "only son" reference is repeated again in the following verse, after God told Abraham to stop:

He said, 'Do not stretch out your hand against the lad, and do nothing to him; for now I know that you fear God, since you have not withheld your son, your only son, from Me.' Genesis 22:12

The Qur'anic and biblical accounts are similar in that Abraham was prepared to sacrifice his son, before God called on him to stop, informing him it was a test of his submissiveness and that Abraham had passed it with flying colors. The Qur'an follows that narration by saluting him, "Peace and salutation to Abraham" (37:109). Abraham was thus exalted and also was promised multiple nations as his followers, and that they too would be blessed:

Then the angel of the LORD called to Abraham a second time from heaven, and said, 'By Myself I have sworn, declares the LORD, because you have done this thing and have not withheld your son, your only son, indeed I will greatly bless you, and I will greatly multiply your seed as the stars of the heavens and as the sand which is on the seashore; and your seed shall possess the gate of their enemies. In your seed all the nations of the earth shall be blessed, because you have obeyed My voice.' Genesis 22:15–18

Ishmael (Ismail): Abraham's First Son

Ishmael is one of the highly revered prophets in the Qur'an. He is often mentioned in association with his father, Abraham. In addition to some of the verses already quoted, he is frequently mentioned elsewhere in high esteem:

Also mention in the Book (the story of) Ismail: He was (strictly) true to what he promised, and he was a messenger (and) a prophet. He used to enjoin on his people prayer and charity, and he was most acceptable in the sight of his Lord. 19:54–55

   And Ishmael and Elisha, and Jonas, and Lot: and to all We gave favor above the nations: 6:86

ISHMAEL IN THE TORAH

Ishmael is mentioned in the Torah several times. In his first covenant, God promises Abraham a great number of descendants and then gives the news of a son (Genesis 17:5). Before Ishmael was born, God promised

Abraham that He would make a great nation out of Abraham. The following narration is at the time of news of the birth of Ishmael, long before the angels gave the news of Isaac's birth to Abraham:

> *After these things the word of the LORD came to Abram in a vision, saying, 'Do not fear, Abram, I am a shield to you; Your reward shall be very great.' Abram said, 'O Lord GOD, what will You give me, since I am childless, and the heir of my house is Eliezer of Damascus?' And Abram said, 'Since You have given no offspring to me, one born in my house is my heir.' Then behold, the word of the LORD came to him, saying, 'This man will not be your heir; but one who will come forth from your own body, he shall be your heir.'* Genesis 15:1–5

The New Living Translation version translates the last verse as:

> *No, your servant will not be your heir, for you will have a son of your own who will be your heir.*

The following chapter of Genesis then goes on to describe the birth of Ishmael.

MUHAMMAD, A DESCENDANT OF ISHMAEL: GOD'S PROMISE TO MAKE A GREAT NATION FROM ISHMAEL

The Torah also mentions that God promised Hagar that He would make a great nation from Ishmael's descendants. However, according to the Bible, God's covenant was to be confirmed with Isaac and his descendants, and not with Ishmael:

> *And Abraham said to God, 'Oh that Ishmael might live before You.' But God said, 'No, but Sarah your wife will bear you a son, and you shall call his name Isaac; and I will establish My covenant with him for an everlasting covenant for his descendants after him.* **As for Ishmael, I have heard you; behold, I will bless him, and will make him fruitful and will multiply him exceedingly. He shall become the father of twelve princes, and I will make him a great nation.'** Genesis 17:18–20

Later as Ishmael grows, Sarah gets upset when Ishmael is said to have made fun of Isaac during his weaning celebration, so Sarah asked Abraham to take them away:

> *Therefore she [Sarah] said to Abraham, 'Drive out this maid and her son, for the son of this maid shall not be an heir with my son Isaac.' The matter distressed Abraham greatly because of his son. But God said to Abraham, 'Do not be distressed because of the lad and your maid; whatever Sarah tells you, listen to her, for through Isaac your descendants shall be named. And of the son of the maid I will make a nation also, because he is your descendant.'* Genesis 21:10–13

Zamzam Well in the Torah

Though not mentioned by name, the Zamzam well is described in the Old Testament, when Abraham takes young Ishmael and Hager away to eventually arrive in Mecca:

> *So Abraham rose early in the morning and took bread and a skin of water and gave them to Hagar, putting them on her shoulder, and gave her the boy, and sent her away. And she departed and wandered about in the wilderness of Beersheba. When the water in the skin was used up, she left the boy under one of the bushes. Then she went and sat down opposite him, about a bowshot away, for she said, 'Do not let me see the boy die.' And she sat opposite him, and lifted up her voice and wept. God heard the lad crying; and the angel of God called to Hagar from heaven and said to her, 'What is the matter with you, Hagar? Do not fear, for God has heard the voice of the lad where he is. Arise, lift up the lad, and hold him by the hand, for I will make a great nation of him.' Then God opened her eyes and she saw a well of water; and she went and filled the skin with water and gave the lad a drink. God was with the lad, and he grew; and he lived in the wilderness and became an archer.* Genesis 21:14–20

Isaac: Abraham's Second Son and the Father of Jacob

Isaac (Ishaq, as he is known in the Qur'an) is one of the highly revered prophets in Judaism, as well as in Christianity and Islam. The second son of Abraham and father of Jacob, God chose him, and his half-brother, Ishmael, to carry the legacy of Abraham, though most of the prophets were from Isaac's progeny. His name is mentioned fifteen times in the Qur'an and eighty times in Genesis. Isaac is buried in the cave of the patriarchs, also known by Muslims as the Mosque of Abraham (*Masjid al-Ibrahimi*), in the city of Hebron in the West Bank. The graves of the other patriarchs and matriarchs are also located there (Abraham, Sarah, Rebecca (Isaac's wife), Jacob, and Leah (Jacob's wife)). Thus the city of Hebron is considered the second holiest city in Judaism after Jerusalem. It is also considered the fourth holiest city in Islam (after Mecca, Medina, and Jerusalem). The news of his birth was given to Abraham and Sarah by the angels, as it appears in the Bible (Genesis chapter 18). The following is the narration in the Qur'an:

> *And his wife was standing (there), and she laughed: But we gave her glad tidings of Isaac, and after him, of Jacob. She said: 'Alas for me! shall I bear a child, seeing I am an old woman, and my husband here is an old man? That would indeed be a wonderful thing!' They said [the angels to Abraham]:' Do you wonder at Allah's bidding? The mercy of Allah and His blessings are on you, O people of the house, surely He is Praised, Glorious.' 11:71–74*

Isaac's righteousness and the prophethood in his progeny have been narrated elsewhere in the Qur'an.

> *And We gave (Abraham) Isaac and Jacob, and ordained among his progeny prophethood and Revelation, and We granted him his reward in this life; and he was in the Hereafter (of the company) of the Righteous. 29:27*
>
> *And I [Joseph] follow the ways of my fathers, Abraham, Isaac, and Jacob; and never could we attribute any partners whatever to Allah: that (comes) of the grace of Allah to us and to mankind: yet most men are not grateful. 12:38*

ISAAC IN THE TORAH

Yishaq in Hebrew mean "he laughs," or "will laugh." The Testament of Isaac is part of the Old Testament's apocrypha. In it, the Archangel Michael is said to have visited Isaac before his impending death, and he visited heaven and hell. Compared to some of the other prophets, especially other patriarchs, Isaac's story and incidents are rather unremarkable, the family feud notwithstanding.

Isaac's wife was Rebekah, mother of Jacob and Esau. According to the calculation of Rabbi Solomon Izhaqi (a.k.a. Rashi, a well-respected eleventh-century Jewish scholar), Rebekah was three years old when she married Isaac. They were married for twenty years when they had Jacob and Esau (Genesis 25:20). Another lesser-known source puts Rebekah's age at marriage at fourteen years. This may seem strange, and a parallel can be drawn to the controversy surrounding the age of Aisha (one of Muhammad's wives), which at the time of her marriage is said to be anywhere from seven to about sixteen years. Obviously, we are not on firm historical ground when discussing the traditional dates and ages lived in these ancient texts. These are examples of sacred history where the message and moral of the stories is primary.

The feud between their mothers apart, there is no suggestion of animosity between Isaac and Ishmael. Chapter 25 of Genesis describes Abraham's death and says that Ishmael returned to Hebron to bury his father along with his half-brother Isaac.

> *Then his sons Isaac and Ishmael buried him in the cave of Machpelah, in the field of Ephron.* Genesis 25:9

Jacob (Ya'qub)

Jacob (Ya'qub, as he is known in the Qur'an) carried the progeny of Abraham and Isaac. His nickname in Arabic was Israeel (Is-ra-eel), which is derived from two words: "Isra" and "eel," translating to Abdullah, meaning "servant of God." Israel (Iz-ra-eel), or Ysra'el as he is known in the Hebrew Bible, also means something similar: "man of God." Israel is variously translated as "prince of God" (from the King James Version), "he who strives with God" (New American Standard Bible), and "God fights" (New Living Translation). According to Genesis 32:28, his name was changed from Jacob to Israel. His progeny and descendants are known in the Qur'an as *Bani Israeel,* meaning "children of Israel," and are frequently mentioned in references to the stories of the Israelites and Moses. The Qur'an describes

Jacob as faithful, a possessor of power and vision, and a man in submission of God. Jacob taught the message of God to his twelve sons, who eventually made up the twelve tribes of Israel. The three patriarchs of Judaism (Abraham, Isaac, and Jacob) are a frequent subject of the Qur'an. In the following verses, they are mentioned simultaneously:

> *And commemorate Our Servants Abraham, Isaac, and Jacob, possessors of Power and Vision. Verily We did choose them for a special (purpose)—proclaiming the Message of the Hereafter. They were, in Our sight, truly, of the company of the **Elect** and the **Good**. 38:45–47*

The words bolded above are *mustafayn,* meaning "elite" (as translated by Yuksel) or "the elect" (as translated by Shakir, Pickthall, and Yousuf Ali), and *khyar,* meaning "the best," "the chosen," or "the good" (as translated by Shakir, Pickthall, and Yousuf Ali, respectively). Sarwar translates *mustafayn* as "the chosen" and *akhyar* as "the virtuous." These verses are followed by references to Ishmael, Elisha, and Ezekiel as the best and the virtuous also, but they do not use the word, *mustafayn.*

Jacob's story in the Qur'an is mentioned usually in association with other prophets but mostly with his twelve sons, specially his most beloved son, Joseph:

> *When God commanded him [Abraham] to submit, he replied, 'I have submitted myself to the Will of the Lord of the universe.' Abraham left this legacy to his sons and, in turn, so did Jacob saying, 'God has chosen this religion for you. You must not leave this world unless you are a Muslim (submitted to the will of the Lord of the Universe).' Were you (believers) there when death approached Jacob? When he asked his sons, 'Whom will you worship after my death?' They replied, 'We will worship your Lord, the Lord of your fathers, Abraham, Ishmael, and Isaac. He is the only Lord, and to Him we have submitted ourselves.' 2:131–133 (Sarwar)*

JACOB IN THE TORAH

Jacob's birth is described in Genesis chapter 25. He was the twin brother of Esau. Esau was the first one to be born, and he was red and hairy (*Esau* means "rough" or "hairy"). It is narrated that Jacob was born with his hand on the heel of Esau (*Ya'aqob* or *Ya'aqov* in Hebrew means "heel-catcher"). The Torah describes in much more detail many of his life struggles including hatred of his twin brother Esau, his deception of Isaac to receive his blessings (rather than Esau receiving it), him being more loved by his mother, the death of his favorite wife, Rachel, the rape of his daughter, Dinah, and his battle with an angel, who eventually gave the news of his name change from Jacob to Israel:

> *Then God appeared to Jacob again when he came from Paddan-aram, and He blessed him. God said to him, 'Your name is Jacob; You shall no longer be called Jacob, But Israel shall be your name.' Thus He called him Israel.* Genesis 35:9–10

Most of these stories (except for Joseph's) are not mentioned in the Qur'an. Jacob's stories and struggles are covered over many chapters in the book of Genesis, culminating in his death, when he gathered his twelve sons and gave them his will and wishes to be buried in the cave where Abraham and Isaac were buried:

> *When Jacob finished charging his sons, he drew his feet into the bed and breathed his last, and was gathered to his people.* Genesis 49:33

The book of Genesis takes sort of a detour between the narration of the birth of Jacob (chapter 25) and his death (chapter 49) to describe briefly the story of Esau and then Joseph (chapters 37 through 47).

Joseph (Yusuf), Son of Jacob

Joseph (Yusuf, as he is known in the Qur'an) was the eleventh son of Jacob and the only prophet among his twelve sons, according to the Islamic traditions. He is one of the most highly regarded prophets in Islam, Christianity, and Judaism. The Qur'an talks about Joseph along with other revered prophets in the following verse:

> *We gave him [Abraham] Isaac and Jacob: all (three) guided: and before him, We guided Noah, and among his [Abraham's] progeny,*

David, Solomon, Job, Joseph, Moses, and Aaron: thus do We reward those who do good. 6:84

Though he is mentioned in many chapters in the Qur'an, the story of Joseph is told in a chapter named after him (Surah al-Yusuf), in a rare continuous stream that is stunningly beautiful, formed, and heart-felt. Unlike many other chapters in the Qur'an named after other prophets, the chapter "Joseph" is almost entirely dedicated to his story, which in large part is similar to the story as told in Genesis. According to the Qur'an and the Bible, Joseph is a righteous person, following the footsteps of his forefathers Abraham, Isaac, and Jacob, and believes in One God and submits to His will. Jacob had twelve sons. Two of them, Joseph and Benjamin, were from Jacob's favorite wife, Rachel (Rachel and Benjamin are not mentioned by name in the Qur'an). Because of this, both the Qur'an and the Bible narrate how his other brothers grew jealous of him.

The Surah al-Yusuf of the Qur'an almost immediately starts by a proclamation about a story to be told by the Almighty.

We relate to you the best of stories through this Qur'an by Our revelation to you (O Muhammad), though before this you were one of those who did not know. 12:3 (Malik)

Yousuf Ali has translated the underlined word as "most beautiful" for the Arabic word *ahsan,* used in the verse. This beautiful story starts with a young Joseph telling his father Jacob about a dream he had, and ends with the reunion of Joseph with his father, to complete the interpretation of the dream. The story that starts in verse 4 ends with a prayer by Joseph in verse 101.

*My Lord! You have given me of the kingdom and taught me of the interpretation of sayings: Originator of the heavens and the earth! You are my guardian in this world and the hereafter; **make me die a Muslim [submitter] and join me with the good**. 12:101* (Malik)

The last part of the verse is in line with many such verses in the Qur'an, where many prophets, from Abraham to Isaac and Jacob and others, have prayed and identified themselves as "Muslims," or submitters. As noted thought this book, various scholars have translated the Arabic word *Muslimeen* as either "Muslims" or "submitters."

Chapter 12 of the Qur'an ("Joseph") has one hundred and eleven verses. The actual story is told in verses 12:4-12:101. There is an intro in verse 12:3: *We narrate to you the best of the stories,* with a short epilogue after the story in verse 12:102: *This is of the announcements relating to the unseen (which) We reveal to you, and you were not with them when they resolved upon their affair, and they were devising plans* (Shakir). A reading of the entire chapter is highly recommended.

JOSEPH'S DREAM

> *When Joseph said to his father: O my father! Surely I saw eleven stars and the sun and the moon—I saw them prostrating to me.* 12:4

When young Joseph tells his dream to Jacob, he is delighted, realizing this is a sign from God that the promise of the prophecy in Abraham's lineage will be fulfilled. Knowing that his ten half-brothers are jealous of him, Jacob tells him not to tell this dream to his brothers.

BROTHERS PLOT AGAINST HIM

Tired of Jacob's relentless love for Joseph, the half-brothers plot against Joseph. They ask Jacob if they could take Joseph with them on a hunting trip, and during the trip, they consider killing him but instead decide to throw him in a well. They return to Jacob and tell him that a wolf ate Joseph, showing him his shirt that they had stained with wolf's blood as proof. Jacob does not believe them but is deeply saddened nonetheless to lose his dear son. Joseph ends up being picked up by a caravan on the way to Egypt and is sold to the king of Egypt; he ends up in the household of his chief, who bought him.

> *The man in Egypt who bought him, said to his wife: 'Make his stay (among us) honorable: maybe he will bring us much good, or we shall adopt him as a son.' Thus did We establish Joseph in the land, that We might teach him the interpretation of stories (and events). And Allah*

has full power and control over His affairs; but most among mankind know it not. 12:21

JOSEPH BEING SEDUCED

Joseph grows into a handsome, attractive young man of immense masculine beauty. The chief's wife, who is not named in the Qur'an but is said to be Zulaikha by Jewish and Islamic traditions, wants to have intimate relations with Joseph but he keeps resisting. One day when they were alone in the house, she makes advances toward him but he refuses again, citing fear of disobedience to God's rules as the reason for his resistance:

> *And she in whose house he was, sought to make himself yield (to her), and she made fast the doors and said: 'Come forward.' He said: 'I seek Allah's refuge, surely my Lord made good my abode: Surely the unjust do not prosper.' 12:23 (Shakir)*

Joseph starts to run for the door but is grabbed from behind by the chief's wife, ripping his shirt in the process. They find her husband at the door, and he naturally becomes furious. Joseph tells him it was his wife who was making the advances, and upon the advice of her family member, the torn shirt is shown as the proof of his innocence. The husband believes his version:

> *So when he [the husband] saw his shirt rent from behind, he said: 'Surely it is a guile of you women; surely your guile is great: O Joseph! turn aside from this; and (O my wife)! ask forgiveness for your fault, surely you are one of the wrong-doers'. 12:28–29 (Shakir)*

A while later, when the wife's lady friends mock her obsession with Joseph, she arranges for the ladies to cut oranges with a knife and calls on Joseph. The women get so spellbound by Joseph's beauty that they cut their fingers rather than the oranges. The wife then reminds her friends why she is so obsessed, as she has to deal with Joseph's beauty every day, since Joseph lives in the same household:

She said: 'This is he with respect to whom you blamed me, and certainly I sought his yielding himself (to me), but he abstained, and if he does not do what I bid him, he shall certainly be imprisoned, and he shall certainly be of those who are in a state of ignominy.' He said: 'My Lord! The prison house is dearer to me than that to which they invite me; and if You turn not away their device from me, I will yearn toward them and become (one) of the ignorant.' 12:32 (Shakir)

And despite proving his innocence, Joseph ends up in the jail after all.

JOSEPH INTERPRETS DREAMS IN THE PRISON

While in prison with two other inmates, Joseph correctly interprets their dreams, and he reaffirms his faith in the one God to the inmates:

And I follow the ways of my fathers, Abraham, Isaac, and Jacob; and never could we attribute any partners whatever to God: that (comes) of the Grace of God to us and to mankind: yet most men are not grateful. O my two companions of the prison! (I ask you): are many lords differing among themselves better, or the One God, Supreme and Irresistible? 12:38–39

When one of them is released, he tells the king (*Malik*, as he is noted in verses 43, 50, and 54) of Joseph's unique ability to correctly interpret dreams. The king himself had a dream of seven fat cows being eaten by seven skinny ones and seven ears of corn being replaced with shriveled ones, but none of his advisors could interpret it, and he decides to call on Joseph, who correctly informs the king of an impending draught that will last seven years, followed by a year of abundant rain. This impresses the king.

THE WIFE AND HER WOMEN FRIENDS FINALLY CONFESS

The chief's wife and her friends eventually retract their story and Joseph is exonerated:

And the king said: 'Bring him to me.' So when the messenger [Joseph] came to him, he said: 'Go back to your Lord and ask him, what is the case of the women who cut their hands; surely my Lord knows their guile'. He said: 'How was your [addressing the lady friends] affair when you sought Joseph to yield himself (to you)?' They said: 'Remote is Allah (from imperfection), we knew of no evil on his part.' The chief's [Aziz's] wife said: 'Now has the truth become established: I sought him to yield himself (to me), and he is most surely of the truthful ones'. 12:50–51 (Shakir)

The king forgives Joseph and appoints him as one of his top aides, giving him a lot of authority:

And the king said: 'Bring him to me, I will choose him for myself.' So when he had spoken with him, he said: 'Surely you are in our presence today an honorable, a faithful one.' 12:54 (Shakir)

JOSEPH'S BROTHERS VISIT EGYPT

Joseph's brothers travel to Egypt for grain. Joseph instantly recognizes them but they don't know it is him. He asks them to bring him their half brother (Benjamin). The brothers go back to their home and tell Jacob they have to take Benjamin to Egypt:

He [Jacob] said: 'Shall I trust you with him with any result other than when I trusted you with his brother aforetime? But God is the best to take care (of him), and He is the Most Merciful of those who show mercy!' 12:64

Jacob fears another plot like the one that took Joseph away from him, but eventually he relents. The half-brothers then take Benjamin back to Egypt. Joseph reveals himself to his only real brother. He places his measuring cup in Benjamin's bag as his people distribute the grain. His people then call out that the chief's measuring cup has been stolen and the thief will be held back. The brothers' bags are searched and lo and behold, the measuring cup is found in Benjamin's bag. His brothers plead to Joseph's men that their brother is not a thief. They eventually return to their homes to Jacob, and once again break his heart by telling him that Benjamin had to be left behind. Jacob is deeply grief stricken.

JOSEPH FINALLY REVEALS HIMSELF TO HIS BROTHERS

Jacob asks the brothers to go back and find both Joseph and Benjamin. The brothers once again return to Egypt and plead with Joseph for the return of the two brothers:

> Then, when they came (back) into (Joseph's) presence they said: 'O exalted one. Distress has seized us and our family: we have (now) brought but scanty capital: so pay us full measure (we pray you), and treat it as charity to us: for Allah does reward the charitable.' He (Joseph) said: '(Do you) know how you dealt with Joseph and his brother, not knowing (what you were doing)?' 12:88–89

Then Joseph finally reveals his identity to his brothers:

> They said: 'Are you indeed Joseph?' He said: 'I am Joseph and this is my brother; Allah has indeed been Gracious to us; surely he who guards (against evil) and is patient (is rewarded), for surely Allah does not waste the reward of those who do good.' 12:90

The brothers then admit their wrongdoing and feel guilty and ask for forgiveness. Joseph forgives them and gives them his shirt to take back to Jacob. He asks them to rub it on Jacob's eyes as a healing, as he had gone blind weeping incessantly in Joseph's absence.

JOSEPH AND JACOB FINALLY REUNITE

The brothers take the shirt back to Jacob, who is not able to see much; he nonetheless smells the scent of Joseph's shirt as they near his house and announces that Joseph may be near. People think he is growing senile. Jacob indeed gets his eyesight back when Joseph's shirt is rubbed on his eyes:

> When the caravan left (Egypt), their father said: 'I do indeed scent the presence of Joseph: No, think me not a dotard' (or weak in judgment). They said: 'By Allah! truly you are in your old wandering mind.' So when the bearer of good news came he cast it on his face, so forthwith

he regained his sight. He said: 'Did I not say to you that I know from Allah what you do not know?' They said: 'O our father! ask forgiveness of our faults for us, surely we were sinners.' 12:94–97

Jacob too forgives the sons and informs them that God also forgave them, since "He is the Forgiving, Compassionate." Jacob then enters Egypt, and finally there is a long-awaited reunion with his most beloved son, Joseph.

THE DREAM IS FULFILLED

Then when they entered the presence of Joseph, he provided a home for his parents with himself, and said: 'Enter Egypt (all) in safety if Allah wills.' And he raised his parents upon the throne and they fell down in prostration before him, and he [Joseph] said: 'O my father! this is the significance of my vision of old; my Lord has indeed made it to be true; and He was indeed kind to me when He brought me forth from the prison and brought you from the desert after the Satan had sown dissensions between me and my brothers, surely my Lord is benign to whom He pleases; surely He is the Knowing, the Wise.' 12:99–100

The story ends with a prayer from Joseph in verse 12:101, as noted in the beginning of this section. The short epilogue to the story of Joseph then follows:

This is of the announcements relating to the unseen (which) We reveal to you [Muhammad] and you were not with them when they resolved upon their affair, and they were devising plans. 12:102 (Shakir)

Muslim scholars believe the chapter was revealed in its entirety in Mecca when the pagans of Mecca challenged the Qur'an's divinity and asked Muhammad about the story of Joseph in order to humiliate him. Though Genesis already had a description of Joseph's story, they were stunned when Muhammad narrated the story that was fairly unknown within the pagan Arabs in Mecca.

The Torah's Accounts of the Story of Joseph

Joseph's life story is told in great detail starting in chapter 37 of Genesis, with his father Jacob settling in the land of Canaan. It ends with Joseph's death at the age of 110 years in chapter 50, which is the end of Genesis. By and large, the story of Joseph is very similar as told in the Torah and the Qur'an. They both hold Joseph in high esteem, mention his unique power to correctly interpret dreams, and portray him as the most beloved son of Jacob. The brothers are jealous and sell him to a caravan, Joseph ends up in Egypt where the chief's wife tries to seduce him, and he resists. He is put in jail, where he uses his ability as a dream interpreter on the inmates, and this skill gets him out of prison when he correctly interprets the king's dreams. The accounts of the two dreams the king had are the same in the Qur'an and the Torah (the seven fat cows eating seven thin ones, and the seven green ears of corn replaced with seven dry ones). He eventually is pardoned and rises up in the ranks quickly and holds a high post in the Egyptian kingdom. His brothers visit Egypt and don't recognize him. He holds his real brother ransom, sends his shirt back to his father, Jacob, who had been missing him dearly, and eventually leads to a happy family reunion, wherein Joseph forgives his brothers. Both the Qur'an and the Torah tell a continuous stream of events, a unique feature for the Qur'an, and a long narration in the Torah, even from biblical standards.

Some variations do exist in the story as told by the Qur'an and the Torah:

- The Qur'an uses the specific term *malik* (with a short "a"), meaning "the king" or "the ruler," to describe the ruler in Egypt. The Qur'an uses the word *pharaoh* (*fir'awn* in Arabic) for the king of Egypt during the times of Moses and never used this term to describe the Egyptian ruler in the story of Joseph (or Abraham). Genesis frequently refers to the Egyptian ruler as Pharaoh in Joseph's story. Though modern writers have used the term Pharaoh to describe all rulers of ancient Egypt, according to historical sources, the title Pharaoh for the rulers of Egypt was not used until the New

Kingdom period of ancient Egypt (comprised of the eighteenth through the twentieth Egyptian dynasties), which started in the sixteenth century B.C.E.[2] By the time of the rule of Thutmose III in 1479 B.C.E., it became a common way of addressing the king. Until this time, the term "Pharaoh" was used to describe the royal palace. According to timelines by biblical scholars, Joseph died in the year 1805 B.C.E., well before the title was in use to indicate the Egyptian ruler. In fact, Genesis uses the title Pharaoh as early as the Abrahamic period, when Abraham took Sarah to Egypt.

Pharaoh's officials saw her and praised her to Pharaoh; and the woman was taken into Pharaoh's house. Genesis 12:15

And in the story of Joseph, Genesis once again calls the king of Egypt a Pharaoh:

Meanwhile, the Midianites sold him in Egypt to Potiphar, Pharaoh's officer, the captain of the bodyguard. Genesis 37:36

The Qur'an refers to the man who took Joseph to his house by the generic word, "chief" (*Aziz*). True to its tradition of being specific, the Torah mentions his name as Potiphar, the captain of the guards of the Pharaoh, as noted in the verse above.

- In the Bible, when the advancing wife tears Joseph's shirt, Potiphar believes the wife's version and imprisons Joseph. The wife tells the story and blames Joseph instead for the advances when Potiphar came home *later that day*. In the Qur'an, the chief is described as being *at the door*, when Joseph is trying to flee, and he initially believes Joseph's defense for his innocence.
- The story about the lady friends cutting their fingers is not described in the Torah.
- The Torah names Benjamin as Joseph's only real brother. The Qur'an does not name any of his brothers.

Discussion Points for Dialogue and Healing

- Abraham is considered the father of the monotheistic faiths of Islam, Christianity, and Judaism and is highly revered by all three. Abraham, Isaac, and Jacob are considered the patriarchs by all three religions. The Qur'an calls them among the elite prophets. The Qur'an proclaims Abraham "friend of God" *(Khalíl Allah)*—a very high rank.

- God promised Abraham great progeny through Isaac. The Hebrew prophets' lineage is through Isaac and Jacob. Muhammad's lineage is traced back to Ishmael. That makes Jews, Christians, and Muslims cousins, belonging to the same Abrahamic family. The "Hebrew prophets" are considered prophets by Christians as well as Muslims.

- Ka'aba, the holiest shrine in Islam, located in the city of Mecca was originally built by Abraham and Ishmael.

- The Torah also refers to Hagar and Ishmael in reverence, promising Abraham a "great nation" from Ishmael.

- Zamzam (well) water located near Ka'aba is considered holy by Muslims. It is part of the ritual of the Hajj for Muslims to circle around ka'aba, and drink Zamzam water. It is ironic that the Qur'an does not make a reference to Zamzam water or Hagar's search for the water in the desert, but the Hebrew Bible does (in the book of Genesis).

- According to the Qur'an, Islam is the faith of Abraham, and in addition to the progeny from Isaac, Abraham, and Ishmael prayed for a prophet from *their* progeny while building *Ka'aba*. Abraham, Jacob, and Joseph all asked their sons to be Muslims, or "submitters."

- Though the relationship between the two wives of Abraham, Sarah and Hagar, was not the most cordial, the Qur'an holds both of them in high esteem. The Torah also reassures Hagar in the wilderness and sends angels to help her and her young son, Ishmael.

- The story of Joseph is remarkably similar in the Qur'an and the Bible. Both scriptures describe his story in unusually long passages.

- Feel free to ponder on the points noted below and add your own.

Time to Ponder

- Jews, Christians, and Muslims consider Abraham their forefather and hold him and his progeny in high esteem. Why has this (along with the belief in the same God) not translated into a better relationship between the Jews, Christians, and Muslims?
- Islam is categorized as the religion of Abraham (*Din al-Ibrahimi*) in the Qur'an, which then was completed by Muhammad. What makes many Muslims (as well as people of other faiths) view Islam as a religion mainly limited to the days of Muhammad and afterwards?

CHAPTER 10
Moses (Musa, Moshe)

Every mother is like Moses. She does not enter the promised land.
She prepares a world she will not see.
Pope Paul VI

This chapter mainly reviews the life of Moses, but in the end it briefly goes over the story of David, a highly regarded king of Israel and a prophet of Islam.

Moses (*Moshe* in Hebrew, or *Musa* in Arabic) is the prophet most often mentioned by name in the Qur'an (136 times). The Torah is the holy book revealed to him by God. *Musa* means "drawn out of water." His Hebrew name, *Moshe*, also means something similar: "to draw out." They both refer to him being drawn out of the Nile River, where his mother had left him as an infant in a basket. Moses is considered the prophet with the highest status in Judaism. Christianity also recognizes him as a highly revered prophet. He is known in the Qur'an as a messenger (*rasul*), an exalted prophet, and a lawgiver.

> *Also mention in the Book (the story of) Moses: for he was specially chosen, and he was a messenger (and) a prophet, and we called him from the right (blessed) side of Mount Sinai, and made him draw near to us, for mystic (converse). 19:51–52*

His story, especially in reference to the pharaoh of Egypt and the children of Israel, is the most frequently told story in the Qur'an. Similarly, in the New Testament, Moses is mentioned more often than any of the other Old Testament prophets.

In a departure from the norm in this book, the life of Moses as told in the Bible will be reviewed first, before the Qur'anic narrations on the same subject. The life struggles and teachings of Moses are described in detail in the Torah, starting with the book of Exodus, and continuing on in Leviticus and Numbers, and ending with Moses' death in the book of Deuteronomy.

BIRTH

According to the biblical sources, Moses was from the genealogy of Levi, one of the twelve sons of Jacob (Israel), and was born in Egypt, described anywhere from one hundred to four hundred years after the death of Joseph. When Joseph passed away, the children of Israel, or Israelites, were living rather well. However, that changed before Moses was born. By now, the king of Egypt, a cruel person, had enslaved the Israelites. Thutmose I, of the eighteenth Egyptian dynasty, is said to be the pharaoh at the time of Moses' birth, though other candidates have been put forth. The Israelites were oppressed and subjected to harsh labor. The children of Israel had multiplied, and there was a population explosion. According to some accounts, they numbered over half a million to about one million at the time. The Pharaoh got concerned that the Israelites might take over the Egyptians, and he passed an executive order to kill all the Israeli baby boys. Moses' mother, fearing that he too will be killed, puts him in a basket and drops it in the Nile River, so he could float to safety, while his sister Miriam watches from the riverbank. Eventually, the Pharaoh's daughter finds Moses. Feeling pity for the crying baby, she takes him to the Pharaoh's palace. (According to Islamic historians, it was Pharaoh's wife, *Asiya*, who picked him up and later adopted him.) She knew the baby was a Jewish boy and looks for an Israeli woman to breastfeed him. Miriam approaches the Pharaoh's daughter and offers to find someone suitable to breastfeed him, and lo and behold finds Moses' real mother to do that. Moses then grows up in the Pharaoh's palace.

MOSES FLEES EGYPT FOR MIDIAN

Very little is mentioned about Moses' youth in the book of Exodus. As he reached young adulthood, he starts to go outside the palace and realizes his people are mistreated. One day he sees an Egyptian beating up an Israelite slave. Moses gets angry and hits the Egyptian, who falls and dies. Moses eventually fears for his own life and flees Egypt and ends up in Midian, which is considered to be in the north of the Red Sea. There he meets his future wife and lives for many years, tending to the livestock of his father-in-law. This is when his life changed, and that of a whole nation that followed.

THE BURNING BUSH TALKS TO MOSES

One day while tending to his normal business, Moses sees a burning bush near Mount Sinai. He becomes curious as he sees the bush burn without being consumed. As he approaches the bush, God calls his name out and asks him to take his shoes off, since he is approaching holy ground (Exodus 3:4). This is the beginning of his prophecy and a long ordeal. God reminds Moses that while he is living comfortably with his family in Midian, the rest of the Israelites are still suffering in slavery in Egypt under the cruel rule of the Pharaoh. God tells Moses to go to the Pharaoh and ask for the release of the Israelites. According to the accounts in Exodus, after initial reluctance, Moses agrees but asks for his brother Aaron, also a prophet, to go with him to help. This is when God gave Moses the staff that can turn into a snake as well as the miracle in his hand that turns very bright (or very white). God endowed Moses with these miracles to convince the children of Israel, as well as the Pharaoh, that he is a prophet sent by God to deliver the divine message. Armed by his belief in God, these two powerful tools, and Aaron, Moses returns to Egypt.

Upon his return, Moses relates to the Israelites what God had instructed him: there is no god but God and to worship no one but Him and that he (Moses) has returned to liberate them. He then asks the Pharaoh to release the Jews, giving him the same message about the One God. The Pharaoh does not take him seriously, even when he demonstrates the miracles bestowed upon his hand and the staff. Instead, the Pharaoh becomes even crueler to the Jewish slaves, and their affliction only worsens. The children of Israel start to blame Moses for their sufferings, saying they wished he had never returned. Moses goes back to God for guidance, who then promises ten plagues upon the Egyptians to convince them to release the Israelites. These are the ten plagues mentioned in the book of Exodus:

1. The Nile turns to blood. (7:14–24)
2. Frogs come out of the Nile. (8:1–15)
3. Gnats, or lice, erupt from the ground. (8:16–19)
4. Flies swarm Egypt. (8:20–32)
5. A mysterious disease affects Egyptian livestock and kills them. (9:1–7)
6. Boils break out on Egyptians and their livestock. (9:8–12)
7. A hailstorm hits Egypt. (9:13–35)
8. Locusts kill the remaining crops of the Egyptians. (10:1–20)
9. Darkness covers Egypt for three days, except Goshen, where Israelites live. (10:21–29)
10. Firstborns (humans and animals) die. (11:1)

FIRST EVER PASSOVER, LEADING TO EXODUS

God goes on to instruct Moses to tell the children of Israel to sacrifice a lamb or a goat and smear its blood on their doors for identification. Detailed instructions are given regarding how the animals are to be slaughtered and eaten. The promise was that God would strike the first-born of the Egyptians but pass over the Israelites' homes, sparing them.

The same night of the Passover, Pharaoh loses his firstborn son and relents to let the Israelites leave Egypt. Led by Moses and Aaron, the Israelites leave quickly. The book of Exodus describes how God guides Moses, in the form of a dark cloud during the day, and a large pillar of fire during the night, to show him the way. This path initially leads to the Red Sea, and eventually leads to the Promised Land—but not until after the death of Moses under the leadership of Moses' successor, Joshua.

THE PARTING OF THE RED SEA

After letting the Israelites go, the Pharaoh changes his mind and decides to chase them down with a huge army. He meets them near the Red Sea. Israelites are caught between the Pharaoh's army on one side and the Red Sea on the other.

> *As Pharaoh drew near, the sons of Israel looked, and behold, the Egyptians were marching after them, and they became very frightened; so the sons of Israel cried out to the LORD. Then they said to Moses, 'Is it because there were no graves in Egypt that you have taken us away to die in the wilderness? Why have you dealt with us in this way, bringing us out of Egypt? Is this not the word that we spoke to you in Egypt, saying, "Leave us alone that we may serve the Egyptians?" For it would have been better for us to serve the Egyptians than to die in the wilderness.'* Exodus 14:10–12[1]

Moses raises his miraculous staff and the sea parts, allowing Moses and the Israelites to pass on dry land and reach the other side of the sea.

> *Then Moses stretched out his hand over the sea; and the LORD swept the sea back by a strong east wind all night and turned the sea into dry land, so the waters were divided. The sons of Israel went through the midst of the sea on the dry land, and the waters were like a wall to them on their right hand and on their left.* Exodus 14:21–22

The Pharaoh and his army follow, but by this time the water recedes and they drown in the Red Sea.

> *Then the Egyptians took up the pursuit, and all Pharaoh's horses, his chariots, and his horsemen went in after them into the midst of the sea.* Exodus 14:23
>
> *Then the LORD said to Moses, 'Stretch out your hand over the sea so that the waters may come back over the Egyptians, over their chariots and their horsemen.' So Moses stretched out his hand over the sea, and the sea returned to its normal state at daybreak, while the Egyptians were fleeing right into it; then the LORD overthrew the Egyptians in the midst of the sea. The waters returned and covered the chariots and the horsemen, even Pharaoh's entire army that had gone into the sea after them; not even one of them remained. But the sons of Israel walked on dry land through the midst of the sea, and the waters were like a wall to them on their right hand and on their left.* Exodus 14:26–29

ISRAELITES COMPLAIN

After successfully evading the Pharaoh and his army, Moses and the Israelites wander in the desert for forty years in search of the Promised Land (Canaan). While wandering in the desert, people grumble more and more and openly complain that they were getting a raw deal. Exodus chapters 16 and 17 describe their frequent complaining. They complained about the rough life in the desert and not having the food they were used to eating:

> *Then they [Israelites] set out from Elim, and all the congregation of the sons of Israel came to the wilderness of Sin, which is between Elim and Sinai, on the fifteenth day of the second month after their departure from the land of Egypt. The whole congregation of the sons of Israel grumbled against Moses and Aaron in the wilderness. The sons of Israel said to them, 'Would that we had died by the LORD'S hand in the land of Egypt, when we sat by the pots of meat, when we ate bread to the full; for you have brought us out into this wilderness to kill this whole assembly with hunger.' Exodus 16:1–3*

The Bible describes how manna (a sticky bread-like substance) and *salwa* (quails) descended from the sky to feed the Israelites. They also complain of not having enough water, so God told Moses to strike a rock with his staff and water gushes forth.

> *Then all the congregation of the sons of Israel journeyed by stages from the wilderness of Sin, according to the command of the LORD, and camped at Rephidim, and there was no water for the people to drink. Therefore the people quarreled with Moses and said, 'Give us water that we may drink.' And Moses said to them, 'Why do you quarrel with me? Why do you test the LORD?' But the people thirsted there for water; and they grumbled against Moses and said, 'Why, now, have you brought us up from Egypt, to kill us and our children and our livestock with thirst?' So Moses cried out to the LORD, saying, 'What shall I do to this people? A little more and they will stone me.' Then the LORD said to Moses, 'Pass before the people and take with you some of the elders of Israel; and take in your hand your staff with which you*

struck the Nile, and go. Behold, I will stand before you there on the rock at Horeb; and you shall strike the rock, and water will come out of it, that the people may drink.' And Moses did so in the sight of the elders of Israel. Exodus 17:1–6

ARRIVING AT MOUNT SINAI

Two months into the journey from Egypt, Moses leads the Israelites to the wilderness of Sinai. He then ascends Mount Sinai and receives God's message, to make a covenant with God.

> *Moses went up to God, and the LORD called to him from the mountain, saying, "Thus you shall say to the house of Jacob and tell the sons of Israel: 'You yourselves have seen what I did to the Egyptians, and how I bore you on eagles' wings, and brought you to Myself. Now then, if you will indeed obey My voice and keep My covenant, then you shall be My own possession among all the peoples, for all the earth is Mine.'"* Exodus 19:3–5

The Israelites respond as follows, promising they will follow God's commands:

> *All the people answered together and said, 'All that the LORD has spoken we will do!'* Exodus 19:8

MOSES RECEIVES THE TEN COMMANDMENTS AT MOUNT SINAI

Moses leaves Aaron to look over the children of Israel in Sinai and ascends the mountain as God had instructed him to do. At first he receives the Ten Commandments. He later receives a number of other instructions that became law for the Jewish nation. All in all the five Books of Moses (the Torah) contain 613 laws. The Ten Commandments were inscribed on a tablet. Later on, God asks Moses to make two copies of the tablets (Exodus chapter 34). The Ten Commandments are:

1. I am the Lord, your God.
2. You shall have no gods before me. You shall not make yourself an idol.

3. Do not take Lord's name in vain (misuse His name).
4. Remember the Sabbath and keep it holy.
5. Honor your mother and father.
6. You shall not kill or murder.
7. You shall not commit adultery.
8. You shall not steal.
9. You shall not bear false witness.
10. You shall not covet your neighbor, their house, wife, male or female servants, ox or donkey, or anything else.

It should be noted that the imperatives known as the Ten Commandments appear twice in the Bible, initially in Exodus 20:1–17 and then repeated in Deuteronomy 5:6–21. The imperatives are the same but various religions have parsed them slightly differently. The Ten Commandments quoted above are from the Jewish (Talmudic) version. For example, Roman Catholics lump together the first two commandments mentioned above, whereas the last commandment is broken into two: 9: "Do not covet your neighbor's wife" and 10: "Or any other belonging of the neighbors."

ISRAELITES MAKE THE GOLDEN CALF

Moses was up on Mount Sinai for forty days, receiving the law; meanwhile, the Israelites grew impatient and asked Aaron to make an idol to worship. According to the biblical accounts, Aaron gathered gold jewelry from them, melted it, and carved it into a calf. The children of Israel, or at least some groups, started to worship the calf. God then asks Moses to go down quickly, as he was getting very angry with the people.

> Aaron said to them, 'Tear off the gold rings which are in the ears of your wives, your sons, and your daughters, and bring them to me.' Then all the people tore off the gold rings which were in their ears and brought them to Aaron. He took this from their hand, and fashioned it with a graving tool and made it into a molten calf; and they said, 'This is your god, O Israel, who brought you up from the land of Egypt.' Now when Aaron saw this, he built an altar before it; and Aaron made a proclamation and said, 'Tomorrow shall be a feast to the LORD.'

So the next day they rose early and offered burnt offerings, and brought peace offerings; and the people sat down to eat and to drink, and rose up to play. Then the LORD spoke to Moses, 'Go down at once, for your people, whom you brought up from the land of Egypt, have corrupted themselves.' Exodus 32:2–7

When Moses descends after receiving the Ten Commandments and the Torah, he gets furious when he sees many of his people worshiping the idol. He throws the tablets to the ground in disgust and burns the idol, grinds it into a powder, and throws it in the water and forces the people to drink it. When Moses asks Aaron what happened under his command, he essentially deflects the blame on to the Israelites. Moses then gets the people on the Lord's side—all Levites—to separate from the rest of the Israelites and asks the tribe of Levites to kill the rest of them. According to Exodus 32:28–29, "about 3,000 people died that day," in order to restore the truth and prevent the corruption of the rest of the Israelites by those who transgressed.

THE TABERNACLE AND THE ARK

Exodus goes on to talk about Moses building a place—a movable tent—to worship God. It describes in elaborate detail what it looked like—its dimensions and various compartments. In it were stored the tablets that were inscribed with the Ten Commandments; they were stored in a container called the Ark of the Covenant. The Ark contained many other relics from Moses and Aaron. The place that housed the Ark is called "the Holy of the Holies" (*Mishkan* in Hebrew).

ISRAELITES FIGHT MANY BATTLES

Between this time and Moses' death, there were many wars between the Israelites and other groups on their way to the Promised Land. These included battles with communities like Canaanites and King Sihon of the Ammonites. These were battles for the establishment of truth and justice, rather than land. It is ironic that Moses himself never set foot in the Promised Land.

MOSES PASSES AWAY

Though Moses could not deliver the Israelites to the Promised Land, he accomplished a lot according to biblical commentators. He liberated the children of Israel from slavery, gave them a code of ethics and law from God, and brought them to the edge of the Promised Land, to the plains of Moab. Only the Jordan River separated them from the Promised Land: Canaan (in current Israel). There in Moab, after God promised that he would lead the Israelites to the Promised Land, Moses passes away at the age of 120. The book of Deuteronomy (the last book of the Torah) ends by praising Moses:

> *Since that time no prophet has risen in Israel like Moses, whom the LORD knew face to face, for all the signs and wonders which the LORD sent him to perform in the land of Egypt against Pharaoh, all his servants, and all his land.* Deuteronomy 34:10–11

Moses in the Qur'an

Moses is known by the nickname of *Kalim Allah,* meaning "One who spoke with God," obviously considered a great honor.

> *Of some messengers We have already told thee the story; of others We have not; and to Moses Allah spoke direct.* 4:164

THE STORY OF MOSES IN THE QUR'AN

Chapter 20 tells the story of Moses. Verses 9 through 98 cover many aspects of his life, starting from the time when God first spoke to him from the burning bush, asking him to go back to Egypt to liberate the Israelites and reminding Moses of his birth and upbringing in the Pharaoh's palace. It narrates his interaction with the Pharaoh, the Pharaoh's tyranny, Moses rescuing the children of Israel from slavery, the Isrealites' frequent complaints, and ends with their worshipping the golden calf. This is probably the second longest sequence in the Qur'an (the longest being the one on Joseph in chapter 12). This sequence ends before the delivery of the Ten Commandments. That part of Moses' prophecy is mentioned elsewhere on various occasions. Most of the story told here is in chronological order (except the flashback to Moses' birth and the killing of the Egyptian, resulting in his escape to Midian). The verses are quoted here without much commentary. The following translation is compiled by Shakir, who uses the Arabic *Musa* for Moses and *Allah* for God:

TALKING TO THE BURNING BUSH

And has the story of Musa come to you? When he saw fire, he said to his family: Stop, for surely I see a fire, haply I may bring to you there from a live coal or find guidance at the fire. So when he came to it, a voice was uttered: 'O Musa: Surely I am your Lord, therefore put (take) off your shoes; surely you are in the sacred valley, Tuwa, And I have chosen you, so listen to what is revealed: Surely I am Allah, there is no god but I, therefore serve Me and keep up prayer for My remembrance: Surely the hour is coming—I am about to make it manifest—so that every soul may be rewarded as it strives: Therefore let not him who believes not in it and follows his low desires turn you away from it so that you should perish'. 20:9–16

GOD THEN GIVES MOSES TWO MIRACLES

'And what is this in your right hand, O Musa!' He said: 'This is my staff: I recline on it and I beat the leaves with it to make them fall upon my sheep, and I have other uses for it.' He said: 'Cast it down, O Musa!' So he cast it down; and lo! it was a serpent running. He said: 'Take hold of it and fear not; We will restore it to its former state: And press your hand to your side, it shall come out white without evil: another sign: That We may show you of Our greater signs.' 20:17–23

GOD INSTRUCTS HIM TO GO TO PHARAOH

Go to Firon [Pharaoh], surely he has exceeded all limits. He said: 'O my Lord! Expand my breast for me, And make my affair easy to me, And loose the knot from my tongue, (That) they may understand my word; And give to me an aider (helper) from my family: Haroun, [Aaron] my brother, Strengthen my back by him, And associate him (with me) in my affair, So that we should glorify You much, And remember You often. Surely, You are seeing us.' He [Allah] said: 'You are indeed granted your petition, O Musa.' 20:24–36

GOD THEN REMINDS MOSES OF HIS MOTHER

And certainly We bestowed on you a favor at another time; When We revealed to your mother what was revealed; Saying: 'Put him into a chest, then cast it down into the river, then the river shall throw him on the shore; there shall take him up one who is an enemy to Me and enemy to him, and I cast down upon you love from Me, and that you might be brought up before My eyes; When your sister went and said: Shall I direct you to one who will take charge of him? So We brought you back to your mother, that her eye might be cooled and she should not grieve.' 20:37–40

MOSES KILLS THE EGYPTIAN

Note: He is not mentioned as an "Egyptian" in the Qur'an:

And you killed a man, then We delivered you from the grief, and We tried you with (a severe) trying. Then you stayed for years among the people of Madyan [Midian]; then you came hither as ordained, O Musa. 20:40

MOSES ASKS FOR AARON AND PLEADS TO PHARAOH:

And I have chosen you for Myself: Go you and your brother with My communications and be not remiss in remembering Me; Go both to Firon, surely he has become inordinate; Then speak to him a gentle word haply he may mind or fear. Both said: "O our Lord! Surely we fear that he may hasten to do evil to us or that he may become inordinate." He [Allah] said: "Fear not, surely I am with you both: I do hear and see. So go you both to him and say: 'Surely we are two messengers of your Lord; therefore send the children of Israel with us and do not torment them! Indeed we have brought to you a communication from your Lord, and peace is on him who follows the guidance; surely it has been revealed to us that the chastisement will surely come upon him who rejects and turns back.'" 20:41–48

MOSES DELIVERS GOD'S MESSAGE TO THE PHARAOH

[When Moses and Aaron went to Pharaoh and delivered this message], Pharaoh said: 'And who is your Lord, O Musa?' He [Moses] said: 'Our

Lord is He Who gave to everything its creation, then guided it (to its goal).' He [Pharaoh] said: 'Then what is the state of the former generations?' He [Moses] said: 'The knowledge thereof is with my Lord in a book, my Lord errs not, nor does He forget; Who made the earth for you an expanse and made for you therein paths and sent down water from the cloud; then thereby We have brought forth many species of various herbs. Eat and pasture your cattle; most surely there are signs in this for those endowed with understanding. From it We created you and into it We shall send you back and from it will We raise you a second time.' 20:49–55

PHARAOH DISBELIEVES, CHALLENGES MOSES

Verses 20:56–64 then go on to describe the Pharaoh's contempt and disbelief; he calls Moses and Aaron "two magicians" and invites them to a duel with his own magicians. Moses accepts the challenge, and the duel takes place on the "day of the festival."

DUEL WITH PHARAOH'S MAGICIANS

They [magicians] said: 'O Musa! Will you cast, or shall we be the first who cast down?' He said: 'No! Cast down.' Then, lo! their cords and their rods—it was imaged to him on account of their magic as if they were running. So Musa conceived in his mind a fear. We [God] said: 'Fear not, surely you shall be the uppermost, And cast down what is in your right hand; it shall devour what they have wrought; they have wrought only the plan of a magician, and the magician shall not be successful wheresoever he may come from.' And the magicians [seeing the miracle of Moses] were cast down making obeisance (in prostration); they said: 'We believe in the Lord of Haroun and Musa.' (Firon) said: 'You believe in him before I give you leave [permission]; most surely he is the chief of you who taught you enchantment, therefore I will certainly cut off your hands and your feet on opposite sides, and I will certainly crucify you on the trunks of the palm trees, and certainly you will come to know which of us is the more severe and the more abiding in chastising.' They said: 'We do not prefer you to what has come to us of clear arguments and to He Who made us, therefore decide what you are going to decide; you can only decide about this world's life. Surely we believe in our Lord that He may forgive us our sins and the magic to which you compelled us; and Allah is better and more abiding.' 20:65–73

PARTING OF THE SEA, PHARAOH DROWNS

And certainly We revealed to Musa, saying: 'Travel by night with My servants, then make for them a dry path in the sea, not fearing to be overtaken, nor being afraid.' And Pharaoh followed them with his armies, so there came upon them of the sea that, which came upon them. And Pharaoh led astray his people and he did not guide (them) aright. 20:77–79

CHILDREN OF ISRAEL ARE LIBERATED, RECEIVE MANNA AND SALWA

O children of Israel! Indeed, We delivered you from your enemy, and We made a covenant with you on the blessed side of the mountain, and We sent to you the manna and the quails. Eat of the good things We have given you for sustenance, and be not inordinate with respect to them, lest My wrath should be due to you, and to whomsoever My wrath is due he shall perish indeed. And most surely I am most Forgiving to him who repents and believes and does good, then continues to follow the right direction. 20:80–82

ISRAELITES START WORSHIPPING THE GOLDEN CALF

Verses 20:83–89 describe God telling Moses to go down from Mount Sinai, as the Israelites had made a golden calf and started worshipping it; these verses also describe Moses' anger over them.

MOSES IS UPSET WITH AARON OVER THE GOLDEN CALF ISSUE

And certainly Haroun had said to them before: "O my people! You are only tried by it, and surely your Lord is the Beneficent (Gracious) Allah, therefore follow me and obey my order." They said: "We will by no means cease to keep to its worship until Musa returns to us." (Moses) said: "O Haroun! What prevented you, when you saw them going astray, So that you did not follow me? Did you then disobey my order?" He said: "O son of my mother! Seize me not by my beard nor by my head; surely I was afraid lest you should say: 'You have caused a division among the children of Israel and not waited for my word.'" He [Moses] said: "What was then your object, O Samiri?" [the person who asked the Israelites to make the calf]. He said: "I saw Gabriel, what they did not see, so I took a handful (of the dust) from the footsteps of the messenger, then I threw it in the casting; thus did my soul commend to me." 20:90–96

The sequence ends with Moses' proclamation:

'Your Allah is only Allah [Your god is only God], there is no god but He; He comprehends all things in (His) knowledge.' 20:98

OTHER PASSAGES ON MOSES

There is yet another long passage about Moses in chapter 7 (*Al-A'raf* or "The Heights") that extends from verse 103 to 171. This set of verses mentions Moses' conversation with God on Mount Sinai and the deliverance of the Ten Commandments on the tablets and the Torah; it also covers some parts mentioned in chapter 20, verses 9–98. After mentioning the Torah's deliverance to Moses, the Qur'an interrupts the story of Moses to claim that Muhammad was mentioned in both the Torah and the Gospel and that he was sent as the messenger for all mankind. The long narration starts with the following verse:

Then after them We sent Moses with Our signs to Pharaoh and his chiefs, but they wrongfully rejected them: So see what was the end of those who made mischief. 7:103

According to the Qur'an, Moses goes to the Pharaoh and not only asks for the release of the children of Israel, but starts by the proclamation that he is the messenger of the Lord of the worlds:

Moses said: 'O Pharaoh! I am a messenger from the Lord of the worlds, One for whom it is right to say nothing but truth about Allah. Now have I come unto you (people), from your Lord, with a clear (Sign): So let the children of Israel depart along with me.' 7:104–105

THE PLAGUES ON THE EGYPTIANS

The chapter then goes on to narrate the plagues that were cast on the Pharaoh's people. However, the Qur'an does not mention every single plague mentioned in the book of Exodus.

We punished the people of Pharaoh with years (of droughts) and shortness of crops; that they might receive admonition. But when good (times) came, they said, 'This is due to us'; When gripped by calamity, they ascribed it to evil omens connected with Moses and those with him! Behold! In truth the omens of evil are theirs in Allah's sight, but most of them do not understand! They said [to Moses]: 'Whatever be the Signs you bring, to work therewith your sorcery [magic] on us, we shall never believe in you.' So We sent (plagues) on them: Wholesale death, locusts, lice, frogs, and blood: Signs openly self-explained: but they were steeped in arrogance, a people given to sin. Every time the penalty fell on them, they said: 'O Moses! On your behalf call on your Lord in virtue of his promise to you: If thou wilt remove the penalty from us, we shall truly believe in you, and we shall send away the children of Israel with you.' But every time We removed the penalty from them according to a fixed term which they had to fulfill, Behold! they broke their word! 7:130–135

MOSES ASKS TO SEE GOD ON MOUNT SINAI

When Moses came to the place appointed by Us, and his Lord addressed him, He said: 'O my Lord! Show (Yourself) to me, that I may look upon You.' Allah said: 'By no means can you see Me (direct); But look upon the mount; if it abide in its place, then shall you see Me.' When his Lord manifested His Glory on the Mount, He made it (turned) as dust. And Moses fell down in a swoon. When he recovered his senses he said: 'Glory be to You! To You I turn in repentance, and I am the first to believe.' (Allah) said: 'O Moses! I have chosen you above (other) men, by the mission I (have given you) and the words I (have spoken to you): take then the (revelation) which I give you, and be of those who give thanks.' 7:143–144

MOSES RECEIVES TORAH ON TABLETS

And We ordained laws for him in the tablets in all matters, both commanding and explaining all things, (and said): 'Take and hold these with firmness, and enjoin your people to hold fast by the best in the precepts: soon shall I show you the homes of the wicked.' 7:145

Verses 7:152–155 go on to describe the golden calf worshipping and Moses' disgust.

The Qur'an interrupts the story here to claim that Muhammad was mentioned in the Torah in verses 157–158, which will be addressed later in chapter 12 ("Muhammad"). After this, the Qur'an returns to the story of Moses by claiming:

Of the people of Moses, there is a section who guide and do justice in the light of truth. 7:159

Qur'anic versus Torah's Accounts of the Story of Moses

As one can gather from the two accounts presented, the basic story as told in the Torah and the Qur'an is very similar, though there are some differences that are outlined below.

THE SIMILARITIES ARE SUMMARIZED FIRST:

- Prebirth: The ruthlessness of the pharaoh of Egypt, and his mistreatment of the Israelites. He enslaved the Israelites and ordered their male newborn babies to be killed. The Pharaoh was a transgressor, a nonbeliever, and a tyrant.
- Moses' mother puts him in a basket in the Nile, his sister offers a Jewish woman to breastfeed him, and that woman turns out to be his real mother. And he ends up being raised in the Pharaoh's palace.
- Moses kills an Egyptian, when he sees him mistreat a Jewish slave, eventually fleeing to Midian, and there he meets his future wife and raises his family.

- At Mount Sinai, God talks from the burning bush to Moses for the first time, telling him to go back to Egypt and liberate the Israelites.
- Moses receives the two miracles: the staff and the bright white hand. Moses talks about his speech impediment and a request to be "strengthened" by Aaron, his brother and another prophet. His request is granted.
- The Pharaoh refuses to let go of the Israelites at first. The plagues hit Egyptians. (The Bible mentions ten of them, the Qur'an only a few of them by name.) The Pharaoh eventually lets the Israelites leave Egypt.
- The Pharaoh then decides to chase them down; Moses parts the Red Sea, letting the Israelites and himself cross, but the Pharaoh and his army drown.
- The Israelites wander in the desert (for forty days, according to Bible; however, the Qur'an, true to its style, does not mention the exact duration). The Israelites constantly grumble and complain. Manna and salwa descend from the sky. The Israelites (or at least many of them) remain ungrateful. They make a golden calf and start worshipping it, while Moses is up on the mountain for forty days receiving the tablets on which the Torah is written. Moses gets furious at the Israelites for the idolatry and gets upset with Aaron, as he had left him in charge of the Israelites when he was away.
- The Torah is a source of mercy to the children of Israel (the Qur'an adds the word *furqan*, or "the criterion"). Both the Qur'an and the Bible use the words "guidance" and "law" frequently in reference to the Torah.

THE FOLLOWING ARE SOME OF THE DIFFERENCES:

- The entire story of Moses, the twelve tribes and their genealogy, and the laws of the Torah are described in much more detail in the Old Testament than the Qur'an. For example, the Torah describes the Tabernacle, the holy place for worship, in great detail, along with the religious laws or commandments. In total, 613 commandments are described; 248 are considered "positive" (i.e., Dos) and 365 are considered negative (Don'ts). The Qur'an makes many general references to the laws (*And We ordained laws for him in the tablets in all matters, both commanding and explaining all things. 7:145*).

- The Torah talks about baby Moses being picked up by the Pharaoh's sister. The Qur'an does not mention who picked him up, but many Muslim commentators and historians believe it was the Pharaoh's wife, Asiya. The Qur'an specifically refers to her as a pious lady.

And Allah sets forth, as an example to those who believe the wife of Pharaoh: Behold she said: 'O my Lord! Build for me, in nearness to You, a mansion in the Garden, and save me from Pharaoh and his doings, and save me from those that do wrong.' 66:11

- The Torah mentions Moses' father-in-law in Midian by two names: *Jethro* and *Ruel*. The Qur'an does not call him by name, but he is believed to be *Shu'ayb*, considered a prophet in Islam.
- In the Torah, Aaron helps the Israelites build the golden calf, which is then used for idol worship. In the Qur'an, Aaron is described as a prophet; he didn't help the Israelites with the idol, though Moses was upset with him for not preventing it. Aaron responds by basically stating he tried but feared for his life and thus didn't intervene with fuller force, as he was following Moses' command to maintain peace while he was gone.
- In the Qur'an, the Pharaoh when drowning tried in vain to declare his belief in God just as he saw death approach him, but he was told it was too late for that kind of trickery:

And We made the children of Israel to pass through the sea, then Pharaoh and his hosts followed them for oppression and tyranny; until when drowning overtook him, he said: 'I believe that there is no god but He in Whom the children of Israel believe and I am of those who submit.' (And it was said to him), 'What? Now! And indeed you disobeyed before and you were of the mischief-makers. This day shall We save you in the body, that you may be a sign to those who come after you! But verily, many among mankind are heedless of Our Signs!' 10:90–92 (Shakir).

Many Muslim scholars feel that the Qur'an is referring to the mummi-fication and preservation of the Pharaoh's body. The Bible does not have such mention of his last minute attempted reversal, or God's promise to save his body as a sign for generations to come.

- In the Qur'an, Moses, while on Mount Sinai, wished to see God, and He warns Moses that he will not be able to sustain the sight (7:142–144). The Torah makes no mention of this event.
- In the Torah, Moses passes away before ever entering the Promised Land. The Qur'an makes no mention of this. Indeed the Qur'an does not address the passing away of Moses at all.

David (Dawud)

David (*Daveed* in Hebrew and *Dawud* as he is known in the Qur'an) is yet another important and highly regarded prophet in the Qur'an and the Bible. He is a messenger (*rasul*) and a righteous king: the second king of the nation of Israel. He is among the select group of messengers who received a named scripture, known as *Zabur* in the Qur'an (Biblical psalms). He was a soldier in the army of Saul (the first king of Israel) and eventually took over the reign. He is given special powers by God as a judge and is famous for singing the praises of the Lord along with the birds and the mountains. He is perhaps most famous for killing a much bigger opponent, Goliath (*Jalut*), a famous warrior in the pagan Philistine army.

> *Bear patiently what they say, and remember Our servant David, the possessor of power; surely he was frequent in returning (to Allah). Surely We made the mountains to sing the glory (of Allah) in unison with him at the evening and the sunrise, And the birds gathered togeth-er; all joined in singing with him. And We strengthened his kingdom and We gave him wisdom and a clear judgment.* 38:17–20 (Shakir)

DAVID'S MELODIOUS SINGING OF GOD'S PRAISES

As mentioned above, David sings the praises of God, and the birds and the mountains join in. In addition to verse 38:18, David's singing of His praises along with the mountains and birds is narrated in chapter 34 as well. It is not entirely clear in what physical form the birds and the mountains joined David in singing, except that it was indeed one of the miracles bestowed on David.

> We bestowed Grace aforetime on David from ourselves: O you Mountains! Sing back the Praises of Allah with him! And you birds (also)! And We made the iron soft [supple] for him. 34:10

Pooya Yazdi, in his commentary of verse 34:10 writes:

> Dawud had been gifted with an enchanting melodious voice, and whenever he sang the glory of Allah the mountains around him would echo his praise, and the birds would join him in chorus. Allah made iron, one of the hardest metals, soft and pliant in his hands, so that without heating the metal he was able to manufacture coats of mail. It is said that Dawud was the first to manufacture coats of mail. As a prophet of Allah he only manufactured armor which is the means of defense, and not swords, which are the implements of aggression.[2]

> And remember David and Solomon, when they gave judgment in the matter of the field into which the sheep of certain people had strayed by night: We did witness their judgment. To Solomon We inspired the (right) understanding of the matter: to each (of them) We gave Judgment and Knowledge; it was Our power that made the hills and the birds celebrate Our praises, with David: it was We Who did (all these things). 21:78–79
>
> It was We Who taught him the making of coats of mail for your benefit, to guard you from each other's violence: will you then be grateful? 21:80

DAVID VS GOLIATH

The Qur'an dubs the battle between David and Goliath as the battle between good and evil—between believers and non-believers.

When they advanced to meet Goliath and his forces, they [the army of Saul and David] prayed: "Our Lord! Pour out constancy on us and make our steps firm: Help us against the unbelieving people." 2:250 (Shakir).

So they put them to flight by Allah's permission. And David slew Goliath, and Allah gave him kingdom and wisdom, and taught him of what He pleased. 2:251 (Shakir)

David in the Old Testament

The Bible holds David in high esteem and, as is customary, describes his life in more detail than the Qur'an does. However, the Old Testament also talks about his sins and adultery with Bathsheba, wife of Uriah, who David had sent to the battlefield. According to the Old Testament, Bathsheba conceives a child, and David later marries her, but God was furious with David and sends Nathan, another prophet, to tell David about his sins. David later repents (Psalm 51:1–12 and 2 Samuel 12:1–15). David receives three rather graphic punishments that are referenced in 2 Samuel 12:11–12. The Qur'an clearly rejects all notions of any sins attributed to prophets, especially major sins like adultery, and holds David, one of the more revered prophets, above such sins.

Discussion Points for Dialogue and Healing

- During Jewish-Muslim dialogue, Muslims should remind their Jewish counterparts that Moses is considered one of the five most exalted prophets in Islam. He is the prophet mentioned the most often by name in the Qur'an. His nickname in the Qur'an is *Kalim Allah,* or "one who spoke with God" (directly)—a great honor indeed.
- His mother and sister, as well as Pharaoh's wife (named *Asiya* in Islamic traditions), are also mentioned with reverence in the Qur'an. Muslims often add, "Peace be upon him" after Moses' name to show respect (as they do with other prophets' names).
- According to both the Qur'an and the Bible, Pharaoh was an evil tyrant. The Israelites (children of Israel) were enslaved and are viewed as victims of his tyranny. After their release, the Israelites frequently

grumbled and complained about the hardship as they wandered in the desert, in search of the Promised Land. Some of the children of Israel reverted to idol worshipping and received the wrath of Moses and God. The Qur'an and Torah are highly critical of this group of Israelites.

- The Ark of Moses containing various relics is considered holy in Torah, as well as the Qur'an. The Qur'an declares that the ark is a source of tranquility.

- The Qur'an refers to David as one of the holiest prophets. He is highly regarded in the Bible and the Qur'an. The scriptures revaled to him are in the form of songs and prayers, known as Psalms in the Hebrew Bible and as *Zabur* in the Qur'an.

- The Qur'an labels Goliath and his army, who came to fight David, as *kafirs* or nonbelievers (infidels). The Bible holds David in high esteem but also mentions David's transgressions (adultery). The Qur'an does not, as it typically holds the prophets above such fallible acts.

- Feel free to ponder on the points noted below and add your own.

Time to Ponder

- The Qur'an is at times frowned upon by non-Muslims for its criticism of the Jews and even accused for being anti-Semitic. Are the accounts of the similar stories on the Israelites in the Torah any less harsh? Was Jesus any less critical of the Jewish leadership of his time? Why are the Torah and the New Testament then not considered "anti-Semitic"?

- Does this criticism in all three scriptures extend to *all* Jews of *all* generations?

- In the Qur'an, David's (a Jewish prophet) battle with Goliath is dubbed as *jihad*, and Goliath's army is labeled *kafir* or infidels. Is that consistent with the prevailing perception of *jihad* and infidels?

CHAPTER 11

Jesus (Isa) and Mary (Maryam)

*For Jesus, there are no countries to be conquered, no ideologies
to be imposed, no people to be dominated. There are only
children, women and men to be loved.*
Henri Nouwen

This chapter will cover the life and teachings of Jesus Christ and his mother
Mary, known in the Qur'an as *Isa* and *Maryam*, respectively. The mother
and the son are inseparable, like no other in history. In both the Qur'an
and the Gospel, the two hold a very high and exalted status. Mary, though
not described as a prophet in the Qur'an, is mentioned with reverence
that is reserved for only the most exalted prophets.

Jesus Christ (Isa)

Jesus is also known as *Messiah* in the Qur'an and known as *Yasu* among
Arabic-speaking Christians. He is a messenger (*rasul*), a lawgiver, and
an exalted prophet. Muslims add, "Peace be upon him" after his name
as a sign of utmost respect. He was sent to the children of Israel and
was given the Holy Book, *Injil*, or Gospel. The Qur'an mentions Jesus
twenty-five times by name but he is referred to numerous other times
without naming him. The specific details of his childhood and other
teachings are not mentioned in detail like the Gospel does. However,
his miraculous birth is the focus of many sections of the Qur'an. Most
of the references to Jesus revolve around his birth, his mother Mary,
his prophecy, and his miracles. In the Qur'an, like all other prophets,
he is considered to be a Muslim, or a submitter (to the will of God), and

believed to have taught his followers the same message: that there is One God without any partners.

THE MIRACLES OF JESUS

The Qur'an refers to Jesus Christ as *Ruh Allah,* or "the spirit of God," in that God endowed him with many unique miracles, reflecting some of God's attributes. God bestowed these miracles upon him as a sign to prove his prophecy:

- Jesus speaks as a newborn from his cradle to defend the honor of his mother, Mary, and to proclaim his prophethood.
- He breathes life into clay and makes it into a bird.
- He cures the lepers.
- He cures the blind.
- He brings the dead back to life.

THE KEY BELIEFS TAUGHT BY THE QUR'AN REGARDING JESUS

1. He was born of a miraculous birth, without a father. The Qur'an gives a parallel with Adam's birth.
2. He was a prophet and a messenger of God. He was the word of God, the spirit of God, and the Messiah. All people in this world will honor him, and he will be honored in the hereafter.
3. However, he was neither divine nor the Son of God.
4. He did not die on the cross, but rather God made him ascend to the heavens to protect his honor. He will return to earth before the Day of Judgment, bringing peace and justice to earth.
5. Jesus preached the unity of God.
6. He performed many miracles, as noted above, all of them *by the will of God,* and thus the ultimate power and supremacy lies with God.

HOLY SPIRIT

The Qur'an repeatedly refers to Jesus as "son of Maryam" and says that God strengthened Jesus with *Ruh al-Quds,* or "Holy Spirit."

We gave Moses the Book and followed him up with a succession of messengers; We gave Jesus the son of Mary clear (signs) and strengthened him with the holy spirit. 2:87

Those messengers We endowed with gifts, some above others: To one of them [Moses] Allah spoke; others He raised to degrees (of honor); To Jesus the son of Mary We gave clear (signs), and strengthened him with the Holy Spirit. 2:253

The following verse refers to the Holy Spirit as well as the miracles that Jesus performed (moreover, the Qur'an insists he performed the miracles with God's permission):

Then God will ask: 'O Isa, son of Maryam! Recall my favor upon you and to your mother, how I strengthened you with the Holy Spirit, so you could speak to the people in cradle and in old age, how I taught you the Book, Wisdom, the Torah, and the Gospel. How you were able to make the figure of a bird out of clay, by My permission, how you breathed into it and changed it into a real bird, by My permission. How you could heal the born-blind and the lepers by My permission. How you could bring the dead body back to life by My permission. How I protected you from the violence of the children of Israel when you came to them with clear signs and the unbelievers among them said: 'This is nothing but a clear sorcery.' 5:110 (Shakir)

What or who is this Holy Spirit? On the surface, it resembles the Holy Spirit (Holy Ghost) component of the Trinity doctrine. In verse 16:102, the words *Ruh al-Quds* (Holy Spirit) is once again used, but this time it is not in relation with Jesus Christ:

*Say [addressing Muhammad]: The **Holy Spirit** has revealed it [the Qur'an] from your Lord with the truth, that it may establish those who believe and as a guidance and good news for those who submit. 16:102 (Shakir)*

Qur'an commentators take the Holy Spirit to mean Archangel Gabriel. Verse 16:102 confirms that belief. The previous verses mentioning the "strengthening" of Jesus "with the Holy Spirit" would then indicate that God empowered Jesus to perform his miraculous acts, or more specifically empowered him with words, through the Archangel Gabriel.

THE ANNUNCIATION AND THE BIRTH OF JESUS

Much like the angels visiting Abraham and giving him the glad tidings about Isaac's birth, Jesus' birth was also announced in advance. In this case, it was Archangel Gabriel who made the announcement. In both cases, the mothers were surprised: Sarah because of old age, and Mary because she was a virgin. The following is the narration from chapter 19, named after Mary (*Surah Maryam*):

> *O Muhammad, relate to them the story of Maryam in the Book (the Qur'an) when she withdrew from her family to a place in the East. She chose to be secluded from them. We sent to her Our angel and he appeared before her as a grown man. She said: "I seek Rahman's (The Gracious-God's) protection against you, leave me alone if you are God fearing." He said: "Don't be afraid, I am merely a messenger from your Rabb [Lord] to tell you about the gift of a **holy son**." She said: "How shall I bear a son, no man has ever touched me nor am I unchaste?" The angel replied: "So shall it be—Your Lord says: "It is easy for Me. We wish to make him a Sign for mankind and a blessing [mercy] from Us—and this matter has already been decreed." So she conceived the child and she retired with him to a remote place. The pains of childbirth drove her to the trunk of a palm-tree. She cried in her anguish: "Ah! Would that I had died before this, and been long forgotten!" Then (the child) called out to her from beneath her: "Grieve not, surely your Lord has made a stream to flow beneath you. If you shake the trunk of this palm-tree, it will drop fresh ripe dates in your lap. So eat, drink, and refresh yourself. If you see anyone, tell him: 'I have vowed a fast to Rahman (The Gracious-God), so I will not speak to anyone today.'"*
> 19:16–26 (Malik)

JESUS TALKS IN THE CRADLE

The newborn baby Jesus then surprises everyone by speaking in the cradle and announcing his prophethood: a unique miracle that had never been seen before (or since). Though to the outside world, this was the first time a newborn spoke, but this seemingly is not the first time Jesus spoke. The verses 19:23–24 quoted above mention something that the Bible does not: the matter of Mary's giving birth to Jesus Christ and the labor pains, indicating the "normalcy" of a human birth. Moreover, *Then (the child) called out to her from beneath her* (or *the voice beneath her called out* as some other Muslim scholars have translated the verse) indicates that Jesus spoke to his mother even *before* his birth.

> *At length she [Mary] brought the (baby) to her people, carrying him (in her arms). They said: 'O Mary! Truly an amazing thing hast thou brought! O sister of Aaron! Your father was not a man of evil, nor your mother a woman unchaste!'* **But she pointed to the baby.** *They said: 'How can we talk to one who is a child in the cradle?' He (Jesus) said: 'I am indeed a servant of Allah: He has given me revelation and made me a prophet; And He has made me blessed wheresoever I be, and has enjoined on me prayer and charity as long as I live; (He) has made me kind to my mother, and not overbearing (or hard to deal with);* **So peace is on me the day I was born, the day that I die, and the day that I shall be raised up to life (again)!**' *Such (was) Jesus the son of Mary: (it is) a statement of truth, about which they (vainly) dispute.* 19:27–34

Note the first bolded segment in the verses. When questioned, she points to her baby to respond to the critics and doubters. How would she have known that the newborn could talk? Once again, the point made about Jesus talking before his birth would make more sense now. (The other possibility would be a prior divine revelation to her about Jesus' ability to speak as a newborn, as noted below in verse 3:45–46.) Also note that Mary is referred to as a sister of Aaron in these verses. This refers to her ancestry, rather than being a biological sister of Aaron. Zechariah was an uncle of Mary and her guardian. Zechariah's wife (known as Elizabeth in the Bible) and Mary were related and were descendants of Aaron, according to Muslim scholars.

The Qur'an then goes on to announce and make very clear that God does not have a son:

> It is not befitting to (the majesty of) God that He Himself should beget a son! He is far above this; for when He decrees a matter He need only say: 'Be' and it is. (Jesus declared), 'Verily God is my Lord and your Lord: therefore serve Him. This is the Right Way.' In spite of this, the sects from among them are divided concerning Jesus. 19:35–37[1]

JESUS THE MESSIAH

Jesus' birth is once again narrated in another set of verses in chapter 3, showing that not only did Mary know about Jesus' ability to talk from the cradle, she also knew what her son would mean to the world; her son would be the long-awaited Messiah:

> Behold! The angels said: 'O Mary! Allah gives you glad tidings of a Word from Him: his name will be Christ [masiyah, messiah] Jesus, the son of Mary, held in honor in this world and the Hereafter and of (the company of) **those nearest to Allah**; He shall speak to the people in childhood and in maturity. And he shall be (of the company) of the righteous.' 3:45–46

According to the Qur'an, Jesus was sent to confirm what's in the Torah and to make some of the things lawful that were previously forbidden. Many of Jesus Christ's teachings are not directly quoted but are mentioned in the form of God's foretelling Mary of his birth, what he will teach, and his miracles.

> She said: "O my Lord! How shall I have a son when no man has touched me?" He said: "Even so: Allah creates what He wills: When He has decreed a plan, He but says to it, 'Be,' and it is! And Allah will teach him the Book and Wisdom, the Law [Torah] and the Gospel, And (appoint him) a messenger to the children of Israel, (with this message): 'I have come to you, with a Sign from your Lord, in that I make for you out of clay, as it were, the figure of a bird, and breathe into it, and it becomes

*a bird by Allah's leave: And I heal those born blind, and the lepers, and I quicken the dead, by Allah's leave; and I declare to you what you eat, and what you store in your houses. Surely therein is a Sign for you if you did believe; (I have come to you), to attest the Law which was before me. And to make lawful to you part of what was (Before) forbidden to you; I have come to you with a Sign from your Lord. **So fear Allah, and obey me. It is Allah Who is my Lord and your Lord; then worship Him. This is a Way that is straight.***" 3:47–51

"Fear Allah" is according to the translation by Yousuf Ali. However, other translators have interpreted this differently, generally to mean to serve and worship him: "Worship Him" (Malik, Mir Ali, and Unal), "keep your duties to Allah" (Pickthall), "be aware of God" (Yuksel), and "serve Him" (Emerick and Shakir).

As noted in many of the verses quoted in this section, Jesus repeatedly declares that God (Allah) is his Lord and commands his followers to worship Him.

While the Qur'an mentions the miracles of Jesus and his high status, the emphasis is clearly on God's ultimate authority. As with other prophets, the Qur'an's underlying teachings are about God's supremacy, whether the matter in question is his miraculous birth or miracles shown by Jesus Christ.

THE DISCIPLES

The Qur'an does not name the disciples or indicate their number but mentions them as true believers. The disciples, when asked by Jesus, go on to pledge their allegiance to Jesus and declare that they believe him and his message to submit to One God.

*When Jesus found unbelief on their part He said: 'Who will be my helpers to (the work of) Allah?' Said the disciples: 'We are Allah's help-ers: **We believe in Allah, and you bear witness that we are Muslims [Submitters]**.'* 3:52

Once again, the Qur'an uses the word *Muslims* in a broader sense here than what is typically perceived. It affirms the Qur'an's teachings that

Islam is the same, universal religion taught by all prophets and thus their followers are submitters, or Muslims.

After the attestation of their faith in God, the disciples then went on to plead to God:

> *Our Lord! We believe in what You have revealed, and we follow the Messenger; then write us down among those who bear witness.* 3:53

ASCENSION

Muslims believe that Jesus did not die on the cross but rather ascended to heaven in bodily form, only to return in his second coming before the Day of Judgment, when he will bring peace, rule the world with justice, and kill the antichrist. They believe that he was made to appear to die on the cross. Who actually died on the cross is not mentioned in the Qur'an, and commentators widely vary in their opinion, from Judas Iscariot to Simon of Cyrene.

> *Behold! Allah said: 'O Jesus! I will take you and raise you to Myself and clear (purify) you (of the falsehoods) of those who blaspheme; I will make those who follow you superior to those who reject faith, to the Day of Resurrection: Then shall you all return unto me, and I will judge between you of the matters wherein you dispute.'* 3:55

According to the commentary by Pooya Yazdi, the followers of Jesus believed his message and accepted him as a prophet of God, believed in his teachings, and his prophecy about the coming of Muhammad.

> *That they said (in boast), We killed Christ Jesus the son of Mary, the Messenger of Allah; but they killed him not, nor crucified him, but so it was made to appear to them, and those who differ therein are full of doubts, with no (certain) knowledge, but only conjecture to follow, for of a surety they killed him not. Nay! God took him up to Himself; and God is Mighty, Wise.* 4:157–158
>
> *And they contrived and Allah contrived and Allah is best of the contrivers.* 3:54 (Fakhry)

Most translators use the word "planned" for "contrived."

The majority of Muslim scholars and interpreters of the Qur'an believe the message in the Qur'an is that God will not allow His faithful servant to suffer and succumb to the enemies' plots and allow the enemies of Jesus, and in turn of God, a final victory. Thus his whole life was a miracle—from his conception, to his life, to the miracles he performed, and to his (apparent) death, or ascension.

Jesus in the Gospels

The story of Jesus' life and teachings are captured in much more detail in the four Gospels. Even the Synoptic Gospels are said to have different perspectives on the life of Jesus. Like in the Qur'an, Jesus is also known as the Messiah in the Gospels. Messiah comes from a Hebrew word *Mashiach*, meaning "anointed one." In Greek, this word is *Christos*, which became "Christ" in English.

THE ANNUNCIATION AND BIRTH OF JESUS IN THE GOSPEL

Like the Qur'an, the Gospel speaks about the announcement of the birth of Jesus. However, the announcement from Archangel Gabriel to Mary is mentioned in the Gospel of Luke only. Matthew talks about an unnamed angel approaching Joseph, who was engaged to be married to Mary. The verses 26 to 36 from Luke, chapters 1, are quoted below:

> In the sixth month of Elizabeth's pregnancy, God sent the Angel Gabriel to Nazareth, a village in Galilee, to a virgin named Mary. She was engaged to be married to a man named Joseph, a descendant of King David. Gabriel appeared to her and said, '**Greetings, favored woman!** The Lord is with you!'
>
> Confused and disturbed, Mary tried to think what the angel could mean. '**Don't be afraid, Mary,**' the angel told her, 'for you have found favor with God! You will conceive and give birth to a son, and you will name him Jesus. He will be very great and will be called the son of the Most High. The Lord God will give him the throne of his ancestor David. And he will reign over Israel forever; his Kingdom will never end!' Mary asked the angel, '**But how can this happen? I am a virgin.**'

> *The angel replied, 'The Holy Spirit will come upon you, and the power of the Most High will overshadow you.* **So the baby to be born will be holy***, and he will be called the son of God. What's more, your relative Elizabeth has become pregnant in her old age! People used to say she was barren, but she's now in her sixth month.* **For nothing is impossible with God.***' Luke 1:26–36

Though not using the exact words, there are striking similarities (bolded in the quotes above) in this account and the Qur'anic verses quoted earlier. Both refer to the angel appearing to Mary, her being afraid, the angel talking about a holy son, and Mary's questioning as to how that is possible since she is a virgin.

According to the Gospel, Mary at the time of the annunciation was living in Nazareth; later she moved to Bethlehem, where Jesus was born. The Gospel, unlike the Qur'anic account, does not mention Jesus talking in the cradle. The Gospels go on to mention his circumcision when he was eight days old—a common practice among the Jews. After this, the Gospels are relatively quiet about his childhood till he was about twelve years old, when his family traveled to Jerusalem for Passover festivities.

JESUS, THE KING OF ISRAEL AND THE SAVIOR

The Gospel refers to Jesus as the king of Israel from David's progeny, who will liberate the Israelites once again—this time from the evil Roman Empire—and that he was the fulfillment of the prediction for the Davidic Messiah.

BAPTISM AND TEMPTATION BY SATAN

Jesus was baptized by John the Baptist. Though John was surprised that Jesus asked him to be baptized, since Jesus was sinless, he proceeded with it anyway. Jesus then goes into a desert, where he fasts for forty days. There Satan appears to him and tempts him three times—by asking him to turn stones into bread, by asking him to jump off the top of Jerusalem's temple, and lastly by asking Jesus to worship him. Every time, Jesus quotes verses from scripture, and in the end, he tells Satan to leave:

"Get out of here, Satan," Jesus told him. "For the scriptures say, 'you must worship the LORD your God and serve only Him.'" Matthew 4:10

HIS TEACHINGS AND THE DISCIPLES

The rest of the Gospels then go on to describe the teachings of Jesus and the establishment of his ministries: how he starts to gather large crowds, and his showing of miracles, including curing lepers, giving eyesight to the blind, and giving life to the dead. The Roman Empire, as well as the religious leadership at the time, became alarmed by his teachings and popularity and began plotting against him, eventually leading to his crucifixion.

The twelve disciples are named in the Gospel. Judas and Peter were among the twelve. Judas is said to have betrayed Jesus when he informed the authorities of his whereabouts for thirty pieces of silver. Judas later commits suicide. However, Peter backs off when approached by the authorities and interrogated about Jesus' whereabouts. He responds by saying he does not know Jesus (as was foretold by Jesus), and provides no information. Peter later cries and repents and becomes a cornerstone for the early church. The Gospel describes the last week of Jesus Christ's life in significant detail, including his seclusion, Judas' betrayal, his last supper with the disciples, his trial by the religious authorities and Roman Empire, and his sentencing.

THE CRUCIFIXION

The cross was set up on a mountaintop. Jesus was put on the cross with nails through his hands and feet. On the way to the cross, he was beaten repeatedly; he was bloodied and made to carry his own cross. While on the cross, many people mocked him, including the chief priests. On the cross, Jesus then shouts out his final words:

At about three o'clock, Jesus called out with a loud voice, 'Eli, Eli [Eloi, Eloi, according to Mark], lema sabachthani?' which means 'My God, my God, why have you abandoned me?' Matthew 27:46, Mark 15:34

True to his character and tradition, even at this tumultuous time, he asks God's forgiveness for the people, for "they don't know what they are doing."

JESUS APPEARS TO HIS DISCIPLES AND OTHER PEOPLE

It's reported that after the crucifixion, Jesus appears to many people, including Mary Magdalene (John 20:10–18), Peter, and other disciples (John 21:1–23). Many of them note that the tomb that was supposed to contain his body was empty. Jesus also suddenly appears to two men walking in a village near Jerusalem:

> And just as they were telling about it, Jesus himself was suddenly standing there among them. '**Peace be with you,**' he said. But the whole group was startled and frightened, thinking they were seeing a ghost. Luke 24:36–37

It is interesting to note that Jesus greets these two people by "Peace be with you," which is strikingly similar to what Muslims typically say to greet each other (*Assalamu Alaikum*). The Arabic translations of the New Testament for this verse also bear striking resemblance to Islamic greetings.

ASCENSION

Jesus is said to have appeared to some five hundred people after his resurrection. He then ascends to heaven as his disciples look on.

The Muslim Jesus

There is relatively little known collection of the sayings and stories ascribed to Jesus Christ in the Islamic history, collected in the premodern period. This is considered the largest non-Christian collection on the life and sayings of Jesus Christ and is nicely reported by Tarif Khalidi in his book *The Muslim Jesus*. He appropriately calls the collection "Muslim Gospels."[2] Many of the sayings are similar to the stories in the canonized Gospels as well as the Gnostic Gospels. I am quoting a small sample here: "Christ passed by a group of Israelites who insulted him. Everytime he spoke a word of evil, Christ answered with good. Simon the pure said to him, 'Will you answer them with good each time they speak evil?' Christ said, 'Each person spends of what he owns.'"[3]

Compare this to a similar command in the Quran in how to respond to the insults and taunts of the enemy.

And the servants of (Allah) Most Gracious are those who walk on the earth in humility, and when the ignorant address them, they say, 'Peace! (Salam)' 25:63

The quotes above revolve around some of the same concept referenced in the Gospels, well known to the Gospel scholars, including prohibition to look at women with lust.

You have heard the commandment that says, 'You must not commit adultery.' But I say, anyone who even looks at a woman with lust has already committed adultery with her in his heart. Matthew 5:27–28

Another passage in the "Muslim Gospel" quoted by Tarif Khalidi has striking resemblance to the last supper mentioned in the Gospel of John: "Jesus prepared food for his desciples. When they had eaten, he washed their hands and feet. They said to him, 'Spirit of God, it is we rather, that should do this.' He replied, 'I have done this so that you would do it to those whom you teach.'"[5]

Trinity

A review of Jesus Christ's life cannot be complete without mentioning the Trinity. The following discussion is undertaken objectively, but with the utmost care and sensitivity, realizing its central importance among many Christian denominations.

The word "Trinity" is derived from Latin *trinitas*, meaning "number three" or "a triad." The Trinity is a widely debated doctrine; near and dear to most Christians, while opposed by Judaism and Islam as well as some Christian churches. It is accepted and vigorously defended by most Christians, including Roman Catholics and most Protestants. The gist of this doctrine is that God exists in three persons: God the father, God the Son, and God the Holy Spirit, but He is really One divine being who merely exists in three forms. All three aspects represent the nature of God.

Jesus Christ, according to the dogma, represents all three. God the Father is God the Creator. He is All-Powerful and All-Knowing. God the Son is in the form and flesh of Jesus Christ, who was both man and God at the same time (or God appearing in flesh). God the Holy Spirit (or Holy Ghost) is the Spirit of God as an inner presence and describes how God touches human affairs. It holds that the Holy Spirit descends on people. Whatever attributes God the Father has, God the Son and God the Holy Spirit have as well.

THE HISTORY

Though the concept of the Trinity probably started in the Pauline era, in the early Church there were various competing views of Jesus Christ: from being only a prophet to being God in the flesh. The doctrine of Trinity did not have its roots firmly established until a Christian church council in 325 C.E. in Nicaea (a village in the current Turkey) fixed the Christian belief of Jesus being the same substance as the Father and the son; several decades later, in 381, a council in Constantinople added the Holy Spirit in the Trinity as having the same substance as God. Triune scholars take the position that even though the doctrine was not established till the late fourth century, it existed in various forms starting with the Pauline era. Modern non-trinitarian groups still exist; perhaps the most well known are Reformist Protestant groups such as Jehovah's Witness and Unitarians, as well as Christian Scientists and the United Church of God (although these groups represent a minority Christian viewpoint). Christian scholars acknowledge that the Trinity is a complex and difficult concept to comprehend, especially for non-Christians. Michael Lodahl, a Christian scholar and professor of theology, defends the Trinity teaching, but in his book *Claiming Abraham*, he acknowledges, "Orthodox Christian teaching in fact does not encourage the idea that God is Jesus, the Messiah, period."[6] He goes on to further state:

> It is not difficult to comprehend the logic of divine power as pre-sented in the Qur'an. This is the God of sheer Omnipotence; the God worshiped not only by Muslims but also by many Jews and Christians—and a great many others, for that matter. It is, however, more difficult to comprehend the logic of divine power in John's

Gospel. This God is indeed the Creator of all things, and in an important sense does indeed exercise "power over everything" and yet this God has "given all things into [Jesus'] hands."[7]

He returns to the subject of the Trinity later in the book and points out, "The doctrine [of the Trinity] itself, of course, did not come ready-made from the Bible but required centuries of reading, reflection, and dispute within the Christian community."[8]

Though "Trinity" does not appear in the New Testament, triune scholars cite numerous passages from the Gospel to support the doctrine:

> Then the eleven disciples left for Galilee, going to the mountain where Jesus had told them to go. When they saw him, they worshiped him but some of them doubted! Jesus came and told his disciples, 'I have been given all authority in heaven and on earth. Therefore, go and make disciples of all the nations, baptizing them in the name of the Father and the Son and the Holy Spirit.' Matthew 28:16–19
>
> After his baptism, as Jesus came up out of the water, the heavens were opened and he saw the Spirit of God descending like a dove and settling on him. And a voice from heaven said, 'This is my dearly loved Son, who brings me great joy.' Matthew 3:16–17

The above passage is also mentioned in John 1:32 and Luke 3:22. There are numerous other mentions of God, the son, and the Holy Spirit that are interpreted by many Christian scholars and theologians as references to the Triune God. The Gospel of John is viewed as the one that most emphasizes the divinity of Jesus Christ:

> Jesus replied, 'I have already told you, and you don't believe me. The proof is the work I do in my Father's name. But you don't believe me because you are not my sheep. My sheep listen to my voice; I know them, and they follow me. I give them eternal life, and they will never perish. No one can snatch them away from me, for my Father has given them to me, and he is more powerful than anyone else. No one can snatch them from the Father's hand. The Father and I are

one.' Once again the people picked up stones to kill him. Jesus said, 'At my Father's direction I have done many good works. For which one are you going to stone me?' They replied, 'We're stoning you not for any good work, but for blasphemy! You, a mere man, claim to be God.' John 10:25–33

The Christian scholars are quick to point out that the Trinity is *not* tritheistic idolatry and that the doctrine calls for One God, who appeared in three forms.

ARGUMENTS AGAINST THE TRINITY

Those arguing against the concept of the Trinity point out that the concept only took firm root centuries after Jesus Christ and was introduced to please the Greco-Roman culture of paganism, when gods had many worldly attributes. They argue that the Old Testament, the Qur'an, and even the New Testament do not support it. The following are among the verses quoted in support of their argument:

OLD TESTAMENT

Hear O Israel, the Lord is our Lord, One Lord. Deuteronomy 6:4

This is what the Lord says, Israel's King and Redeemer, the Lord of Heaven's Armies: 'I am the First and the Last; there is no other God.' Isaiah 44:6

I am the Lord; there is no other God. Isaiah 45:5

NEW TESTAMENT

"Get out of here, Satan," Jesus told him. "For the scriptures say, 'you must worship the LORD your God and serve only Him.'" Matthew 4:10

Once a religious leader asked Jesus this question: "Good Teacher, what should I do to inherit eternal life?" "Why do you call me good?" Jesus asked him. "Only God is truly good. But to answer your question, you know the commandments: You must not commit adultery. You must not murder. You must not steal. You must not testify falsely. Honor your father and mother." Luke 18:18–19

SON OF GOD AS A METAPHOR?

Those against the Trinity further argue that the Jews before Jesus Christ often referred to people as "sons of God" to mean the servants of God. The sons of God served God and worked in His cause to please Him and to seek His nearness. Therefore "son of God" should not be taken in its literal sense to mean a biological son. "Son of God" and "Sons of God" are metaphorically mentioned numerous times in the Old and New Testaments:

> *Then the people began to multiply on the earth, and daughters were born to them. The sons of God saw the beautiful women and took any they wanted as their wives.* Genesis 6:1–2
>
> *And the Lord told Moses, "When you arrive back in Egypt, go to Pharaoh and perform all the miracles I have empowered you to do. But I will harden his heart so he will refuse to let the people go. Then you will tell him, 'This is what the Lord says: Israel is my firstborn son. I commanded you, Let my son go, so he can worship me. But since you have refused, I will now kill your firstborn son!'"* Exodus 4:21–23
>
> *God blesses those who work for peace, for they will be called the children of God.* Matthew 5:9

Before the last supper, when Jesus washed the feet of his disciples, he gave some last minute advice. Among other instructions, he told his disciples:

> *I tell you the truth, slaves are not greater than their master. Nor is the messenger more important than **the one** who sends the message.* John 13:16

JESUS' LINEAGE AND THE TRINITY

After describing his baptism, the Gospel of Luke, in keeping with the Bible's tradition of outlining the lineage of the prophets in detail, describes Jesus' lineage all the way to Adam:

> *Jesus was about thirty years old when he began his public ministry. Jesus was known as the son of Joseph. Joseph was the son of Heli. Heli*

was the son of Matthat. Matthat was the son of Levi. Levi was the son of Melki. Melki was the son of Jannai. Luke 3:23–24

The rest of the verses (23–38) continue in the same fashion and end like this:

Enosh was the son of Seth. Seth was the son of Adam. Adam was the son of God. Luke 3:38

Opponents of the Trinity doctrine point out again the reference to Adam as the son of God as a metaphor. They further ask why there is such a long lineage if one is to accept the "Jesus, the son of God" dogma. In that case, the description should have started and ended without anyone in between.

JESUS ACTED WITH GOD'S WILL
I can do nothing on my own. I judge as God tells me. Therefore, my judgment is just, because I carry out the will of the one who sent me, not my own will. John 5:30
So Jesus told them, 'My message is not my own; it comes from God who sent me.' John 7:16

These verses seem to concur with the ones quoted earlier from the Qur'an indicating the miracles were shown by God's permission.

JESUS THE MESSIAH
Then he [Jesus] asked them [his disciples], 'But who do you say I am?' Peter replied, 'You are the Messiah sent from God!' Luke 9:20

The above verse essentially states that Jesus was the *anointed* (Messiah) and God was the *anointer*.

The Qur'an and the Trinity
Like Judaism and many other religions, Islam does not believe in the doctrine of the Trinity. The Qur'an specifically rejects the notion that Jesus is God, or

the Son of God. It states that the birth of Jesus was similar to the birth of Adam, different only in that Adam was born without a father *and* a mother.

> *The similitude of Jesus before God is as that of Adam; He created him from dust, then said to him: 'Be'. And he was.* 3:59

The Qur'an mentions that Jesus was a prophet who taught the oneness of God (*tawhid*), a fundamental belief taught by the Abrahamic scriptures.

> *They take their priests and their anchorites to be their lords in derogation of Allah, and (they take as their Lord) Christ the son of Mary; yet they were commanded to worship but One God: there is no god but He. Praise and glory to Him: (Far is He) from having the partners they associate (with Him).* 9:31
>
> *The Messiah, son of Mary is but a messenger; messengers before him have indeed passed away; and his mother was a truthful woman.* 5:75
>
> *O People of the Book! Do not exceed the limits in your religion, and do not speak (lies) against God, but (speak) the truth; the Messiah, Jesus son of Mary is only a messenger of God and His Word which He communicated to Mary and a spirit from Him; believe therefore in God **and** His messengers, and say not, Three. Desist, it is better for you; God is only one God; far be It from His glory that He should have a son, whatever is in the heavens and whatever is in the earth is His, and God is sufficient for a Protector.* 4:171 (Shakir)
>
> *Say: He is God, the One and Only; God, the Eternal, Absolute; [or Self-sufficient]. He begets not, nor is He begotten. And there is none like unto Him.* 112:1–4

Another parallel between the Qur'an and the Gospel can be drawn in the following passages about Jesus and his disciples (God speaks in the first person in the Qur'anic passage quoted below):

> *And when I revealed to the disciples, saying, 'Believe in Me and My messenger,' they said: 'We believe and bear witness that we submit.'* 5:111 (Shakir)

Once again, the Qur'anic focus is on Jesus' teachings on belief in God *and* his messenger (Jesus), indicating they are two separate entities. Compare that to the Gospel of John, when Jesus instructs his disciples:

> *Let not your heart be troubled: you believe in God, believe **also** in me.*
> John 14:1

CHRISTIAN SECULAR ARGUMENTS AGAINST THE TRINITY:

As noted earlier, recent scholarship is showing that there was great diversity of views among early Christians and that the viewpoints of those Jewish Christians who lost the theological wars to the Catholic Church were preserved in groups like the Ebionites whose Christology is more aligned with that of the Qur'an. In *The Complete Gospels,* over two dozen Biblical scholars examine the four New Testament gospels as well as many gospels that did not make the cut as canonical writings such as the Q Gospel and the Gospels of Thomas, Judas, and Mary. Their research sheds light on the diversity of opinion about Jesus' sayings and his divinity. The Q Gospel refers to the early collection of the sayings of Jesus that most scholars believe the authors of Matthew and Luke used in writing their gospels.[9] Its views on Jesus are more similar to the Quranic teachings than the canonized gospels. "Jesus appears in Q as a wise teacher and prophet. In fact, Jesus implicitly links himself to the prophets of Israel's past, who Q says, consistently rejected, even killed." The chapter on the Q Gospels goes on to state:

> Jesus' death is presumed in Q (13:34-35), but not described. It is seen as evidence of the unbelief of the people, not as an act that brings salvation. Jesus' disappearance is hinted at in 13:35, which some scholars see as reference to Jesus' assumption into heaven. If so, then in Q Jesus is not raised from the dead but "taken up" in somewhat the same way as Enoch (Gen 5:24) and Elijah (2 Kgs 2:1,11). From there, Jesus is to return, at some unpredictable time, as the "Human One" (e.g., Q 12:40 and 17:24).[10]

These views are strikingly similar to the teachings of the Qur'an than the four gospels.

Other scholars who do not believe that the gospels are unaltered, or in Jesus' divinity, include Reza Aslan, the author of *Zealot*, as well as Bart D. Ehrman, one of the most renowned Bible scholars and the James A. Gray distinguished professor of Religious Studies at University of North Carolina at Chapel Hill. Ehrman is author of several books looking at the historical perspective of the early church and the compilation of the gospels as well as the development of the doctrine of the Trinity. "The more I studied the manuscript tradition of the New Testament, the more I realized just how radically the text had been altered over the years at the hands of the scribes, who were not only conserving scriptures but also changing it."[11] In another of his book on this subject, he writes, "As a historian I am no longer obsessed with the theological question of how God became a man, but with the historical question of how a man became God."[12] He goes on to point out that what the earliest Christians meant by saying "Jesus is God" may not have meant what later Christians came to associate with that belief. Even though he now considers himself an agnostic after being an evangelical Christian for years, Ehrman's research is once again more in line with the Islamic view of Jesus as a prophet.

Mary (Maryam) in the Qur'an

Like her son Jesus Christ, Mary (Maryam as she is known in the Qur'an) is held in very high esteem, and though not considered a prophetess, or divine, she is mentioned with utmost respect. Many of the Quranic verses quoted in the prior section also refer to Mary. She is known to have spoken with angels, a great honor in itself, usually reserved for messengers and prophets. The Qur'an defends her vigorously and testifies to her chastity. Jesus himself is repeatedly mentioned in the Qur'an as "Jesus, son of Mary." She is one of only eight people in the Qur'an to have a chapter named after them (and the only woman). She is mentioned by name more often in the Qur'an than the New Testament. In fact, she is the *only* woman mentioned by name in the Qur'an. She is among the four holiest women mentioned in sayings of Muhammad (*hadith*). The other three are Fatima (his daughter), Khadijah (his first wife), and Asiya (pious wife of Pharaoh of Exodus, who picked Moses out of the Nile).

Mary's father was Amram (known as *Imran* in Arabic and *Joachim* in Christian literature). It is said that Mary's mother prayed to God to give what's "in her womb" in service of God. Mary was raised by her uncle, Zechariah, and she often secluded herself to temple in remembrance of God, where, it was said, she received food from the angels.

> *Behold! a woman of Imran said: 'O my Lord! I do dedicate unto You what is in my womb for Your special service: So accept this of me: For You hear and know all things.' When she was delivered, she said: 'O my Lord! Behold! I am delivered of a female child! And Allah knew best what she brought forth. And no wise is the male like the female. I have named her Mary, and I commend her and her offspring to Your protection from the Evil One, the Rejected.'*
>
> *Graciously did her Lord accept her: He made her grow in purity and beauty: To the care of Zechariah was she assigned. Every time that he entered (her) chamber to see her, He found her supplied with sustenance. He said: 'O Mary! Where (comes) this to you?' She said: 'From Allah: for Allah Provides sustenance to whom He pleases without measure.'* 3:35–37

CHOSEN ABOVE ALL WOMEN AND PURIFIED BY GOD

The Qur'an declares that Mary was chosen above all women of the world—a declaration not found in the New Testament. While announcing the birth of Jesus to Mary, the proclamation is made:

> *'Behold!' the angels said: 'O Mary! God has chosen you and purified you, chosen you above the women of all nations.'* 3:42

Shia Muslim scholars and commentators like Pooya Yazdi go on to state that Fatima, daughter of Muhammad, was given the status and the title of the "leader of the ladies of the worlds" *(Syedatun Nisa)*, for chastity and purity, citing many authentic hadith to support that belief. The last part of Qur'anic verse 33:33 is often quoted in support of that belief as well. Nonetheless, Mary retains a very high stature and is highly regarded among all Muslims.

MARY WAS A DEVOUT WORSHIPER AND GUARDED HER CHASTITY

The Qur'an testifies to Mary's pious character and her chastity, leaving no doubts in the mind of followers and readers of the Qur'an. The Qur'an refers to this perhaps more strongly and more often than the New Testament itself.

> *O Mary! Worship your Lord devoutly: Prostrate yourself, and bow down (in prayer) with those who bow down. 3:43*
>
> *And Mary the daughter of Imran, who guarded her chastity; and We breathed into (her body) of Our spirit; and she testified to the truth of the words of her Lord and of His Revelations, and was one of the devout (servant). 66:12*
>
> *And (remember) her who guarded her chastity: We breathed into her of Our spirit, and We made her and her son a sign for all peoples. 21:91*

GOD MADE MARY (AND HER SON) A SIGN FOR ALL PEOPLE

In addition to the verse quoted above, here is another one with the same declaration:

> *And We made the son of Mary and his mother a symbol [of Our grace], and provided for both an abode in a lofty place of lasting restfulness and unsullied springs. 23:50*

It is interesting to note that in the verse above, Jesus is referred to as the "son of Mary" without naming him; and Mary herself is referred to as "his mother" without naming her.

The Qur'an does not mention much about Mary's whereabouts at the time of the crucifixion, or about her death. The Qur'an also does not mention her betrothal to Joseph. (Betrothal, also called espousal, is a formal state of engagement to be married, a Jewish tradition that has been practiced since the times of Abraham). In fact, the Qur'an is entirely quiet about any mention of Joseph, who, the New Testament says, married Mary after the miraculous conception of Jesus.

Mary in the Gospels

Highly revered by all Christian groups, some more than others, Mary is mentioned by name fewer than nineteen times in the New Testament, most often in the Gospel of Luke (twelve times by name). The Gospel of Matthew mentions her by name five time, Mark's Gospel once, and once in the book of Acts, whereas John's Gospel does not mention her by name at all, though "the mother of Jesus" is mentioned on a couple of occasions. There are two nativity accounts in the Gospels. Matthew tells the story from Joseph's perspective, whereas Luke narrates it with the focus on Mary—something that it shares with the Qur'an. (Please see section above under "Jesus in the Gospels" and Luke 1:26–36.) John's Gospel says that Mary witnessed the crucifixion of her son, Jesus Christ:

> But standing by the cross of Jesus were his mother and his mother's sister, Mary the wife of Clopas, and Mary Magdalene. When Jesus saw his mother and the disciple whom he loved standing nearby, he said to his mother, 'Woman, behold, your son!' John 19:25–26

Mary is mentioned as a caring, loving, and concerned mother. Her motherly side is evident from the passage in Luke when Jesus accompanies her to Jerusalem at the age of twelve and went to a temple during the Passover festival, apparently without her knowledge, and she gets very anxious when she does not find him around.

> When they couldn't find him, they went back to Jerusalem to search for him there. Three days later they finally discovered him in the Temple, sitting among the religious teachers, listening to them and asking questions. All who heard him were amazed at his understanding and his answers. His parents didn't know what to think. 'Son,' his mother said to him, 'why have you done this to us? Your father and I have been frantic, searching for you everywhere.' Luke 2:45–48

Mary's high position varies somewhat among Christians. The Roman Catholics highly revere her (but do not consider her divine); they ask her for intercession, believe in her assumption (taken up in to heavens), and believe in her perpetual virginity. These views are also shared by Eastern Orthodox Christians. Protestants, on the other hand, believe in the virgin birth of Jesus and that she was an ordinary, but a highly pious woman devoted to God. They believe that Jesus had brothers and sisters, thereby opposing the view of her perpetual virginity. All groups agree on her being a very pious lady, one who is highly regarded in God's view. Mary is believed to have lived for a varying period after the ascension of Jesus, from three days to twenty-four years.

Discussion Points for Dialogue and Healing

- Jesus Christ (Isa, as he is known in the Qur'an) is highly revered both in the New Testament and the Qur'an. In Islam, he is considered one of the five most exalted, or *ulu'l azm*, prophets. The Qur'an calls Jesus the Messiah. Muslims add "Peace be upon him" whenever saying Jesus' name (as they do with other prophets' names in a show of respect).

- During Christian-Muslim dialogue, it is important to point out that there is no other religion, besides Christianity, where Jesus is held in such high esteem. The same goes with his mother, Mary, known as Maryam in the Qur'an.

- During Jewish-Christian dialogue, it is important to point out that though Jesus in the Gospels was critical of the Jewish religious leadership at the time, this was not meant to be a flat condemnation of all Jews of all times.

- The Qur'an gives Jesus the prophetic name of *Ruh Allah*, meaning "Spirit of God." He is also referred to as "the word of God." He is mentioned by name numerous times in the Qur'an, besides narrations of his miraculous birth without a father, his teachings, and his miracles, such as giving life to the dead, giving vision to the blind and curing the lepers. The Qur'an portrays that as a sign of God's supremacy, rather than Jesus' divinity. He is frequently referred to as the "son of Maryam."

- The doctrine of the Trinity didn't take firm root until a few centuries after Jesus, though it had an undeveloped form starting from the

Pauline era. According to the doctrine, God presented Himself in three personas: the Father, the Son, and the Holy Spirit. Christian theologians point out that the Trinity does not mean tritheistic idolatry. The Qur'an, like many non-Christian faiths, opposes the doctrine of the Trinity.

- During Christian-Muslim dialogue, the subject of trinity should be brought up with extreme caution. The Muslims should realize that despite the Qur'an's clear opposition to the doctrine, this is a subject near and dear to many (Trinitarian) Christians, along with the subject of salvation and crucifixion. The subject should be discussed only when the groups have established a good relationship with each other, making a scholarly debate as a means of "getting to know each other," rather than pointing out "who is right and who is wrong." It is important to remember that both the Qur'an and the Bible have mentioned in various places that only God will decide that, since he is the ultimate Judge. This principle is applicable in any situation when approaching issues of divergent views.

- Mary, the only woman mentioned by name in the Qur'an, is highly revered and "chosen among the women of all nations." In fact, there is an entire Surah, or chapter, named after her (*Surah Maryam*). The Qur'an emphasizes her chastity and though she is not considered a prophetess, God spoke often to her through angels, including giving her the glad tidings of the birth of Jesus.

- John the Baptist, known as *Yahya*, in Islam, is considered a prophet. He is also highly revered and is said to have carried the teachings of Jesus.

- Feel free to ponder on the points noted below and add your own.

Time to Ponder

- While the Qur'an gives elite status to Jesus, what is the purpose of its denial of the account of Jesus dying on the cross and the proclamation that he was raised to heaven?

- Some argue that the God of Christians is not the same as the God of Muslims on account of the doctrine of the Trinity. Is that an argument between Islam and Trinitarian Christianity, or between Trinitarian Christianity and the rest of the religious traditions?

CHAPTER 12

Muhammad

I have studied him—the wonderful man—and in my opinion far from being an anti-Christ, he must be called the Savior of Humanity.
George Bernard Shaw

If we could view Muhammad as we do any other important historical figure we would surely consider him to be one of the greatest geniuses the world has known.
Karen Armstrong

Many non-Muslims, as well as many Muslims, often think of Muhammad as the "founder" of Islam. The Quranic view is that Islam (or submission to God) is the universal message revealed to humanity through a series of prophets and that Muhammad was the *last* prophet in that chain of prophethood. Muhammad was sent with a set of religious laws, or shariah, making him a *nabi*, or messenger (similar to other messengers like Moses and Jesus). The Quranic view is that Muhammad did not bring a "new religion" per se, but rather *completed* the religion of other prophets before him—that religion being Islam, or submission. The singularity of the religion will be discussed in more detail in chapter 13.

NAMES OF MUHAMMAD

The name *Muhammad* means "the praised one" or "worthy of praise." He was also known as *Ahmad*, with similar meanings: "most worthy of praise" or "highly praised." He was also known as *Mustafa*, meaning the "chosen one." Other names Muhammad is known by include *Rahmat* al-alamayn ("blessing for all the worlds"), and *Habib Allah* ("the beloved of God").

PBUH

You might see the acronym "PBUH" following Muhammad's name, which stands for "Peace be upon him." This is derived from the Qur'anic verses whereby God instructs followers to send their peace and blessing unto him.

> *God and His angels send blessings on the Prophet [Muhammad]: 'O you who believe! Send your blessings on him, and salute him with all respect.'* 33:56
>
> *He it is Who sends blessings on you [Muhammad], (as do) His angels, that He may bring you [believers] out from the depths of darkness into light: and He is Full of Mercy to the Believers.* 33:43

As noted before, in a show of respect, Muslims use the words "peace be upon him" after the names of all prophets. Though I have not always used these words in this book while mentioning the prophets, the respect for them is always intended and never ignored.

Brief Life History

In order to understand the Qur'an fully, it is critically important to study and understand the life of Muhammad. Without it, it would be like trying to understand the Torah without knowing the life history of Moses and the children of Israel, or to understand the Gospel without knowing the history involving Mary and Jesus Christ. Many books on the life and legacy of Muhammad have been written in recent times including *Muhammad: A Prophet For Our Time* by Karen Armstrong, *The First Muslim: The Story of Muhammad* by Lesley Hazelton, *Misquoting Muhammad: The Challenges and Choices of Interpreting the Prophet's Legacy* by Jonathan A.C. Brown, and *Muhammad: His Life Based on the Earliest Sources* by Martin Lings among my favorite readings.

Though often seen as "controversial" in the west, Muhamamd is highly revered by Muslims and admired by many secular western scholars. "As a paradigmatic personality, Muhammad has important lessons, not only for Muslims, but also for western people. His life was a jihad: as we shall see, this word does not mean 'holy war,' it means 'struggle.' Muhammad literally sweated with the effort to bring peace to war-torn Arabia, and we need people who are prepared to do this today. His life was a tireless campaign against greed, injustice, and arrogance."[1]

Lesley Hazelton, an agnostic from a Jewish background writes, "The parallels between Muhammad and Jesus are striking. Both were impelled by a strong sense of social justice; both emphasized unmediated access to the divine; both challenged the established power structure of their times. As with Jesus, theology and history travel side by side in any account of Muhammad's life, sometimes as closely as train tracks, at others widely divergent."[2]

Deepak Chopra, a thinker and spiritualist explained the reasons for his attraction to Muhammad: "He appeals to me most because he remade the world by going inward. That's the kind of achievement only available on the spiritual path. In the light of what the Prophet achieved, he raises my hopes that all of us who lead everyday lives can be touched by the divine. The Koran deserves its place as a song of the soul, to be celebrated wherever the soul matters."[3]

A brief synopsis is submitted here. His life can be summarized in three parts: From birth to the first revelation at age forty, his prophetic life in Mecca, and lastly the post-emigration (*hijra*) years in Medina.

BIRTH TO THE ANNOUNCEMENT OF PROPHECY (570 C.E. TO 610 C.E.)
Muhammad was born in the city of Mecca in the year 570 C.E. His lineage is from Abraham through his first son Ishmael through Kedar (Qedar), one of the twelve sons of Ishmael. In those days, Mecca was a trade center and a trade route from Yemen in the south to Syria in the north. Muhammad was born in a clan known as Quraysh. Most Meccans were pagans and polytheists. The Ka'aba, the holiest shrine in Islam built by Abraham and Ishmael, was by now riddled with many idols. The chief god's name was Hubal. Allah was considered one of the gods and was called upon only in crisis; there was not the same monotheistic concept of Allah as the Muslims have now, or as taught by prior prophets. In addition, there were three goddesses in Ka'aba named al-Lat, Manat, and al-Uzza. The pagans considered them daughters of Allah. Despite

being covered with gods by the pagans, in violation of the monotheistic intentions of its founders, the Ka'aba retained its sacred status (though for entirely different deities) and was a vital center for pilgrimage.

Muhammad's father, Abdullah, died before his birth. His mother, Amina, and grandfather, Abd al-Muttalib, raised him. His mother passed away when he was six years old, and two years later, his grandfather also passed away, leaving him with one of his uncles, Abu Talib, as his guardian and, as we will see, his protector. Abu Talib was a trader and highly respected tribal leader in Mecca.

Muhammad's noble character and high ethical and moral standards were apparent well before his announcement of prophethood. He accompanied his uncle on many trade caravans. During these journeys, Muhammad encountered diverse people and came to learn about the wider world. He was always interested in religion and spoke whenever possible with Jewish and Christians religious leaders. Throughout this period of his life, people respected him for his honesty, kindness, and trustworthiness. It was a common practice for people to leave their earnings and other valuable belongings in his possession without any witnesses or agreements, trusting him that he would return it without any issues and thus received the nicknames *Al-Sadiq* (the truthful) and *Al-Amin* (the trustworthy).

One of the wealthiest persons in all of Arabia, a tradeswoman named Khadijah, became aware of his attributes and employed him to lead her trade caravan. She sent a trusted employee to observe him. His report was nothing short of stellar for Muhammad's honest dealings, and he spoke highly of his ethical standards and manners. Impressed by these attributes, it's reported that she eventually proposed to Muhammad, and he accepted. It was by all means a very happy marriage, built on mutual respect and love. Khadijah and Muhammad were very supportive of each other. Muhammad did a lot of his own household chores, like preparing food, sewing his clothes, and repairing his shoes.

FIRST REVELATIONS (610 C.E.)

The Meccans were mostly illiterate, though they excelled in poetry. The pre-Islamic culture of Mecca was not pretty; it is known as *Jahiliyyah*, or "the age of ignorance." In addition to idol worshipping, fights were common among the tribes for petty issues. A newborn daughter brought shame to a family's honor, and many were buried alive or abandoned. Women had practically no rights, and neither did slaves. Muhammad wanted no part of it and often went on reclusive trips for days to a cave near Mecca on Mt. Hira. He meditated deeply and worshipped God for long periods of time. Then one day his whole life changed, which started a new chapter in the history of religions, when the first five verses of the Qur'an were revealed to him through Archangel Gabriel.

> Read! In the name of your Lord Who created—created man from a clot. Read! Your Lord is the Most Honorable, Who taught by the pen. Taught man what he knew not. 96:1–5 (Shakir)

The question "when did he 'become' a prophet?" is somewhat controversial. Most Muslims believe he "became" a prophet at this time. Others believe that, like all other prophets, he was sinless and was born a prophet. Regardless, all Muslims agree that the message he received at the age of forty was the start of the revelations of the Qur'an and his ministry.

EARLY PREACHING

Muhammad initially kept his prophecy to his own circle of family and close friends. The first one to hear about the experience was Khadijah herself. Soon thereafter his cousin, Ali, and other family members confirmed his prophetic station. As one might guess, his first public announcement didn't go very well. He gathered the pagans of Mecca and asked them, "If I told you there is an army waiting behind these mountains to attack you, would you believe it?" They responded, "Of course, you are *Al-Sadiq* (the truthful) and you never lie." Muhammad then followed up by saying something to the effect of, "Then let me tell you that there is no god but God (Allah) and I am his messenger." The animosity shown by the Meccan pagans was instantaneous. The "truthfulness" and "trustworthiness" he earned over decades of immaculate character dissolved quickly after this declaration. Despite this, Muhammad continued to preach the unity of God and asked the pagans to stop worshipping powerless gods. Meanwhile, his uncle, Abu Talib, continued to protect and support him.

NEW CONVERTS ARE PERSECUTED

Since Muhammad was relatively protected at this time due to the reputation and status of Abu Talib, the wrath of the pagans fell on the new converts. The main persecutors were leading members of the Quraysh tribe that controlled the economic fortunes of Mecca and the region. The Ka'aba was both a place of worship and trade, and it was thought by the Quraysh leaders that any disruption of idol worship would have a negative impact on their economic fortunes. These leaders began torturing Arabs who converted to Muhammad's message. Among them was an African slave named Bilal, from Ethiopia. He was dragged on hot desert sand, heavy rocks were put on his chest, and he was asked to recant his newfound belief. He, like all other converts, refused. The Quraysh called for a social and economic boycott of Muslims, and many Muslims, especially those who were poor and vulnerable, died due to insufficient food and other hardships. This difficult experience took a heavy toll on Muhammad and his family, and in the year 619, both Khadijah and Abu Talib died due to failing health caused by the boycott. This year is called "the Year of Sorrow," as he lost two of his most beloved and staunch supporters.

CHRISTIAN RULER GRANTS REFUGE IN ABYSSINIA (ETHIOPIA)

In the difficult times preceding the deaths of Khadijah and Abu Talib, around the year 615, Muhammad allowed the immigration of about eighty converts to Abyssinia (currently Ethiopia). A group of Meccan Quraysh tribesmen followed them. Their pagan leader brought gifts to the ruler and met them in the palace of the Christian king named Ashama Ibn Abjar (commonly known in Islamic traditions as Al-Najashy); they asked him to extradite the immigrant Muslims to Mecca, so they could be persecuted. He described the immigrants as unruly people who disobeyed the gods of Mecca, explaining that they preached oneness of God. The Christian ruler, known for his mercy and fairness, brought the Muslims back to the palace to respond. Ja'far ibn Abi Talib, Muhammad's cousin and one of the Muslim leaders, went on to plead his case. He stated that they were ignorant people before Muhammad's message, worshipping idols and acting like wild animals. "We acted badly," he admitted, adding that they abandoned relatives and mistreated their neighbors. "Strong oppressed the weak." he stated.

After this background, Ja'far goes on to describe how Muhammad changed them, in that he invited them to worship one God, to be honest and truthful, to visit their relatives, to be good neighbors, to give in charity, to avoid committing atrocities, and to prevent spreading evil against women or taking orphans' money. He went on to describe how this resulted in their persecution and torture by the pagan Meccans, resulting in their escape to Abyssinia as they preferred this king over many others, knowing he would treat them justly.

Al-Najashy then asked Ja'far if this prophet had brought any revelations, to which Ja'far quoted the following verses from the chapter 19 (Surat al-Maryam) of the Qur'an (these were also quoted in the previous chapter):

And mention Maryam [Mary] in the Book when she drew aside from her family to an eastern place. So, she took a veil (to screen herself) from them; then We sent to her Our Spirit, and there appeared to her a well-made man (an angel). She said: 'Surely I fly for refuge from you to the Beneficent God, if you are one guarding (against evil)'. He said:' I am merely a messenger from your Lord to tell you about the gift of a holy son.' She said: 'When shall I have a boy and no mortal has yet touched me, nor have I been unchaste?' He said: 'Even so; your lord says: It is easy to me: and that We may make him a sign to men and a mercy from us; and it is a matter which has been decreed.' So, she conceived him; then withdrew herself with a remote place and the throes (of childbirth) compelled her to take herself to the trunk of a palm tree. She said: 'Oh, would that I had died before this, and had been a thing quite forgotten!' Then (the child called out to her from beneath her): 'Grieve not, surely your lord has made a stream to flow beneath you. And shake toward you the trunk of the palm tree, it will drop on you fresh ripe dates. So, eat and drink and refresh the eye. Then if you see any mortal, say: Surely I have vowed a fast to the Beneficent God.' 19:16-26

It is said that by now, the Christian ruler Al-Najashy was in tears. Ja'far went on to recite more verses; last segment is quoted below (after people questioned Mary about the baby Jesus):

> *But she pointed to him. They said: 'How should we speak to one who was a child in the cradle?' He said: 'Surely I am Allah's servant; he has given me the Book and made me a prophet, and has made me blessed wherever I may be, and he has enjoined on me prayer and poor-rate so long as I live and dutiful to my mother; and he has not made me insolent, unblessed and peace be on me on the day I was born, and on the day I die, and on the day I am raised to life.' 19:29-33*

It is reported that the priests and the monks wept humbly, too. At this time, Al-Najashy angrily told the Qurasyh pagans that he believed the Muslims' story and he returned their gifts. He then asked Ja'far, "How do you greet each other?" Jafar responded, "By saying *Assalamu Alaikum* (Peace be upon you)." At which time, Al-Najashy said, "*Assalamu Alaikum.* You are welcome to stay in my land."

The stories of most other Muslim converts were not nearly as cordial or heart-warming, as they were severely persecuted by Meccan pagans.

MIRAJ/ISRA (ASCENSION TO HEAVEN/NIGHT JOURNEY): 620 C.E.
Following the "year of sorrow," Muhammad is said to have ascended to heaven one night, a journey called *Miraj*. To this day, that night, on the eve of the 27th of Rajab (the seventh month of the Islamic calendar), is observed in many Muslim countries as "the night of Miraj." According to the Islamic traditions, in the first part of the trip, called *Isra*, Muhammad was taken by Gabriel on Buraq, the mythological steed, from Ka'aba to the "farthest mosque," or the Al-Aqsa mosque in Jerusalem. From there he was taken into heaven. At each station of heavens, he met various prophets from Adam to Abraham to Moses to Jesus, accompanied by Archangel Gabriel. He was then led directly in close proximity to God, so close that it's reported that even the Archangel Gabriel had to excuse himself. There, Muhammad spoke directly to God at a distance of "two bows or less," according to the Qur'an as noted below. The matters of Islamic jurispru-

dence were handed to him. It is widely believed by Muslims that the Miraj was to honor and reward him for his hard work, to show him God's signs, and also to boost him when he was feeling down following the deaths of his two dearest supporters: Khadijah and Abu Talib. After his dialogue with God, Muhammad was brought back on Buraq to Mecca and his bed. It is said that the time it took on earth for his door chain to swing only once is the time it took for the entire night's journey.

Whether this journey was physical or spiritual is a matter of debate among the scholars. Ibn Ishaq, the author of the first biography on Muhammad, believed the journey was spiritual, whereas later authors, like Ibn Kathir and Al-Tabari, believe the journey was physical. "He saw only God's signs and symbols—not God himself, and latter mystics emphasized the paradox of this transcendent insight, in which Muhammad both saw and did not see the divine essence."[4] Karen Armstrong goes on to observe that, "Most writers leave the final vision of God in reverant obscurity, because it was literally ineffable, lying beyond the reach of speech. Muhamamd had to abandon ordinary human concepts, going beyond the lote tree, the boundary of mundane knowledge. Even Gabriel could not accompany him on this last stage of his journey. He had to leave everybody and—the latter mytics insisted—even himself behind to lose himself in God."[5] Most of the details are part of the hadith or Islamic history, and the Qur'an does not give many specifics of the night journey. The Miraj is mentioned in the opening verse of chapter 17, named *Al-Isra* ("The Night Journey"):

> *Glory to (Allah) Who did take His servant [Muhammad] for a Journey by night from the Sacred Mosque to the farthest Mosque, whose precincts We did bless, in order that We might show him some of Our Signs.* 17:1

And in chapter 53, the night journey is referred to once again in a bit more detail. The verses assert that the journey was real and the prophet was not dreaming or making it up:

> *Endued with Wisdom: for he appeared (in stately form). While he was in the highest part of the horizon. Then he approached and came*

closer, And was at a distance of two bow lengths or (even) nearer. So did (Allah) convey the inspiration to His Servant, (conveyed) what He (meant) to convey. The (Prophet's) (mind and) heart in no way falsified that which he saw. Will you then dispute with him concerning what he saw? For indeed he saw him at a second descent, Near the Lote-tree beyond which none may pass: (said to be at the farthest end of the seven heavens, beyond which none can pass). Near it is the Garden of Abode. Behold, the Lote-tree was shrouded (in mystery unspeakable!) (His) sight never swerved, nor did it go wrong! For truly did he see, of the Signs of his Lord, the Greatest! 53:6–18

EMIGRATION TO MEDINA OR HIJRA (622 C.E.)

Back in Mecca, life was getting harder for the new Muslims. After the death of his uncle, Abu Talib, the pressure mounted on Muhammad. There were more direct threats to Muhammad's life. He had given permission for many of his followers to immigrate to Medina, known as Yathrib at the time. The enemies were planning an attack on him during his sleep. They surrounded his house. It is reported that God informed him of their plans, and he made his cousin, Ali, lie in his bed, to give the impression Muhammad was home and asleep. He then left his house in the dark, accompanied by his close friend, Abu Bakr. When the pagans entered Muhammad's house, they were surprised and furious to see Ali instead of Muhammad and went on to chase him into the desert. Muhammad and Abu Bakr hid in a cave. Muslim narrations speak of a tree that grew overnight as well as a spider web that spread across the opening of the cave, making the enemies believe no one could be hiding inside the cave. They eventually gave up the chase, and Muhammad safely proceeded to Medina.

The emigration to Medina became a landmark event and is the beginning of the Islamic calendar. The event is known as *Hijra*. The year 2017 C.E. corresponds to 1433 A.H. (after Hijra).

LIFE IN MEDINA

Muhammad was warmly greeted by people in Medina, which means "the city"—the full name being *Medinat al-Nabi*, or "the City of the Prophet."

He quickly became not only a spiritual leader, but a statesman, a military leader, and a strategist as well. He paired each immigrant Muslim with one of the Medinites, called *Ansar* (helper), and declared them brothers. He made joint agreements with the two main Jewish clans in Medina, which stipulated the two groups would support each other if either party came under attack, and started a social system of fairness and justice, as the new religious laws were revealed. There the first Muslim community took roots, with its own set of laws, justice, and religious and social reforms.

The emigration only fueled the hatred and animosity of the pagans of Mecca toward Muhammad and his newfound ministry; this led to many wars between the two parties when the pagans attempted to overcome the new community. These were fought mostly near or around Medina. During his time in Medina, the nature of the revelations in the Qur'an changed from issues related to the unity of God and avoiding polytheism to setting religious and social laws, and verses on interfaith issues as the audience changed from pagan Meccans to a newly formed Muslim community and the Jews and the Christians of Medina.

CONQUERING OF MECCA (630 C.E.)

By now, Islam had spread from a handful of followers to tens of thousands due to rapid conversion, without the use of force. Muhammad entered into an agreement with the Quraysh leaders in Mecca, called the Treaty of Hudaibiyya. It called for a ten-year truce. However, the pagans broke the treaty repeatedly when they continued to attack small groups of Muslims from Medina, which eventually prompted Muhammad to respond with force, in accordance with the terms of the treaty. In January of 630, Muhammad, accompanied by an army of ten thousand, marched into Mecca after the pagans again broke the terms of the treaty. In a nearly bloodless takeover, Muhammad announced general amnesty. However, he continued to live in Medina, his adopted city.

LAST PILGRIMAGE AND DEATH (632 C.E.)

Muhammad led Muslims on a hajj, a pilgrimage to Mecca, where he gathered all the pilgrims in the plains of Arafat for his last sermon. This included part of verse 3 from chapter 5:

This day have I perfected your religion for you, completed My favor upon you, and have chosen for you Islam as your religion.

The Shia Muslims believe that as the crowd started to disperse after the sermon, he called them back at a place called the pond of Khum, and the following verse was revealed, contending this was in reference to the announcement of Ali as his successor:

O Messenger! Proclaim the (message) which has been sent to you from your Lord. If you did not, you would not have fulfilled and proclaimed His mission. And Allah will defend you from men (who mean mischief). 5:67

By now Islam had spread beyond the confines of Arabia. People were highly impressed with Muhammad's humble, benevolent nature and the simple message of fairness, justice, and peace for all, while protecting the rights of the oppressed and neglected (women, blacks, slaves, and orphans, among others). Soon after the return from Mecca, Muhammad fell ill and, after a brief illness, passed away on June 8, 632, at the age of sixty-two. Even to his detractors, his amazing story of establishing a social and religious system within a very short span of twenty-two years that exists till this age, is nothing short of astounding and one of the all-time success stories.

Belief in Muhammad's Prophecy is Essential

The second part of Muslim *shahada* is belief in Muhammad as God's Prophet. It is considered an essential part of the Islamic faith, according to commands directly from the Qur'an.

Say [O Muhammad]: "O mankind! Verily, I am an apostle of God to all of you, [sent by Him] unto whom the dominion over the heavens and the earth belongs! There is no deity save Him; He [alone] grants life and deals death! Believe, then, in God and His Apostle—the unlettered Prophet who believes in God and His words—and follow him, so that you might find guidance!" 7:158 (Asad)

O mankind! The Apostle has now come unto you with the truth from your Sustainer: believe, then, for your own good! And if you deny the truth—behold, unto God belongs all that is in the heavens and all that is on earth, and God is indeed all-knowing, wise! 4:170 (Asad)

And those who disbelieve say: You are not a messenger. Say: Allah is sufficient as a witness between me and you and whoever has knowledge of the Book. 13:43

Only those are Believers who have believed in Allah and His Messenger, and have never since doubted, but have striven with their belongings and their persons in the Cause of Allah: Such are the sincere ones. 49:15

The above verse is preceded by a verse that addresses the Bedouins who claimed belief without attaining it, "for belief has not yet entered" their hearts.

MUHAMMAD ON SOCIAL JUSTICE

One of the messages that endeared Muhammad to the masses was his care for the poor, the destitute and the oppressed. Black people were used as slaves in Pre-Islamic Arabia and the social elites of Mecca could not bear to hear that they were all equal. After performing the hajj (pilgrimage to Mecca), when addressing a large crowd of Muslims during his farewell sermon, Muhammad declared:

All mankind is from Adam and Eve, an Arab has no superiority over a non-Arab nor a non-Arab has any superiority over an Arab; also a white has no superiority over a black nor a black has any superiority over a white—except by piety (God-consciousness) and good action.

MUHAMMAD'S INSTRUCTIONS FOR KINDNESS

He led by example in showing kindness to everyone around him. Note that in the following *hadith*, his instructions are not to be kind just to Muslims, or even people of faith, but to all creations, humans, animals, and plants and by inference, the planet earth:

Those who are kind and considerate to Allah's creatures, Allah bestows His kindness and affection on them. Show kindness to the creatures on the earth so that Allah may be kind to you.

COVENANT OF MUHAMMAD TO THE CHRISTIAN MONKS/FREEDOM OF RELIGION

It is reported that Muhammad used to visit the monastery of St. Catherine located at the foot of Mount Sinai. In a letter he wrote to the Christian monks of St. Catherine Monastery, known as the Covenant of Muhammad, he gave protection to the Christians to freely practice their religion. In a letter that should still serve as a guide to protect the rights of Christian and other religious minorities in Muslim countries, he granted protection to the Christians in wide-ranging areas. It's said the original letter is preserved at the royal treasury in Istanbul, and a copy is displayed at the St. Catherine monastery. Some excerpts are cited below:

> This covenant was written by Muhammad, the son of 'Abd Allah, the proclaimer and warner, trusted to protect Allah's creations, in order that people may raise no claim against Allah after [the advent of] His Messengers for Allah is Almighty, Wise. He has written it for the members of his religion [Muslim] and to all those who profess the Christian religion in East and West, near or far, Arabs or non-Arabs, known or unknown, as a covenant of protection. If anyone breaks the covenant herein proclaimed, or contravenes or transgresses its commands, he has broken the Covenant of Allah, breaks his bond, makes a mockery of his religion, deserves the curse, whether he is a sultan or another among the believing Muslims.
>
> If a monk or pilgrim seeks protection, in mountain or valley, in a cave or in tilled fields, in the plain, in the desert, or in a church, I am behind them, defending them from every enemy; I, my helpers, all the members of my religion, and all my followers, for they [the monks and the pilgrims] are my protégés and my subjects.
>
> I protect them from interference with their supplies and from the payment of taxes save what they willingly renounce. There shall be no compulsion or constraint against them in any of these matters.

A bishop shall not be removed from his bishopric, nor a monk from his monastery, nor a hermit from his tower, nor shall a pilgrim be hindered from his pilgrimage. Moreover, no building from among their churches shall be destroyed, nor shall the money from their churches be used for the building of mosques or houses for the Muslims. Whoever does such a thing violates Allah's covenant and dissents from the Messenger of Allah.

Neither poll-tax nor fees shall be laid on monks, bishops, or worshippers for I protect them, wherever they may be, on land or sea, in East and West, in North and South. They are under my protection, within my covenant,and under my security, against all harm. . . .

If a Christian woman enters a Muslim household [by marriage], she shall be received with kindness, and she shall be given opportunity to pray in her church; there shall be no dispute between her and a man who loves her religion. Whoever contravenes the covenant of Allah and acts to the contrary is a rebel against his covenant and his Messenger.

These people shall be assisted in the maintenance of their religious buildings and their dwellings; thus they will be aided in their faith and kept true to their allegiance.[6]

And to ensure that this covenant is not viewed as limited to the Arabian peninsula or to Muhammad's time, the Prophet concludes with the following:

None of them shall be compelled to bear arms, but the Muslims shall defend them; and they shall never contravene this promise of protection until the hour comes and the world ends.[7]

It would seem that some of the extreme and terror groups in predominantly Muslim countries have not gotten the memo.

References in the Qur'an

Muhammad is referred to by name (Muhammad) only four times in the Qur'an and by his other name, Ahmad, once. However, there are numerous references to him in other passages that start with *qul,* meaning, "say" (O Muhammad), and also by "O, messenger," "O, prophet," and other indirect references, including "you," *Yasin,* and others.

MUHAMMAD, THE PROPHET FOR MANKIND

The Qur'an considers Muhammad a prophet sent for mankind, not just a specific group of people:

> *(O Muhammad,) say: "**O mankind!** I am the apostle of Allah toward all of you from He to whom belongs the kingdom of the heavens and the earth. There is no deity but Him. He brings to life and causes to die. Therefore, believe in Allah and His Messenger, the unlettered Prophet (Muhammad) who believes in Allah and His Word. Follow him so that you may be rightly guided. 7:158 (Malik)*
>
> *We have sent you (O Prophet!), to mankind as a messenger; and God is sufficient as a witness. 4:79 (Malik)*
>
> *O Muhammad! This is a Book which We have revealed to you so that you may bring mankind out of utter darkness to the light, by the leave of their Lord, to the Way of the Mighty, the Praiseworthy. 14:1 (Malik)*

MUHAMMAD: THE ANSWER TO THE PRAYER OF ABRAHAM

Many Muslim scholars believe that Muhammad was the answer to the prayers of Abraham and Ishmael, while building Ka'aba in Mecca. The following verses are the culmination of their prayers:

> *Our Lord! And make us both submissive (Muslims) to You and (raise) from our offspring a nation submitting to You [Muslims], and show us our ways of devotion and turn to us (mercifully), surely You are the Oft-returning (to mercy), the Merciful. Our Lord! And raise up in them a Messenger from among them who shall recite to them Your communications and teach them the Book and the wisdom, and purify them; surely You are the Mighty, the Wise. 2:128–129 (Shakir)*

MUHAMMAD'S CHARACTER

Addressing and referring to Muhammad and dispelling the claim of his opponents, the Qur'an proclaims his noble character:

> *Nay, verily for you [Muhammad] is a reward unfailing: And you (stand) on an exalted standard of character.* 68:3–4

In the times prior to the declaration of his prophecy, the pagans of Mecca had given him the nickname of *al-Amin,* or "the trustworthy." They would leave their valuables in his possession, often without any documentation, knowing fully well that he would honor their trust and return them when needed. Years later after his invitation to worship one God, when he was forced to immigrate to Medina, fearing for his life, he was still in possession of many of the valuables of the Meccans. Rather than keeping them to himself, he asked Ali, who stayed behind in Mecca for a little while, to return them to their rightful owners—the same pagans who were determined to harm him.

MUHAMMAD, MERCY FOR MANKIND

The Qur'an calls Muhammad mercy to the believers:

> *Now has come unto you a Messenger from amongst yourselves: it grieves him that you should perish: ardently anxious is he over you: to the believers is he most kind and merciful.* 9:128

He showed mercy to everyone regardless of their creed. This is based on the many stories of Muhammad's life that show his tender heart and mercy to people, including those who tortured him, his family, and companions. An often-told story about him goes as follows:

Muhammad went to Taif, a town near Mecca, to preach to the locals. The trip was rather discouraging, in that no one took heed, and in fact they mocked and ridiculed him. He was physically attacked, and one old woman threw garbage over him every day when he passed near her house. One day, when he passed through the same street, no one threw garbage on him from that house. He inquired and found out the old woman had fallen ill. He then spent time consoling her, tended to her illness, and cleaned her house, as it had gotten dirty during her illness.

People also threw rocks at him and put thorny bushes in his path so much that his shoes would be filled with blood. Battered and disappointed, he returned to Mecca, and on his way back, it is narrated, the Archangel Gabriel met him and offered to turn the whole town upside down as punishment. Muhammad instead showed his benevolent nature and forgave his tormentors and offered a prayer for them.

Years later, upon his triumphant return to Mecca, the same Meccans who abused him and his supporters, now feared for their lives. But it was a bloodless coup. He asked the Meccan pagans who were awaiting his decision about them, "How do you expect me to treat you?" They responded unanimously: "You are a noble one, the son of a noble one." He then told them, "You may go free! No reproach this day shall be on you; may God forgive you."

MUHAMMAD, A BLESSING AND MERCY FOR ALL THE WORLDS

The Qur'an goes on to proclaim him as mercy, or blessing, not just for Muslims, or mankind, but all of the worlds (plural). This is the verse where Muhammad is called the *Rahmat al-'Alamin,* meaning "mercy to all the worlds."

> And We have not sent you [O Muhammad] but as **a mercy to the worlds.** 21:107 (Shakir)

Yousuf Ali translates this verse as "a mercy to all the creatures."

The hadith is full of narrations of his instructions to show mercy to others, including animals.

NOT DIVINE

Despite his noble character, Muhammad is not believed to be divine. The Qur'an warns those who might be tempted to think otherwise (or who might have lost their belief after Muhammad's death) in the following verse:

> And Muhammad is no more than a messenger; the messengers have already passed away before him; if then he dies or is killed, will you

turn back upon your heels? And whoever turns back upon his heels, he will by no means do harm to Allah in the least and Allah will reward the grateful. 3:144 (Shakir)

DOES NOT SAY ANYTHING ON HIS OWN

Muhammad is believed by Muslims to have said nothing on his own, except what was revealed to him by God through revelations.

By the star when it goes down. Your Companion is neither astray nor being misled. Nor does he say (aught) of (his own) desire. It is naught but revelation that is revealed, the Lord of Mighty Power has taught him. 53:1–5

This in many ways is not different from Jesus proclaiming that his words are not his own but essentially are inspired by God, as told in the Gospel of John:

So Jesus told them, 'My message is not my own; it comes from God who sent me.' John 7:16

*Jesus replied, 'All who love me will do what I say. My Father will love them, and we will come and make our home with each of them. Anyone who doesn't love me will not obey me. **And remember, my words are not my own.** What I am telling you is from the Father who sent me.'* John 14:23–24

OBEY MUHAMMAD, THE JUDGE

Since Muhammad's words are believed to be under divine control, obeying him and obeying God go hand-in-hand. The Qur'an has many verses with the phrase "Obey God and obey the messenger."

O you who believe! Obey God and obey the Messenger and those in authority from among you; then if you quarrel about anything, refer it to God and the Messenger, if you believe in God and the last day; this is better and very good in the end. 4:59 (Shakir)

The following is another verse, in addition to the verse quoted above, asking believers to seek and accept his judgments:

> But no, by the Lord, they can have no (real) faith, until they make you judge in all disputes between them, and find in their souls no resistance against your decisions, but accept them with the fullest conviction. 4:65

MUHAMMAD A WARNER AND BEARER OF GOOD TIDINGS

Like all other prophets before him, the Qur'an refers to Muhammad frequently as a warner and the bearer of glad tidings:

> Surely We have sent you with the truth as a bearer of good news and a warner; and there is not a people but a warner has gone among them. 35:24
>
> Say: I am not the first (new) of the messengers, and I do not know what will be done with me or with you: I do not follow anything but that which is revealed to me, and I am nothing but a plain warner. 46:9 (Shakir)

MUHAMMAD THE LAST PROPHET

A key Islamic belief is that Muhammad is the seal, or the last of the prophets:

> Muhammad is not the father of any of your men, but (he is) the Messenger of Allah, and the Seal of the Prophets: and Allah has full knowledge of all things. 33:40

Muhammad in the Bible

Muslim scholars and commentators of the Qur'an contend that Muhammad was foretold in the Bible, and in fact many Jews and Christians of Arabia were awaiting the coming of the prophet to fulfill the prophecy in the Bible. (Similar to the Christian belief that Jesus was foretold in the Old Testament.) It must be pointed out here, however, that Muhammad is not considered the Messiah. According to most Muslim scholars, the two persons who foretold Muhammad's prophecy (to Muhammad) were Christian monks, first when he was a young boy, accompanying his uncle on a trade journey, and then after the first revelation of Qur'anic verses, when Khadijah is said to have taken him to her cousin, a Jewish Christian, for advice on his experience. (The Shia Muslim commentators disagree with the latter, believing that he did not need a confirmation of his prophecy from another human.) The Qur'an refers to the prophecy being foretold in the Bible in the following verses:

> *And remember, Jesus, the son of Mary, said: 'O children of Israel! I am the messenger of God (sent) to you, confirming the Law [Torah] before me, and giving Glad Tidings of a Messenger to come after me,* **whose name shall be Ahmad**.*' But when he [Muhammad] came to them with Clear Signs, they said, 'this is evident sorcery!' 61:6*

In a long sequence previously quoted in chapter 16, the Qur'an interrupts the story on Moses to proclaim the following:

> *Those who follow the messenger, the unlettered Prophet, whom they find mentioned in their own (scriptures), in the law [Torah] and the Gospel, for he commands them what is just and forbids them what is evil; he allows them as lawful what is good (and pure) and prohibits them from what is bad (and impure); He releases them from their heavy burdens and from the yokes that are upon them. So it is those who believe in him, honor him, help him, and follow the light, which is sent down with him, it is they who will prosper. Say [O Muhammad]: 'O men! [Mankind] I am sent unto you all, as the Messenger of Allah, to Whom belongs the dominion of the heavens and the earth: there is no god but He: it is He That gives both life and death.' So believe in Allah and His Messenger, the Unlettered Prophet, who believes in Allah and His words: follow him that (so) you may be guided. 7:157–158*

These verses naturally sent the Muslim scholars to search for verses in the Bible to find these statements, even though they believe the Bible is in altered form from its original divine revelations.

COMING OF MUHAMMAD

The following are the verses often quoted by Muslim scholars to point out that Moses in the Torah spoke about the coming of Muhammad:

> *The Lord, your God will raise up for you **a Prophet like me** from your midst, **from your brethren**. Him you shall hear. Deuteronomy 18:15*
>
> *And the Lord said to me [Moses]: 'What they have spoken is good. I will raise up for them a Prophet like you **from among their brethren**, and will put My words in His mouth, and He shall speak to them all that I command Him.* Deuteronomy 18:17–18

In the New Testament, Peter while addressing the crowd, made a reference to these passages.

> *Moses said, 'The Lord your God will raise up for you a Prophet like me from among your own people. Listen carefully to everything he tells you.'* Acts 3:22

However, these verses are a subject of controversy and contradictory claims, as outlined in the following sections.

The above translation of the verses from Deuteronomy is from the King James Version. A similar translation is found in the New International Version of 1984. The newer translations of the Old Testament have translated the emboldened words differently:

> *I will raise up for them a prophet like you **from among their fellow Israelites.*** (New International Version)
>
> *I will raise up a prophet like you **from among their fellow Israelites.*** (New Living Translation)

Many Christian scholars argue that the Deuteronomy verses were actually in reference to the coming of Jesus, since he was an Israelite and Muhammad was from the progeny of Ishmael in Arabia. They point out that God indeed put His words in Jesus' mouth and that Jesus *was* the word of God. Matthew Henry in his commentary of Deuteronomy 18:15–18 goes on to quote the following verses in support of the belief that God spoke through Jesus:

Long ago God spoke many times and in many ways to our ancestors through the prophets. And now in these final days, he has spoken to us through his Son. Hebrews 1:1–2

Muslim scholars counter by referring to the older translations, using the word "brethren," rather than "fellow Israelites." Moreover, Jesus' birth was miraculous, without a father, and thus he couldn't have been a "prophet like Moses." The debate goes on. Regardless of who these particular verses refer to, there is a general consensus among Christian and Muslim scholars that the coming of Jesus was also foretold in the Torah and that the Jews were indeed awaiting for the Messiah.

THE LIKENESS OF MOSES AND MUHAMMAD

Muslim scholars go on to point out the similarities between Moses and Muhammad to highlight the verse in Deuteronomy 18:15 ("a prophet like me"), and therefore these references foretold the coming of Muhammad, and not Jesus, as Christian scholars hold. They maintain that Jesus shared some, but not all, of the following attributes of Muhammad and Moses:

- Lawgivers
- Spiritual leaders
- Judge and arbitrator for their communities
- Political leader of their communities
- Military leaders
- Raised by someone other than their parents (at least for most of their early lives)

PARACLETE: THE COMFORTER

In the Gospel of John, Jesus spoke of a comforter, or Paraclete, who will come after him:

> *But I will send you the **Advocate** [Comforter, from the Greek Paraclete], the Spirit of truth. He will come to you from the Father and will testify all about me.* John 15:26
>
> *But the **Comforter,** which is the Holy Ghost, whom the Father will send in my name, he shall teach you all things, and bring all things to your remembrance, whatsoever I have said unto you.* John 14:26

The words above in bold are the English translation of the original Greek word, *peraclytos*. In Christianity, *Paraclete* has been used to mean "a helper," "an advocate," and "an intercessor" (Jesus Christ). Later on, the early church around the fourth century used the word *Paraclete* to mean the "Holy Spirit." Some Muslim scholars have pointed out that the original Greek word used was *Periklytos*, which has almost the same meaning as the Arabic names Muhammad or Ahmad: "the praised one" or "praise-worthy" (Ibn Kathir, David Benjamin Keldani), and in some older Arabic translations of the New Testament, has been translated as "Ahmad." (The current Arabic versions of the New Testament mostly translate the word as *ruh al-quds,* or "Holy Spirit.") They contend that *Periklytos* got replaced with *parakletos* (or Paraclete in English).

Moreover, Muslim scholars claim that the *Paraclete* is spoken of in the future tense and as such couldn't have meant Jesus himself, as Jesus was foretelling a future prophet. (*He will come to you from the Father and will testify all about me.*) Therefore, they conclude that these biblical verses are what the Qur'anic verse 61:6 perhaps refers to (*And remember, Jesus, the son of Mary, said: 'O children of Israel! I am the messenger of God (sent) to you, confirming the Law (Torah) before me, and giving Glad Tidings of a Messenger to come after me, **whose name shall be Ahmad.'**).* Moreover the *spirit of truth*, in John 15:26, Muslims contend, once again refers to Muhammad, whose nickname as mentioned before was *Al-Sadiq* (the truthful). The matter largely remains unresolved without a consensus between Christian and Muslim scholars.

THE GREAT NATION FROM ISHMAEL

According to the Torah, God's first covenant to Abraham about having great numbers of descendants and having an heir occurred before the birth of Ishmael, the ancestor of Muhammad.

Then the Lord took Abram outside and said to him, 'Look up into the sky and count the stars if you can. That's how many descendants you will have!' Genesis: 15:5

The covenant described in Genesis is then followed by the birth of Ishmael in chapter 16. And in narrating the story of Hagar and young Ishmael in the desert crying for water, Genesis refers to creating a great nation from Ishmael:

But God heard the boy crying, and the angel of God called to Hagar from heaven, 'Hagar, what's wrong? Do not be afraid! God has heard the boy crying as he lies there. Go to him and comfort him, for I will make a great nation from his descendants.' Genesis 21:17–18
As for Ishmael, I will bless him also, just as you have asked. I will make him extremely fruitful and multiply his descendants. He will become the father of twelve princes, and I will make him a great nation. Genesis 17:20

The great nation reference, one may contend, tells nothing about Muhammad's prophecy. However, one may wonder, in terms of biblical lineage and legacy of prophecy, how else can a "great nation" from Ishmael be defined *without* a prophet? And if that prophet wasn't Muhammad, then who else was a prophet from Ishmael's lineage with a great nation? Please refer to Qur'an verses 2:127–129, noted earlier in this section, when they prayed for a great nation from their progeny and a messenger.

Discussion Points for Dialogue and Healing

- Muhammad is highly revered by the Qur'an. He is mentioned by name only four times but he is addressed in other ways numerous times. The name *Muhammad* means "the praised one." His other name *Ahmed* means "most worthy of praise" or "highly praised." Even his pagan enemies in Mecca recognized Muhammad's highly ethical and moral practices and gave the nicknames of the truthful (*al-Sadiq*) and the trustworthy (*al-Amin*).
- Just like my advice to the Muslims on the subject of the trinity, it is important for Jews and Christians (and people of other faiths)

to remember during interfaith dialogue, that Muslims revere Muhammad like no other human being. Therefore in order to maintain, or advance interfaith harmony, any potentially critical views should be exchanged only when there is deep understanding and an established relationship between the groups. The underlying objective, once again, is to get to know each other.

- Similarly Muslims should remember that Muhammad preached, and instructed his followers to respect each other's places of worship and in fact commanded his followers to honor freedom of religious expression for people of other faiths, as evident from his letter (covenant) to the Christian monks of St. Catherine monastery near Mt. Sinai. Moreover his command to be kind to others was not just towards Muslims but towards all creations of God. That includes planet earth!

- The taunts and insults thrown at Muhammad are nothing new. In fact he was forced to immigrate to Medina when his life was endangered. However, Muhammad's own response to personal insults and taunts was to show kindness and mercy, even to his worst enemies—a lesson that should still be very valuable to his followers.

- Muhammad's lineage to Abraham is through his first son, Ishmael. The story of Ishmael and Abraham in the book of Genesis refers to a "great nation" from the descendants of Ishmael. The Qur'an insists that the coming of Muhammad was foretold in the Bible, and that his name will be Ahmad (the name given to him by his mother). The Greek word *Paraclete* in the New Testament, has been interpreted by Christians and Muslims to indicate Jesus and Ahmad, respectively.

- The first set of revelations of the Qur'an occurred when Muhammad was forty years old in the year 610 C.E. Among the first to confirm his prophethood were two Christian monks.

- Muhammad is referred to in the Qur'an as a mercy (blessing) to mankind, and all the worlds, not just for Muslims.

- Feel free to ponder on the points noted below and add your own.

Time to Ponder

- Jesus in the Gospel of John (14:26 and 15:26) speaks of a comforter/advocate to come after him and that he *will testify all about me* and *he shall teach you all things.* If one believes it was not a reference to Muhammad, then who else fits the description? If it refers to the second coming of Jesus, why would Jesus testify all about *himself?*
- Is it time for Muslims to ask what their Christians cousins often ask: What would Muhammad do?
- Based on their firm belief in the merciful, kind and forgiving personalities, should the Muslims and Christians also ask what would Muhammad *not* do, and what would Jesus *not* do?

CHAPTER 13

Scriptures and People of the Book

I believe that if Mohammed, Buddha, Jesus, and Moses all got together they would be best of friends because the spiritual basis of all religions is something that builds unity.
Yehuda Berg

This chapter will cover the Qur'anic references to the Qur'an itself and the prior scriptures, specifically the Torah, the Psalms, and the Gospels as well as the references to the "People of the Book" *(ahl al-kitab)*. While presenting here the Qur'anic and biblical viewpoints in an accurate and objective manner, the sensitive nature of this subject is never overlooked.

As I noted earlier, in their basic forms, the three faiths have their roots in Abraham. They all believe in the same God—the Creator of Adam and the heavens and earth; in the Day of Judgment; and in the hereafter. They believe in the prophets, though belief in Jesus and Muhammad are not shared by all religions (belief in Jesus by Jews, belief in Muhammad by Jews and Christians). The moral and ethical values and laws are also very similar in their essence, as discussed later in this book. Where they diverge significantly seem to be in the details of how they interpret religious practices, laws, and rituals as well as on historical perspectives on prophetic stories, and they are often colored by geo-political complexities.

The Qur'an on the Qur'an
Readers of the Qur'an quickly discover a feature unique to the scriptures: the Qur'an refers to itself in various forms. This section will focus on the

Qur'an's self-references and proclamation as a complete guide to mankind and other matters such as the purpose of the revelations.

The word *Qur'an* means "reading" or "recitation" and is derived from the word *qa'ra*, meaning "to read" or "to recite." The Qur'an refers to itself frequently in various forms such as "the Qur'an," "the Revelations," or simply *al-kitab* (the Book).

THE QUR'AN: HEALING FOR MANKIND

The Qur'an boldly proclaims itself as the recipe for healing mankind. It's the spiritual remedy for healing all of the diseases of the heart and mind. To seek peace in the heart and mind and to attain complete spiritual health, the Qur'an instructs the readers to seek the remedy within the teachings of the Qur'an.

> *O mankind! There has come to you a direction from your Lord and a healing for what (diseases are) in your hearts—and for those who believe, a guidance and a Mercy.* 10:57

The word used in this verse for the cure or healing is *shifa,* which is typically used to imply health, recovery, or healing. Note that the verse is addressed to mankind as it relates to the healing aspect and not only to Muslims or people of faith. The disease is the lack of faith and the remedy is in the principles as taught by God in the Qur'an. The "direction" is in reference to the Qur'an itself.

Also note that the verse starts by pronouncing the Qur'an as healing for *mankind* but ends with the statement that the guidance and mercy in it is for *those who believe.* The Qur'an describes ways for the heart's purification through remembrance of God, submitting to the will of God, and following the path prescribed by Him. The Qur'an instructs readers to elevate the spiritual heart to a level that is in awe, as well as in love of God, and is in a state of gratitude and submission so much so that God's will becomes their will. In other words, this state of submission and containment softens the hearts and minds to allow God's light to enter one's soul and change one's perception of the purpose of existence and living to be in complete alignment with the principles of living, as defined and prescribed by God.

There are numerous passages in the Qur'an addressed to mankind, clearly indicating that the revelations are for the purpose of all of humanity, rather than a specific group of people. The word used in Arabic for mankind is *al-nas* and has been variously translated as "mankind" (Pickthall, Asad, Yousuf Ali, Malik), "humankind" (Unal), "men" (Shakir, Asad), and "people" (Yuksel, Mir Ali-Pooya, Fakhry, Emerick).

> *We have explained in detail in this Qur'an, for the benefit of **mankind**, every kind of similitude: but man is, in most things, contentious.* 18:54

The Qur'an is a universal message for all humanity.

> *This is a message unto all mankind. Hence, let them be warned thereby, and let them know that He is the One and Only God; and let those who are endowed with insight take this to heart!* 14:52 (Asad)
>
> *This (revelation) is a means of insight for mankind, and a guidance and grace unto people who are endowed with inner certainty.* 45:20 (Asad)
>
> *This Qur'an is not such as can be produced by other than Allah. On the contrary it is a confirmation of (revelations) that went before it, and a fuller explanation of the Book—wherein there is no doubt— from the Lord of the worlds.* 10:37

As mentioned in the introduction, the Qur'an was revealed in bits and pieces over twenty-three years, rather than all at once, as described in the following verse:

> *(It is) a Qur'an which We have divided (into parts from time to time), in order that you might recite it to men at intervals: We have revealed it by stages.* 17:106

The Qur'an speaks itself as the *Al-Furqa'n,* or "the criterion," between truth and falsehood, right and wrong. In other words, the teachings of the Qur'an shall serve as the criteria for contentious matters:

> *Blessed is the One Who has revealed Al-Furqa'n to His servant*
> *[Muhammad], that he may be a Warner to the worlds.* 25:1 (Shakir)

The Qur'an in Arabic

The Qur'an contains many references not only to the revelation in the Arabic language but to the rationale as well:

> *Thus have we sent down this Qur'an in Arabic and clearly proclaimed*
> *in it some of the warnings so that they may take heed or that it may*
> *serve as a reminder to them. High and exalted be Allah, the True King!*
> *Do not hasten to recite the Qur'an before its revelation is completely*
> *conveyed to you, and then say: 'O Rabb [Lord]! Increase my knowl-*
> *edge.'* 20:113–114 (Malik)
>
> *Surely this Qur'an is a revelation from the Lord of the Worlds. The*
> *trustworthy Spirit [Angel Gabriel] brought it down upon your heart*
> *so that you may become one of those who are appointed by Allah to*
> *warn the people in a plain Arabic language. This fact was foretold in*
> *the scriptures of the former people.* 26:192–196 (Malik)

The phrase "former people" is in references to the people of the Book (Jews and Christians).

> *This Qur'an is revealed by the Compassionate, the Merciful. A Book*
> *whose verses are well explained, A Qur'an in the Arabic language for*
> *people who understand. A giver of good news and admonition: yet*
> *most of the people turn their backs and do not listen.* 41:2–4 (Malik)

The question that can be asked concerning the Qur'an's Arabic language is: If it was meant for mankind, why was it only revealed in the Arabic language? There may not be a simple answer but the same is true for all other scriptures that were revealed in the native language of the prophet and the community it was revealed upon—the idea being for the "primary" audience to learn it and then spread it to others in their own languages with the invitation to eventually learn it in the scripture's original language.

The Qur'an
EASY TO UNDERSTAND

There are many verses that affirm the claim that the Qur'an is easy to understand, despite popular belief to the contrary among non-Muslims (as well as many Muslims).

> *And We have indeed made the Qur'an easy to understand and remember: then is there any that will receive admonition?* 54:17

The same exact verse is repeated three more times in the same chapter: 54:22, 54:32, and 54:40. The following verse refers to the two simple purposes of the scripture clearly spelled out:

> *Praise be to God Who has revealed the Book to His servant and did not make it complicated. It is straightforward so that He may warn about the terrible punishment for the unbelievers from Him and give good news to the believers who do good deeds that they shall have a goodly reward.* 18:1–2 (Malik)

SOME VERSES ARE CLEAR WHILE OTHERS ARE ALLEGORICAL

The following verse acknowledges various levels of complexities within the Qur'an as it pertains to the clarity of the message. Some verses have an obvious meaning and can be literally translated without much interpretation or pondering; others require deeper levels of understanding of the subject matter. Some verses are meant to convey the basic message of the Qur'an; therefore they form the foundation of the book, while others can be fully understood by serious students of the scripture and those "firmly grounded in knowledge." The translation used here is by Yousuf Ali and alternative translations are also noted in parenthesis, as noted by various scholars:

> *He it is Who has sent down to you the Book: In it are verses basic or **fundamental** [translated as decisive by Pooya Yazdi and Shakir, definite by Yuksel, and clear by Pickthall]; **they are the foundation of the Book**: others are **allegorical** [translated as ambiguous by Yazdi and multiple-meaning by Yuksel]. But those in whose hearts is perversity*

follow the part thereof that is allegorical, seeking discord, and searching for its hidden meanings, but no one knows its hidden meanings except Allah and those who are firmly grounded in knowledge; they say: 'We believe in the Book; the whole of it is from our Lord': and none will grasp the Message except men of understanding. 3:7

In his commentary of this verse, Pooya Yazdi explains, "Most of the verses of the Qur'an are clear and decisive. There is no ambiguity in them. They are known as the *muhkamat* (basic, fundamental, decisive). They relate to the fundamentals of the faith, such as the Oneness of Allah, the directions pertaining to the practice of the faith, and the laws governing the day-to-day life of the faithful. They can neither be changed nor modified. Any man of average intelligence can understand and follow them."[1]

Then to explain the allegorical verses, he adds, "The *mutashabihat* (allegorical) are the verses which have been composed in subtle and profound diction and style. They carry implications other than the literal meanings, and therefore, are capable of giving different significations." He goes on to state that the phrase "those who are firmly grounded in knowledge" refers to Muhammad and his noble family, and thus one should use their teachings and examples for a more complete understanding of the Book. However, not understanding these ambiguous verses does not change the foundation of the book, which, according to this verse, is made up of clear and decisive verses.

A BOOK OF WISDOM

Claiming repeatedly that it's a book of wisdom, the Qur'an invites deep thinking and reflection on God's signs that are abundant all around us. It challenges our intellect with the implication that if we contemplate the verses, we will be led to the same conclusions as the teachings of the Qur'an. This wisdom is not necessarily reflected in one's genius as a mathematician or physicist, for example, but sets its own criteria. It provides guidance as it relates to the two paths: the straight path consisting of knowledge of God, surrendering to His will, commands, and laws, being good to others, and the other path consisting of disbelief, denial or disobeying His commands and engaging in evil deeds. The destinations are also clearly spelled out for either path. The wisdom is then defined, not in terms of an IQ number, but whether one takes heed to the guidance and teachings provided therein. The Qur'an does not separate religion from science (or nature), nor science from religion.

> These are the verses of the Book of Wisdom. 10:1
>
> These are verses of the Book of wisdom, a guide and a mercy for the doers of goodness. Those who keep up prayers, pay the poor-rate [zakat or charity] and are certain of hereafter. These are on a guidance from their Lord, and these are they who are successful. 31:1–5 (Shakir)
>
> I swear by the Qur'an, which is full of Wisdom. That you [Muhammad] are indeed one of the messengers. On a straight way. A revelation by the Almighty, the Merciful. 36:1–5 (Shakir)
>
> By the Book that makes things clear, We have made it a Qur'an in Arabic, that you may be able to understand (and learn wisdom). And verily, it is in the Mother of the Book, in Our Presence, high (in dignity), full of wisdom. 43:2–4

Qur'anic View of the other Scriptures

The Qur'an has a clear view of the prior scriptures: The scriptures, as set down by Moses and Jesus and other prophets, are sacred and to be respected but exist today (and as they did in the days of Muhammad) in an altered state from their original divine revelations. Muslims are commanded to "believe" in all scriptures. In the very beginning of the Qur'an, it asks believers to respect the Qur'an and the prior scriptures. The Qur'an is a continuation of the revelations from the same God.

> This Book, there is no doubt in it, is a guide to those who guard (against evil) Those who believe in the unseen and keep up prayer and spend out of what We have given them. And who believe in that which has been revealed to you [Muhammad] and that which was revealed before you and they are sure of the hereafter. 2:2–4 (Shakir)
>
> This Qur'an is not such as can be produced by other than God; on the contrary it is a confirmation of (revelations) that went before it, and a

fuller explanation of the Book—wherein there is no doubt—from the Lord of the worlds. 10:37

The Qur'an, in addition to generic references to "what was sent before," also mentions the Torah and the Gospel by name. In the following verses, the Qur'an confirms the divine source of the Torah, the Gospel, and "the Book" (the Qur'an). The Qur'an declares that the Torah and the Gospel were "guidance and light." The following is a small sample:

*It was We who revealed the law [Torah] (to Moses): **therein was guidance and light**. By its standard have been judged the Jews, by the prophets who bowed (as in Islam) to Allah's will, by the rabbis and the doctors of law: for to them was entrusted the protection of Allah's book, and they were witnesses thereto: therefore fear not men, but fear me, and sell not my signs for a miserable price. If any do fail to judge by (the light of) what Allah hath revealed, they are (no better than) Unbelievers. We ordained therein for them: 'Life for life, eye for eye, nose for nose, ear for ear, tooth for tooth, and wounds equal for equal.' But if anyone remits the retaliation by way of charity, it is an act of atonement for himself.* 5:44–45*
    We gave Moses the Book and followed him up with a succession of messengers.* 2:87
    And remember We gave Moses the scripture and the criterion (between right and wrong): There was a chance for you to be guided aright. 2:53
    *In the past We granted to Moses and Aaron the Furqan and a Light and a Message for those who would do right [**or guard against evil**].* 21:48

It is of note that the Qur'an uses the word *Furqan* for the Torah also, as it has for itself.

Moreover, the Torah is described as a guide for the *muttaqin* ("those who do right", or "guard against evil")—a term often translated as pious, God-concious or in awe of God. In fact this is the same word used in the beginning of the Qur'an in reference to the Qur'an itself.

This Book, there is no doubt in it, is a guide to those who guard (against evil). 2:2 (Shakir)

QUR'AN ON THE GOSPEL (INJIL): GUIDANCE AND LIGHT

In the verses preceding the one quoted below, the Qur'an makes references to the Torah and the prophets that followed Moses, the rabbis who protected the Torah, and Jesus being given the *Injil* and that it was a guidance for the *muttaqin* ("righteous or God-conscious").

*And We sent, following in their footsteps, Jesus, the son of Mary, confirming that which came before him in the Torah; and We gave him the Gospel, in which was guidance and light and confirming that which preceded it of the Torah as guidance and instruction **for the righteous**. And let the People of the Gospel judge by what Allah has revealed therein. And whoever does not judge by what Allah has revealed—then it is those who are the defiantly disobedient.* 5:46-47 (Sahih International)

In the first verse quoted below, the Qur'an addresses Mary in reference to Jesus Christ and says that he was born with the knowledge of the prior scriptures, including the Torah:

And He [God] will teach him [Jesus] the scripture and wisdom, and the Torah and the Gospel. 3:48 (Shakir)

*Then We made Our messengers to follow in their footsteps, and We sent Jesus son of Mary afterwards, and We gave him the Gospel and **We put in the hearts of those who followed him kindness and mercy**.* 57:27 (Shakir)

When Allah will say: O Jesus son of Mary! Remember My favor on you and on your mother, when I strengthened you with the Holy Spirit, you spoke to the people in the cradle and when of old age, and when I taught you the Book and the wisdom and the Torah and the Gospel. 5:110 (Shakir)

It is He Who sent down to you (step by step), in truth, the Book [the Qur'an], confirming what went before it; and He sent down the Law (of Moses) [Torah] and the Gospel (of Jesus) before this, as a guide to mankind, and He sent down the criterion (of judgment between right and wrong). 3:3

People of the Book

The term *ahl al-kitab* or "People of the Book" is used in the Qur'an for the followers of the Torah and the Gospel, implying Jews and Christians. The term also refers to Sabians and Zoroastrians, two other monotheistic faiths that pre-date Islam. This subject tends to be emotionally charged and often a source for criticism of the Qur'an, especially in the West—usually by those who are not scholars of, or well versed in, the Qur'an. The following are a few verses that mention the people of the book:

> *Indeed, those who have believed [in Prophet Muhammad] and those [before Him] who were Jews or Sabeans or Christians—those [among them] who believed in Allah and the Last Day and did righteousness—no fear will there be concerning them, nor will they grieve. 5:69* (Sahih International)
>
> *Indeed, those who have believed and those who were Jews and the Sabeans and the Christians and the Magians [Zoroastrians] and those who associated with Allah—Allah will judge between them on the Day of Resurrection. Indeed Allah is, over all things, Witness. 22:17* (Sahih International)

At times the Qur'an addresses the "children of Israel"—referring to the Israelites, or more directly as "Jews and Christians," usually in references to the Jews and Christians of Medina. In the early days of the prophecy in Mecca, most of Muhammad's interactions, and thus the Qur'anic verses, were related to pagan beliefs and practices. After the *hijra* or emigration to Medina, as the Muslim community took shape, the Qur'an then spells out the new law for this community as well as the guidelines for interactions with the Jews and Christians who lived in and around Medina. And according to the following verse, the fate of all nations will be in the hands of God only:

> *As for those who have faith and do righteous deeds, We shall soon admit them to gardens beneath which rivers flow to live therein for-*

ever. This is the promise of Allah, true indeed, and who can be truer in his words than Allah? The final result will neither be in accordance with your desires nor in accordance with the desires of the People of the Book. He who does evil will be requited with evil: he will find no protector or helper besides Allah. But the one who does righteous deeds, whether a male or a female—and he or she is a believer—shall enter paradise and will not be harmed a speck. 4:122–124 (Malik)

PEOPLE OF THE BOOK VS. THE BOOK OF THE PEOPLE
Based on the above discussion, it can be argued that the Qur'an was revealed as the Book of the People. Alternatively, if one is to believe that the Qur'an was the last of the three Testaments of Abrahamic faith, then a book containing the Torah, the Gospel and the Qur'an may be considered the "Book of the People."

Islam: One Religion from Adam to Muhammad
Many people around the world, including many Muslims, tend to think of Islam as being born in seventh-century Arabia; they consider Muhammad as its "founder," and the Qur'an as its Holy Book. Was Islam a result of Jewish and Christian influence on Muhammad? Did it start as an independent religion and borrow some concepts from the other two monotheistic religions prevalent in Arabia at the time?

> *And We gave Moses the Book, in order that they might receive guidance. And We made the son of Mary and his mother as a Sign: We gave them both shelter on high ground, affording rest and security and furnished with springs.* 23:49–50

After these verses, the essential message contained in the scriptures is put in perspective in the next set of verses. The words in parenthesis are mine, and are used for emphasis.

> *O messengers! (Note the plural used) Eat of pure things and do good deeds, certainly I have knowledge of all your actions. In fact, **your religion is one religion,** and I am your Lord: so fear Me Alone. Yet people have divided themselves into factions and each faction rejoices*

in its own doctrines—well! Leave them in their heedlessness for an appointed time. 23:51–53 (Shakir)

Many secular scholars also recognize the concept of Islam as a continuation of other monotheistic religions, and Deepak Chopra observes this universality in one of his books: "This is also true with Islam, which sees itself as "confirming" the past, meaning that God updated his old message as written in Torah and the New Testament…. Allah wanted the updated message to be complete. As a result, Islam became more than a religion; it's a way of life so all-consuming that nothing has been left to chance."[2]

> **The same religion** *has He established for you [Muhammad] as that which He enjoined on Noah—that which We have sent by inspiration to you—**and that which We enjoined on Abraham, Moses, and Jesus:** Namely, that you should remain steadfast in religion, and make no divisions therein: to those who worship other things than God, hard to the unbelievers is that which you call them to. God chooses to Himself those whom He pleases, and guides to Himself those who turn (to Him).* 42:13
>
> *This day have I perfected for you your religion and completed My favor on you and chosen for you Islam as a religion.* 5:3 (Shakir)
>
> *The religion before God is Islam (submission to His Will).* 3:19
>
> *Typically, Religions are named by their followers after their prophet's departure from this world, but as noted above, Islam was named as a religion by God in the Qur'an. The Qur'an proclaims that the prophets brought one religion, and named it Islam.*
>
> *Do they seek for other than the religion of Allah? While all creatures in the heavens and on earth have, willing or unwilling, bowed to His Will (accepted Islam), and to Him shall they all be brought back. Say (O Muhammad): We believe in God and what has been revealed to us, and what was revealed to Abraham, and Ishmael and Isaac and Jacob and the tribes, and what was given to Moses and Jesus and to the prophets from their Lord; we do not make any distinction between any of them, and to Him do we submit.* 3:83–84

After this broad definition, the Qur'an urges people to accept no other religion:

And whoever desires a religion other than Islam, it shall not be accepted from him. 3:85 (Shakir)

CHAIN OF PROPHETS AND ISLAM

In one very long sequence in chapter 21 of the Qur'an (verses 48-91), many prophets are mentioned, one after another, and at the end, the Qur'an declares that they all belong to the same nation (*umma*).

After mentioning many great prophets, the Qur'an puts it all in perspective:

> *Verily this Islam is your religion, is one religion, and I am your Lord, so worship Me and I am your only Lord, therefore worship Me alone. And they broke their religion (into sects) between them: to Us shall all come back. Therefore, whoever shall do of good deeds and he is a believer, there shall be no denying of his exertion, and surely We will write (it) down for him. 21:92–94 (Shakir)*

ISLAM: RELIGION OF ABRAHAM (DIN AL-IBRAHIM)

The Qur'an describes Islam as a universal religion with a broader meaning as well as the *Din al-Ibrahim*, or the "religion of Abraham." There are numerous references to "this religion" as the "way of Abraham" and that he, as well as his descendants, were Muslims, as defined by the Qur'an.

> *And who forsakes the religion of Abraham but he who makes himself a fool, and most certainly We chose him in this world, and in the hereafter he is most surely among the righteous. When his Lord said to him, Be a Muslim (submit), he said: "I submit myself to the Lord of the worlds." 2:130–131 (Shakir)*

One might find an apparent contradiction in calling Islam the one religion God sent down, as well as the "religion of Abraham." So how about the prophets before Abraham? What religion were they preaching? The Qur'an, as mentioned in preceding discussions, praises Abraham as a noble servant of God, and one may conclude that by referring to the universal religion Islam as the religion of Abraham, the Qur'an intended to highlight Abraham's key role in propagating that religion by linking it to him, who in turn was following the same universal religion.

WHO IS A KAFIR/NONBELIEVER ("INFIDEL")?
Some non-Muslims, as well as some Muslims, assume that Islam considers People of the Book (a typical reference for the Jews and the Christians) and all other non-Muslims as infidels (*kafir*, plural *kuffur*).

The word *kafir* is variously translated as "nonbeliever," "unbeliever," or "disbeliever." A *kafir*, according to the concepts laid out by the Qur'an, is a faithless soul, one who rejects the truth, an anti-submitter. Just like a Muslim is in a state of submission, a *kafir* similarly is in a state of rejection of the truth. The first *kafir* was Satan, when he refused to bow to Adam at God's command.

> *And when We said to the angels: 'Make obeisance (bow down) to Adam' they did obeisance, except Iblis (did it not). He refused and he was proud, and he was one of the unbelievers.* 2:34 (Shakir)

A *kafir* rejects the truth knowingly and disbelieves in God, the angels, the messengers, and the hereafter. This would include pagans, idolaters, polytheists (*mushrikin*), and atheists. The word *kafir* comes from a root word that means "a farmer who covers the seed with soil." *Kafir* in this sense refers to someone who covers the truth. The term "infidel" is in fact not an Islamic term and is derived from the French word *infidèle* and was originally used by Christians in the late fifteenth century. Infidel has been used broadly to describe those who rejected Christianity, or anyone outside of the faith.

Verse 98:1 (*Those who disbelieved from among the people of the Book*) supports the argument that the People of the Book do *not* equate with *kuffur* or disbelievers. Since they are said to have among them disbelievers, therefore they must have believers among them as well. Thus, to refer to the People of the Book as infidels or nonbelievers as a group is *not* in accordance with the Qur'anic teachings.

In fact, the Qur'an calls those who were opposing and fighting against David as unbelievers or *kuffur*.

> *And when they went out against Jalut [Goliath] and his forces they said: Our Lord, pour down upon us patience, and make our steps firm and assist us against the unbelieving people [kafirs].* 2:250 (Shakir)

Alternately, those who were fighting with Moses are called believers in the Qur'an. When Moses led the children of Israel near the edge of the Promised Land, he spoke to his people:

> *And when Musa said to his people: "O my people! Remember the favor of Allah upon you when He raised prophets among you and made you kings and gave you what He had not given to any other among the nations."* 5:20 (Shakir)
> *Two men of those who feared [were God-fearing], upon both of whom Allah had bestowed a favor, said:' Enter upon them by the gate, for when you have entered it you shall surely be victorious, and on Allah should you rely if you are believers.'* 5:23 (Shakir)

The word used for believers is *muminin*, a term often used for pious, God-concious Muslims.

It is clear from the verses noted above that the Qur'an refers to the various factions among the People of the Book (and children of Israel)—some were believers, others were nonbelievers. This account is no different than the Tanakh, which frequently refers to the Israelites who reverted to polytheism; many of them were killed by Moses and the believing Israelites.

Who Is Righteous?

The following verse defines who is righteous without saying if one must be a "Muslim" or a "Jew" or a "Christian." It defines what one must do to be counted among the God-fearing, righteous, pious people. The first part involves beliefs and the second part deals with actions—what one must do to be righteous:

> *It is not righteousness that you turn your faces toward the East and the West, (meaning facing Ka'aba for prayers) but righteousness is*

*this that one should **believe in God** and **the last day** and **the angels** and **the Book** and **the prophets**, AND give away wealth out of love for Him to the near of kin and the orphans and the needy and the wayfarer and the beggars and for (the emancipation of) the captives, and keep up prayer (salat) and pay the poor-rate (zakat); and the performers of their promise when they make a promise (or keep their pledges when they make a pledge), and the patient in distress and affliction and in time of conflicts—these are they who are true (to themselves) and these are they who guard (against evil). 2:177 (Shakir)*

The last underlined phrase is also translated as "pious" (Mir Ali, Malik), "Allah-fearing" (Yousuf Ali, Pickthall), "God-fearing" (many modern translators), or "righteous" (Yuksel). The Arabic word used in the Qur'an is *muttaqun.*

The following verse is not nearly as detailed but revolves around the same theme:

*And they [referring to People of the Book] say: None shall enter the garden [paradise] except he who is a Jew or a Christian. These are their vain desires. Say: Bring your proof if you are truthful. Yes! **Whoever** submits himself entirely to God and he is the doer of good (to others) he has his reward from his Lord, and there is no fear for him nor shall he grieve [on the Day of Judgment]. 2:111–112 (Shakir)*

Interfaith Dialogue as Taught by the Qur'an

The differences and the tensions that currently exist between Jews, Christians, and Muslims are nothing new; they have existed for centuries. The Qur'an acknowledges these conflicts and provides broad guidelines that instruct Muslims on how to approach interfaith dialogue:

*Do not argue with the People of the Book except in the **best manner**— except for those wicked amongst them, and say: "We acknowledge what was revealed to us and in what was revealed to you; Our God and your God is the same. To Him we peacefully surrender." 29:46 (Yuksel)*

The word emboldened above is *ahsan* (with a short "a" sound) and is translated as "by what's best" (Shakir, Mir Ali), "with means better than mere disputation" (Yousuf Ali), "in good taste" (Malik), and "in the best way" (Unal).

This verse served as a catalyst for my engagement in interfaith work. I draw at least two lessons as guiding principles for interfaith dialogue from this verse. First, the dialogue should take place in the best of manners, with civility. Second, the dialogue's focus is on drawing attention to the commonalities we share: *We acknowledge what was revealed to us and in what was revealed to you; Our God and your God is the same. To Him we peacefully surrender.* This is a direct reference I found in the scriptures that says the God of Jews, Christians, and Muslims is the same. Indeed, the transliteration for the last sentence, "To Him we peacefully surrender" is *wanahna lahu muslimun*; essentially indicating we are all Muslims, or submitters, in a more global sense. Additionally, this verse serves as another argument against those who claim that the Qur'an considers Jews and Christians as *kuffur*, or infidels, since "our God and your God is the same" and "To Him we peacefully surrender." We believe and worship the same God, thus we are all believers.

Engaging others in the best manner is not limited to interfaith dialogue. The Qur'an goes on to command Muslims to use the same principles with any dialogue. The Arabic word used for "goodly exortation" in the next verse is *hasana* from the same root as *ahsan*, used in verse 29:46 narrated above, and ending in the same exact word: *ahsan* (best manner).

> *Call to the way of your Lord with wisdom and goodly exhortation, and have disputations with them in the best manner.* 16:125 (Shakir)
>
> *Say: O People of the Book! come to common terms as between us and you: That we worship none but Allah[God]; that we associate no partners with him; that we take not, from among ourselves, Lords and patrons other than Allah.* 3:64

TYPES OF INTERFAITH DIALOGUE, TRIALOGUE, OR POLYLOGUE

Though one may speak of interfaith dialogue as a conversation between two faith groups, it may be more accurate to term this as a *trialogue* as it relates to building bridges between Jews, Christians, and Muslims. In fact some have used the term *polylogue* to describe such conversations between people from multiple faith groups. Nonetheless, the term dialogue is retained here for its more global understanding and use.

Two Vatican documents, *Dialogue and Mission* and *Dialogue and Proclamation,* eloquently describe the many forms interfaith dialogue can take:

1. *The dialogue of life* in which people share their hopes, aspirations, and daily problems in a cordial manner. This is mostly a secular experience such as sharing birthdays, camping trips, etc.
2. *The dialogue of action* where practical collaboration aims to confront situations of social injustice or oppression and promote values such as peace and reconciliation. Examples include working in homeless shelters, clinics for the underprivileged, food banks, etc.
3. *The dialogue of theological exchange* in which we explore together the understanding of each other's doctrinal beliefs and spiritual values.
4. *The dialogue of shared religious experience* with topics in or about prayer, through dialogue in or about prayer, liturgy, contemplation, faith, and ways of searching for God or the Absolute. Examples include attending an interfaith wedding, Friday Muslim prayers, church services, and attending festival of Sukkot in a synagogue.[3]

"I Have a Dream" in the Qur'an: The Qur'an and Diversity

In Washington D.C. on August 28, 1963, in his now legendary "I Have a Dream" speech, Dr. Martin Luther King Jr. shared his vision of a nation where social justice will prevail: "I have a dream that my four little children will one day live in a nation where they will not be judged by the color of their skin, but by the content of their character."

I do not know if Dr. King had studied the Qur'an, but at its core, he was wishing for what the Qur'an had declared over fourteen hundred years ago. The first verse quoted below is addressed to all mankind, reminding us that we are all descendants of the same parents, and that we will be judged by our deeds. The second verse proclaims that, far from discriminating someone based on their language or the color of their skin, we should see this diversity among ourselves as a divine sign and cherish our diversity rather than use it to create prejudice, fear, or hate. The last verse reminds us that God has intentionally made us different, and commands the followers to hasten to do good works for each other.

> O mankind! We created you from a single (pair) of a male and a female, and made you into nations and tribes, **that you may (come to) know each other** (not that you may despise each other). Verily the most honored of you in the sight of Allah is (he who is) the most righteous of you. And Allah has full knowledge and is well acquainted (with all things). 49:13
>
> And one of His signs is the creation of the heavens and the earth and the diversity of your tongues and colors; most surely there are signs in this for the learned. 30:22 Shakir
>
> To each among you have We prescribed a law and an open way. If Allah had so willed, He would have made you a single people, but (His plan is) to test you in what He has given you: so strive as in a race in all virtues (good works). The goal of you all is to Allah; it is He that will show you the truth of the matters in which you dispute. 5:48

People of the Book: Some Were Good, Some Were Not

The Qur'anic narrations involving the children of Israel with Moses are similar in many ways to the biblical accounts. The following is a review of some of these verses, along with some "controversial" verses, cited by some in the West to accuse the Qur'an of "promoting hatred." The Qur'an, like the Torah, is often critical of the Israelites who accompanied Moses in the wilderness in search of the Promised Land. The Qur'an also talks about their favored status:

> O' children of Israel! Remember My favors which I bestowed upon You; that I exalted you above all other nations. 2:47 and 2:122 (Malik)
>
> And there are, certainly, among the People of the Book, those who believe in God, in the revelation to you, and in the revelation to them, bowing in humility to God: They will not sell the Signs of God for a miserable gain! For them is a reward with their Lord, and God is swift in account. 3:199

Not all of them are alike: Of the People of the Book are a portion that stand (for the right): They rehearse [recite] the Signs [revelations] of God all night long, and they prostrate themselves in adoration. They believe in God and the last day, and they enjoin what is right and forbid the wrong and they strive with one another in hastening to good deeds, and those are among the good . . . (As for) those who disbelieve, surely neither their wealth nor their children shall avail them in the least against God; and these are the inmates of the fire; therein they shall abide. 3:113–116

Among the People of the Book are some who, if entrusted with a hoard of gold, will (readily) pay it back; others, who, if entrusted with a single silver coin, will not repay it unless you remain firm in demanding, because, they say, 'there is no call on us (to keep faith) with these Gentiles,' and they tell a lie against God, and (well) they know it. Yea, whoever fulfills his promise and guards (against evil)—then surely God loves those who guard (against evil). (As for) those who take a small price for the covenant of God and their own oaths—surely they shall have no portion in the hereafter, and God will not speak to them, nor will He look upon them on the day of resurrection nor will He purify them, and they shall have a painful chastisement. 3:75–77

The Qur'an on Arabs: Some Were Good, Some Were Not

The Qur'an's criticism is not limited to the pagans and the transgressors among the People of the Book. Similarly the due praise is given to the righteous:

The Arabs of the desert are the worst in unbelief and hypocrisy, and most fitted to be in ignorance of the command which Allah has sent down to His Messenger: But Allah is All-knowing, All-Wise. 9:97

But some of the desert Arabs [Bedouins] believe in God and the Last Day, and look on their payments as pious gifts bringing them nearer to God and obtaining the prayers of the Messenger. Surely it shall be means of nearness for them. Soon will God admit them to His Mercy: for God is Oft-forgiving, Most Merciful. 9:99

THE QUR'AN ALLOWS MARRYING PEOPLE OF THE BOOK

The Qur'an allows believers of the Qur'an and Muhammad (commonly viewed as "Muslims") to marry Jews and Christians with certain conditions:

> *Today all good clean things have been made lawful for you; and the food of the People of the Book is also made lawful for you and your food is made lawful for them. Likewise, marriage with chaste free believing women and also chaste women among the People who were given the Book before you is made lawful for you, provided that you give them their dowries and desire chastity, neither committing fornication nor taking them as mistresses.* 5:5 (Malik)

Conversely, many Jewish sages have argued against interfaith marriages between Jewish and non-Jewish people, citing some Tanakh verses such as Deuteronomy 7:1–5, revealed in reference to how the Israelites should treat other tribes like the Ammonites and Canaanites. The verses for obvious reasons refer to the nonbelievers of the time, predating the followers of the Gospel and the Qur'an:

> *Nor shall you make marriages with them. You shall not give your daughter to their son, nor take their daughter for your son. For they will turn your sons away from following Me, to serve other gods.* Deuteronomy 7:3–4

Is Friendship with the People of the Book Forbidden?

The following verse has been flashed on television screens and is misused by critics of the Qur'an, as well as by some Muslims, to discourage friendships between Muslims, Jews, and Christians. I will quote a common translation first:

> *O you who believe! do not take the Jews and the Christians for friends; they are friends of each other; and whoever amongst you takes them for a friend, then surely he is one of them; surely Allah does not guide the unjust people.* 5:51 (Shakir, and similarly by Pickthall).

There are two points that need to be reiterated here. First, the verses of the Qur'an (like the Bible) should be viewed within the proper context. Second, it must be pointed out that the word used for *friendship* in the verse is *awliya*, which means "allies" or "protector," or "protecting friend," which has a very different connotation than just a "friend." Yuksel thus translates this verse as *do not take the Jews and the Christians for allies* and comments that the word is not to be taken in the context of social, personal, or financial interactions, but rather in the case of religious conflict. In addition, it does not refer to all People of the Book, as will be discussed below.

THE CONTEXT

The verse was revealed in Medina, where the local Jews started to show hostilities against the new converts and the budding Islamic community. According to Muslim historians, they were mocking and ridiculing the new Muslims. This verse was revealed in reference to *these* Jews, not all Jews; and for that matter, not all Jews and Christians "who will ever live." The verses 5:57–58 that followed verse 5:51 (quoted above) address that:

> *O you who believe! Take not for friends and protectors those who take your religion for a mockery or sport [or joke], whether among those who received the scripture before you, or among those who reject Faith; but fear Allah, if you have faith (indeed). 5:57*
>
> *When you proclaim your call to prayer [adhan] they take it (but) as mockery and sport; that is because they are a people without understanding. 5:58*

The Qur'an commands us to be kind and respect those who have not done injustice to the believers.

> *God does not forbid you respecting those who have not made war against you on account of (your) religion, and have not driven you forth from your homes, **that you show them kindness and deal with them justly; surely God loves the doers of justice.** 60:8 (Shakir)*

And one should take the entire Qur'an for a proper context; verse 5:5 on interfaith marriages (quoted above) has significant relevance to the discussion here. Making the "food lawful" in the same verse as allowing marriage with the Jews and the Christians is a call for social interaction between people of faith and implies sharing meals, more than just consuming kosher food. It is a time-honored human custom that promotes good will, and it is harder for people to remain enemies when they break bread together. The allowance of interfaith marriages and promoting social interaction over meals is clearly a far cry from the call of "don't make friends with the People of the Book."

The Torah's Accounts of the Children of Israel

Many in the West criticize the Qur'an for being too harsh on the Israelites, saying that it promotes hatred toward them. However, the Torah seems equally as harsh, if not more so. The Qur'an and the Torah seem to take a similar view: God chose and favored the children of Israel, showing mercy to them. God cursed the enemies of the children of Israel, including the pharaoh and others who fought them on their way to the Promised Land. However, the journey in wilderness from Egypt to the Promised Land was not exactly an easy one.

The Qur'an and the Old Testament describe many stories about the transgressions of the children of Israel, their rebellious nature, and their constant grumbling. Some of the verses related to Israelites' grumblings were quoted earlier in the chapter on Moses. Other Israelites, however, remained pious and steadfast, and they trusted in God despite their adversities.

The Lord told Moses, 'Quick! Go down the mountain! Your people whom you brought from the land of Egypt have corrupted themselves.' Exodus 32:7

Then the Lord said, 'I have seen how stubborn and rebellious these people are. Now leave me alone so my fierce anger can blaze against them, and I will destroy them.' Exodus 32:9–10

RECURRENT REBELLION BY THE CHILDREN OF ISRAEL

A recurring theme of the Hebrew Bible is the frequent backsliding of the

Children of Israel. For example, when nearing the Promised Land, Moses sent two noble spies (Caleb and Joshua) out ahead to investigate. They reported that the people there were giants, making them look like grasshoppers, and said the city had fortified walls. The spies further reported they had no chance against them, except Caleb and Joshua, who maintained that by having trust in God, they could overcome their apparent shortcomings. The Israelites then rebelled against them.

> *Why is the Lord taking us to this country only to have us die in battle?* Numbers 14:3.
>
> *But the whole community began to talk about stoning Joshua and Caleb. Then the glorious presence of the Lord appeared to all the Israelites at the Tabernacle. And the Lord said to Moses, "How long will these people treat me with contempt? Will they never believe me, even after all the miraculous signs I have done among them? I will disown them and destroy them with a plague. Then I will make you into a nation greater and mightier than they are!"* Numbers 14:10–12
>
> *Then the Lord said to Moses and Aaron, "How long must I put up with this wicked community and its complaints about me? Yes, I have heard the complaints the Israelites are making against me. Now tell them this: 'As surely as I live, declares the LORD, I will do to you the very things I heard you say. You will all drop dead in this wilderness! Because you complained against me, every one of you who is twenty years old or older and was included in the registration will die. You will not enter and occupy the land I swore to give you. The only exceptions will be Caleb son of Jephunneh and Joshua son of Nun.'"* Numbers 14:26–30

Israelites' idolatry and sexual relations with Moabite women:

> *While the Israelites were camped at Acacia Grove, some of the men defiled themselves by having sexual relations with local Moabite women. These women invited them to attend sacrifices to their gods, so the Israelites feasted with them and worshiped the gods of Moab. In this way, Israel joined in the worship of Baal of Peor, causing the Lord's anger to blaze against his people.* Numbers 25:1–3

GOSPELS' CRITICISM OF THE RELIGIOUS LEADERS

Not just the Qur'an and the Old Testament, but the New Testament as well, spoke negatively of many of the religious leaders at the time. Jesus often called them hypocrites. Matthew chapter 23 opens up with Jesus calling on his disciples. These are strong words from anyone—especially from someone as kind-hearted, merciful, and loving as Jesus:

> *What sorrow awaits you teachers of religious law and you Pharisees. Hypocrites! For you build tombs for the prophets your ancestors killed, and you decorate the monuments of the godly people your ancestors destroyed. Then you say, 'If we had lived in the days of our ancestors, we would never have joined them in killing the prophets.' But in saying that, you testify against yourselves that you are indeed the descendants of those who murdered the prophets. Go ahead and finish what your ancestor started. Snakes! Sons of vipers! How will you escape the judgment of hell?* Matthew 23:29–33
>
> *Then Jesus said to the crowds and to his disciples, 'The teachers of religious law and the Pharisees are the official interpreters of the law of Moses. So practice and obey whatever they tell you, but don't follow their example. For they don't practice what they teach.'* Matthew 23:1–3

The purpose of these references from the Qur'an, the Old Testament, and the New Testament is not to be critical of any group but to show the consistency of the scriptures in reference to historical events. It is noteworthy that the scriptures also praise the pious and the righteous among these groups, putting their criticism in perspective.

Discussion Points for Dialogue and Healing

- The Qur'an repeatedly refers to the original Torah and the Gospel as "guidance," "light," and "mercy." It also states the original scriptures have been altered, a view shared by many secular Christian and Jewish scholars. The Muslims are still commanded to believe in the divine nature of their scriptures. Once again, my advice is not to bring this last point into interfaith conversations unless the relationship between groups is well established based on mutual respect.

- The Qur'an views Islam as one universal religion and that all prophets, from Adam to Muhammad, preached the same basic religion. Islam is referred to as *Din al-Ibrahimi*, or the "religion of Abraham."
- Guiding principles of interfaith dialogue, according to the teachings of the Qur'an, call for dealing with each other in the best of manners and highlight the common bonds that exist between people of Abrahamic faiths.
- The golden rule of Christianity, Judaism, and Islam calls for treating others as you would like to be treated (it is presumed that we would like to be treated nicely). Jesus taught to "turn the other cheek," and to "love thy enemy," without implying that the Jews, Christians, and Muslims are enemies by default.
- The struggle is not between Jews, Christians, and Muslims. The struggle is between extremists of all faiths on one side, and the decent majority of all faiths on the other side. The decent majority must be at least as active as the vocal minority that threatens to divide us.
- Contrary to the common belief, the Qur'an does not forbid Muslims from being friends with Jews and Christians in terms of daily social and personal interactions.
- In the Qur'an's description of righteousness, Jews, Christians, and Muslims are mentioned side by side, as long as they all meet the prescribed criteria (see verses 2:177 and 5:69).
- The Qur'an and the Bible command believers to leave the judgment involving the differences between various faiths to God (i.e., they should not be the ones judging each other).
- Feel free to ponder on the points noted below and add your own.

Time to Ponder

- The distrust and, at times, frank animosity between Jews, Christians, and Muslims has existed for centuries. In such situations, is the behavior of the followers when approaching interfaith relationships consistent with the teachings and the guidelines established by the scriptures they follow?
- In these situations what would Moses, Jesus, and Muhammad do?

Conversely, what would Moses, Jesus, and Muhammad *not* do? Would they oppress other nations, kill innocent women and children, bomb abortion clinics, and burn Qur'ans?

- Jews, Christians, and Muslims hold the same view of the holy land. Shouldn't this shared respect for the holy land serve as an inspiration to work together to accomplish the common goals of peace and harmony, rather than fight over it?

Part Three

THE QUR'AN
AND DAILY LIFE

CHAPTER 14
Pillars of Islam

Where there is charity and wisdom, there is neither fear nor ignorance.
Francis of Assissi

Overcoming poverty is not a gesture of charity. It is an act of justice.
Nelson Mandela

This section will cover the teachings of the Qur'an and the Bible on social aspects of life in accordance with the divine law. A detailed description of Islamic law and jurisprudence (*fiqh*) is beyond the scope of this book. Most of the topics outlined in this section are mostly relevant to individuals rather than society in general.

Before getting into the specific topics, it is worth emphasizing that the Qur'an's view of religion is much broader than just a set of religious instructions and laws. Islam is viewed as a way of life and covers every aspect of daily life: from "purely religious" instruction like prayers and other mandatory forms of worship, to the laws that govern daily lives like marriage, divorce, inheritance, personal finances, personal behavior, and ethics, as well as the societal issues.

Pillars of Islam
There are five basic, mandatory commandments, or pillars, of Islam, as interpreted by most Muslim jurists, and they are listed as follows:

1. *Shahada*, or Testimony
2. *Salat*, or Daily Prayers

3. *Zakat*, or Helping the Poor (Charity)
4. *Sawm*, or Fasting
5. *Hajj*, or Pilgrimage[1]

SHAHADA (TESTIMONY)

This is the basic statement, or testimony to faith. It simply states:

> *I testify that there is no god but God, and Muhammad is the messenger of God.*

The Qur'an has numerous passages that form the basis for the *shahada*. The first part, "there is no god but God," also forms one of the Ten Commandments and is the basic tenet of the three Abrahamic faiths. The main difference in the creed is the second part: "Muhammad is the messenger of God."

> *There is no god but He: That is the witness of God, His angels, and those endued with knowledge, standing firm on justice. There is no god but He, the Exalted in Power, the Wise. 3:18*
>
> *Say: He is Allah the One and Only. 112:1*

As for the second part of *shahada*, there are numerous passages addressing Muhammad, or referring to Muhammad as the warner or the bearer of glad tidings, or calling him, "O' Prophet." Some examples are noted here:

> *We have sent you (O Prophet!), to mankind as a messenger; and God is sufficient as a witness. 4:79 (Shakir)*
>
> *Muhammad is the messenger of God. 48:29*

Though typically "no god but God" and Muhammad's prophecy are mentioned separately, the following verse combines the two commandments:

> *Say (O Muhammad): 'O mankind! Verily, **I am an apostle (messenger) of God** to all of you (sent by Him) unto Whom the dominion*

*over the heavens and the earth belongs! **There is no deity save Him;
He (alone) grants life and deals death!' Believe, then, in God and His
Apostle—the unlettered Prophet who believes in God and His words—
and follow him, so that you might find guidance!' 7:158 (Asad)*

SALAT (DAILY PRAYERS)

Salat is the ritual prayer that is obligatory for all Muslims. It is more than
"the prayers" as might be perceived by the English translation. It follows
a prescribed pattern and recitation of specific verses and supplications in
a particular sequence. There are five mandatory prayers each day from
dawn to late evening. In each *salat,* there are a prescribed number of *rakat,*
or "cycles." In addition, Muslims also offer the prayers on Friday in congregation and on the occasion of two festivals: *Eid al-Fitr* (after Ramadan)
and *Eid al-Adha* (after Hajj). The congregational prayers on Friday are
emphasized in the following verse:

> *O you who believe! when the call is made for prayer on Friday, then
> hasten to the remembrance of Allah and leave off trading; that is better
> for you, if you know. 62:9 (Shakir)*

The prayers can be done in private (individually), at home and work,
but it's more highly recommended they be offered as a congregation in a
mosque (*masjid*). Before one starts the prayers, one must cleanse with water by performing ablution (*wadu*). Many consider this a spiritual rather
than physical cleansing. Each prayer is announced with a call to prayer,
known as *adhan.*

More than just a set of ritualistic verses or postures, it is considered a way to purify one's soul and attain spiritual health by seeking
nearness to God by worshipping Him and remembering Him often.
The daily prayers are constant reminders of one's duty to God and
are intended to prevent one from getting perverted or deviating from
the right path. One must be entirely devoted and maintain the entire
focus on remembrance of God during *salat,* and not merely fulfill the
mechanical requirements. *Salat* can be viewed as a means for a person to communicate with God, whereas the recitation of the Qur'an

can be considered God talking to the person, completing a two-way communication.

> *Recite that which has been revealed to you of the Book and keep up prayer (salat); surely prayer keeps (one) away from indecency and evil, and certainly the remembrance of Allah is the greatest, and Allah knows what you do. 29:45 (Shakir)*

Salat is often mentioned in combination with *zakat* (charity):

> *And be steadfast in prayer; practice regular charity; and bow down your heads with those who bow down (in worship). 2:43*
> *And be steadfast in prayer and pay the regular charity and whatever good you send before for yourselves, you shall find it with Allah; surely Allah sees what you do. 2:110 (Shakir)*

SALAT WAS ALSO ORDAINED ON ABRAHAM, MOSES, JESUS, AND OTHER PROPHETS

Non-Muslims and many Muslims erroneously believe that *salat* was ordained on Muhammad and subsequently on his followers only. But the Qur'an indicates it was ordained on other prophets as well:

> *And We bestowed on him [Abraham], Isaac, and, as an additional gift, (a grandson), Jacob, and We made righteous men of every one (of them). And We made them leaders [Imams], guiding (men) by Our Command, and We sent them inspiration to do good deeds, to establish regular prayers [salat], and to practice regular charity [zakat]; and they constantly served Us (and Us only). 21:72–73*
> *And mention Ishmael in the Book; surely he was truthful in (his) promise, and he was a messenger, a prophet. And he enjoined on his family prayer and almsgiving [zakat], and was one in whom his Lord was well pleased. 19:54–55 (Shakir)*

Salat and *zakat* were ordained on the children of Israel:

And remember We took a covenant from the children of Israel (to this effect): Worship none but Allah; treat with kindness your parents and kindred, and orphans and those in need; speak fair to the people; be steadfast in prayer [salat]; and practice regular charity [zakat]. 2:83

Similar passages are repeated when recalling prophets prior to Muhammad and their communities: on the children of Israel (2:43, 2:83); on Sho'aib, a prophet in Midian, often said to be described by Muslims as Jethro of the Hebrew Bible (11:87); **on Moses** (*And I have chosen you [referring to Moses], so listen to what is revealed. Verily, I am Allah: There is no god but I: So serve you Me (only), and establish regular prayer for celebrating My praise.* 20:13–14); and **on Jesus** (*He said [referring to Jesus' testimony from the crib]: Surely I am a servant of Allah; He has given me the Book and made me a prophet. And He has made me blessed wherever I may be, and He has enjoined on me prayer* [salat] *and poor-rate* [zakat] *so long as I live.* 19:30–31).

ZAKAT (ALMSGIVING, CHARITY)

There are three forms of charitable giving in Islam. *Zakat* is obligatory. *Sadaqat* is above and beyond the mandatory giving and is highly recommended. *Khums*, according to the Shia Muslim theology only, is also mandatory.

Every religion has some form of charitable giving for religious, social, and educational services. Islam has institutionalized the charitable giving in the name of God. *Zakat* means "to purify" and refers to purifying one's wealth and soul. Purification of the soul implies freedom from selfishness and greed, and to unattach one's self from worldly wealth and to seek nearness to God. It helps fulfill the societal obligations of the individual. It is intended to prevent wealth hoarding and to meet the needs of the poor in the community through altruistic acts.

Zakat is due as a fixed proportion of one's surplus wealth and earnings after meeting one's financial obligations and liabilities. It is mentioned by name thirty times alongside *salat*, in addition to numerous other references to spend in the way of God.

> *And be steadfast in prayer; practice regular charity; and bow down your heads with those who bow down (in worship).* 2:43
>
> *And be steadfast in prayer and regular in charity: And whatever good you send forth for your souls before you, you shall find it with Allah: for Allah sees well all that you do.* 2:110
>
> *Only God is your Guardian [protecting friend or wali] and His Messenger and those who believe, those who keep up prayers and pay the poor-rate while they bow.* 5:5 (Mir Ali)

Shi'a Muslim commentators believe the last part of the verse revealed refers to Ali, Muhammad's son-in-law, who reportedly dropped his ring to a beggar while bowing down during a prayer.

In the following verse, *zakat* and other giving is termed *qarza hasna*, "a loan to God," or "a beautiful loan," which will be paid back on the Day of Judgment in the form of mercy and forgiveness to the donor:

> *Read, therefore, as much of the Qur'an as may be easy (for you); and establish regular Prayer and give regular Charity; and loan to Allah a Beautiful Loan [qarza hasna]. And whatever good you send forth for your souls you shall find it in Allah's Presence—yes, better and greater, in reward and seek the Grace of Allah: for Allah is Oft-Forgiving, Most Merciful.* 73:20

GIVING OPENLY IS FINE; GIVING IN SECRET IS EVEN BETTER
The Qur'an encourages giving openly or secretly, but giving secretly, without showing off, is even better. Giving, for the purpose of showing off, is highly undesirable:

> *Those who (in charity) spend of their goods by night and by day, in secret and in public, have their reward with their Lord: on them shall be no fear, nor shall they grieve.* 2:274
>
> *If you do deeds of charity openly, it is well; but if you bestow it upon the needy in secret, it will be even better for you, and it will atone for some of your bad deeds. And God is aware of all that you do.* 2:271 (Asad)

In fact, one cannot be righteous until he gives in the way of God to the needy:

> *By no means shall you attain to righteousness until you spend (benevolently) out of what you love; and whatever thing you spend, Allah surely knows it.* 3:92 (Shakir)

God is the recipient of charitable giving:

> *Do they not know that Allah accepts repentance from His servants and takes the alms [gifts of charity], and that Allah is the Oft-returning (to mercy), the Merciful?* 9:104 (Shakir)

SAWM (FASTING)

Sawm, or fasting, is mandatory during the month of Ramadan, the ninth month of the Islamic calendar. The fasting starts at dawn with a meal called *suhur*, and lasts till sunset with another meal called *iftar*. During this time, one is not to eat or drink anything. Contrary to a common perception, fasting is considered much more than simply avoiding food and drinks, and in fact is an example where English translation loses the essence of the original concept. It's a time for spiritual healing, strengthening faith, and reflection. The time is spent in remembrance of God, getting near to Him, repenting, avoiding all major and minor sins, and spending for the needy in the way of God. Though at a glance, fasting may seem "unnatural" and harsh, those who fast regularly insist that fasting actually is an uplifting experience. This is the time to renew one's vows and relationship with God. According to Muslim view, fasting teaches the virtues of self-discipline and self-control over bodily desires (hunger, sexual feelings, anger, etc.).

> *O you who believe! Fasting is prescribed for you, as it was prescribed for those before you, so that you may guard (against evil).* 2:183 (Shakir)

The word used in the above verse is "prescribed." Indeed, many Muslim scholars and Muslim physicians point out many health benefits of fasting, including cleansing of the gastrointestinal tract, better control of blood glucose, weight, and cholesterol. In addition, fasting seems to stimulate endorphins, considered an important neurochemical that controls pain and emotional well-being. Religious scholars point out that the physical benefits are just one small, though important, element of fasting, and the real benefit is spiritual growth and healing. The verse also points out that fasting was prescribed before the time of Muhammad. Indeed many other religions and cultures such as Judaism, Christianity, Hinduism, and Buddhism observe fasting in one form or another.

WHAT'S FORBIDDEN DURING FASTING?

- Physical needs: Avoiding food, drink, smoking, and sexual intercourse
- Morals: Avoiding sins, major and minor
- Spiritual: Avoiding distractions that move one away from God

A festival called *Eid al-Fitr* follows at the end of the month. It is not to celebrate the *end* of Ramadan, but Muslims view it as a day to give thanks to God for all the blessings and bounties received during the month of Ramadan.

> The month of Ramadan is that in which the Qur'an was revealed, a guidance to men and clear proofs of the guidance and the distinction; therefore whoever of you is present in the month, he shall fast therein, and whoever is sick or upon a journey, then (he shall fast) a (like) number of other days; Allah desires ease for you, and He does not desire for you difficulty, and (He desires) that you should complete the number and that you should exalt the greatness of Allah for His having guided you and that you may give thanks. 2:185 (Shakir)

According to many Muslim traditions, all good deeds during the month of Ramadan, as an added incentive, are multiplied many times. One particular night, known as the Night of Power (*Lailat al-Qadr*), is of great importance to Muslims. Chapter 97 of the Qur'an is named after that night (*qadr*). It's said that this is the night when the Qur'an was revealed, in its entirety, from God to the lower heaven, and the angels are said to descend upon earth all night till the dawn, to bring peace, mercy, and forgiveness, and all matters for the next year are decreed. Muslims spend the night in prayer, repentance, and seeking His nearness. As mentioned before, in its basic concept, the night has many parallels to the Jewish *Yamim Noraim*, or "Days of Awe" (days of repentance). The translation of the entire chapter is quoted below:

> *Surely We have revealed this (Qur'an) in the night of the power. And what will make you understand, what the night of the power is! The night of the power is better than one thousand months. The angels and the Spirit (Gabriel) come down with every decree, by the leave of their Lord, that night is the night of Peace, till the break of dawn.* 97:1–5 (Malik)

HAJJ (PILGRIMAGE TO MECCA)
Unlike daily prayers, charity, and fasting, the hajj is mandatory only once in a lifetime, for those who are able and can afford to travel to Mecca during the month of *Dhul-Hijja*, the twelfth month of the Islamic calendar. Each year, millions of Muslims from all around the world, from various ethnicities, and socio-economic backgrounds meet in the city of Mecca and perform various rituals in a show of unity, simplicity, harmony, and submission to God.

A life changing experience for many: During this whole month, pilgrims spend time in remembrance of God, supplications, and deeds of charity; they avoid major and minor sins. The experience is considered a purification of mind and soul, and pilgrims after performing the hajj are said to be as pure as a newborn. Most people upon their return from the hajj report that it was a life-changing experience, and that they had never felt so much peace in their hearts before. Malcolm X, in one of the letters he wrote from Mecca during hajj, noted:

> Never have I witnessed such sincere hospitality and overwhelming spirit of true brotherhood as is practiced by people of all color and races here in this ancient Holy land, the home of Abraham,

Muhammad, and all the other prophets of the Holy scriptures. For the past week, I have been utterly speechless and spellbound by the graciousness I see displayed by all around me by people of all colors. There were tens of thousands of pilgrims, from all over the world. They were of all colors, from blue-eyed blondes to black-skinned Africans. But we were all participating in the same ritual, displaying a spirit of unity and brotherhood that my experiences in America had led me to believe never could exist."[2]

A 2008 study conducted in conjunction with Harvard University's JFK School of Government entitled "Estimating the Impact of the Hajj: Religion and Tolerance in Islam's Global Gathering," found that Muslim communities become more open after the hajj experience. The authors of the study concluded that the hajj "increases belief in equality and harmony among ethnic groups and Islamic community and that hajjis (those who have performed the hajj) show increased belief in peace, and in equality and harmony among adherents of different religions. The evidence suggests that these changes are more a result of exposure to and interaction with hajjis from around the world, rather than religious instruction or a changed social role of pilgrims upon return."[3]

The rituals: Most of the rituals are to commemorate and honor the acts of Abraham, Ishmael, and Hagar. For example, walking between the mountains of Safa and Marwa commemorates Hagar's running back and forth in the desert, looking for water for her son Ishmael; drinking from the well of Zamzam; animal sacrifice after Abraham's attempted sacrifice when he received vision from God; and stoning the devil where he is said to have appeared to Abraham to deceive him.

The Bible and the Pillars of Islamic Faith

As mentioned earlier, the Qur'an claims that in their basic forms, the pillars and other acts (or branches) of Islamic faith mentioned above were commanded to other prophets and their communities before Muhammad. A review of the Bible would seem to collaborate this claim. Though not as specific as the Qur'anic references or in conformity with current traditional practices of Muslims, there are numerous references in both the Old and the New Testament to prayers, fasting, charity, doing good, and forbidding evil.

Salat is not mentioned by name in the Old or New Testament but there are references on regular prayers and ablutions (washing before prayers).

- **Ablution/washing before prayers:** The Torah describes Moses, Aaron, and the priests washing their hands and feet before entering the altar:

  Next Moses placed the washbasin between the Tabernacle and the altar. He filled it with water so the priests could wash themselves. Moses and Aaron and Aaron's sons used water from it to wash their hands and feet. Whenever they approached the altar and entered the Tabernacle, they washed themselves, just as the Lord had commanded Moses. Exodus 40:30–32

Not only were they supposed to wash, it was made a permanent law for their descendants:

  Then the Lord said to Moses, "Make a bronze washbasin with a bronze stand. Place it between the Tabernacle and the altar, and fill it with water. Aaron and his sons will wash their hands and feet there. They must wash with water whenever they go into the Tabernacle to appear before the Lord and when they approach the altar to burn up their special gifts to the Lord—or they will die! They must always wash their hands and feet, or they will die. This is a permanent law for Aaron and his descendants, to be observed from generation to generation." Exodus 30:17–22

- **Kneeling (*ruku*) and prostration (*sujud*)** are considered signs of humility before God and part of the rituals of the Muslim prayers. These have been mentioned many times in the Bible, without using the specific terms:

Moses and Aaron turned away from the people and went to the entrance of the Tabernacle, where they fell face down on the ground. Then the glorious presence of the Lord appeared to them. Numbers 20:6

Then Jesus went with them to the olive grove called Gethsemane, and he said, 'Sit here while I go over there to pray.' He took Peter and Zebedee's two sons, James and John, and he became anguished and distressed. He told them, 'My soul is crushed with grief to the point of death. Stay here and keep watch with me.' He went on a little farther and bowed with his face to the ground, praying, 'My Father! If it is possible, let this cup of suffering be taken away from me. Yet I want your will to be done, not mine.' Matthew 26:36–39

- **Praying regularly/prayer times:** Though the regular prayers five times a day are not practiced by Christians and Jews today, there are some references to daily prayers performed at particular hours of the day:

In Caesarea there lived a Roman army officer named Cornelius, who was a captain of the Italian Regiment. He was a devout, God-fearing man, as was everyone in his household. He gave generously to the poor and prayed regularly to God. Acts 10:1–2

It further goes on to describe Cornelius's experience:

Cornelius replied, 'Four days ago I was praying in my house about this same time, three o'clock in the afternoon.' Acts 10:30

(This would roughly correspond to the mid afternoon Muslim prayer time.)

Now Peter and John went up together into the temple at the hour of prayer, being the ninth hour. Acts 3:1 (King James Version)

The New Living Translation's version is as follows:

Peter and John went to the Temple one afternoon to take part in the three o'clock prayer service.

- **The *Qiblah*, or direction of prayers:** In the early days of Muhammad, the first *Qiblah* was Jerusalem (Al Quds Mosque/Dome of the Rock, believed by Muslims to have been built by Solomon). The *Qiblah* was changed to the Ka'aba in Mecca according to the Qur'anic verses 2:142–144. The Bible points out that when Solomon prayed to the Lord, he used to face toward the temple in Jerusalem.

> *May you watch over this Temple night and day, this place where you have said, "My name will be there." May you always hear the prayers I make toward this place. May you hear the humble and earnest requests from me and your people Israel when we pray toward this place. Yes, hear us from heaven where you live, and when you hear, forgive.* 1 Kings 8:29–30

Daniel, another Jewish prophet, used to pray regularly (though three times a day, according to the Bible) and faced Jerusalem during the prayers:

> *But when Daniel learned that the law had been signed, he went home and knelt down as usual in his upstairs room, with its windows open toward Jerusalem. He prayed three times a day, just as he had always done, giving thanks to his God.* Daniel 6:10

It appears then that some form of daily prayers were regularly performed by these biblical figures, with many rituals similar to the Muslim prayers as ordained by the Qur'an, like ablution, kneeling, prostration, and facing the *Qiblah*.

- **Fasting:** Moses fasted for forty days and forty nights. He did it twice, once before receiving the tablets, and the other time when he found out about the idolatry of the children of Israel upon coming down from Mount Sinai:

> *This happened when I was on the mountain receiving the tablets of stone inscribed with the words of the covenant that the Lord had made with you. I was there for forty days and forty nights, and all that time I ate no food and drank no water.* Deuteronomy 9:9

King David fasted to humble himself:

Yet when they were ill, I grieved for them. I denied myself by fasting for them, but my prayers returned unanswered. Psalm 35:13

Jesus fasted for forty days and nights, like Moses did, while he was in the desert and the devil tried to tempt him:

Then Jesus was led by the Spirit into the wilderness to be tempted there by the devil. For forty days and forty nights he fasted and became very hungry. Matthew 4:1–2

The prophet Isaiah teaches what fasting entails and the true spirit of fasting (something that Muslims can readily relate to):

"I will tell you why!" I respond. "It's because you are fasting to please yourselves. Even while you fast, you keep oppressing your workers. What good is fasting when you keep on fighting and quarreling? This kind of fasting will never get you anywhere with me. You humble yourselves by going through the motions of penance, bowing your heads like reeds bending in the wind. You dress in burlap and cover yourselves with ashes. Is this what you call fasting? Do you really think this will please the Lord? No, **this is the kind of fasting I want***: Free those who are wrongly imprisoned; lighten the burden of those who work for you. Let the oppressed go free, and remove the chains that bind people. Share your food with the hungry, and give shelter to the homeless. Give clothes to those who need them, and do not hide from relatives who need your help."* Isaiah 58:3–17

- **Charity:** A hallmark of Christian teaching has always called Christians to acts of charity.

Teach those who are rich in this world not to be proud and not to trust in their money, which is so unreliable. Their trust should be in God, who richly gives us all we need for our enjoyment. Tell them to use their money to do good. They should be rich in good works and generous to those in need, always being ready to share with others. By doing this they will be storing up their treasure as a good foundation for the future so that they may experience true life. 1 Timothy 6:17–19

JESUS TAUGHT TO GIVE IN SECRET, NOT FOR SHOW

*Watch out! Don't do your good deeds publicly, to be admired by others, for you will lose the reward from your Father in heaven. When you give to someone in need, don't do as the hypocrites do—blowing trumpets in the synagogues and streets to call attention to their acts of charity! I tell you the truth; they have received all the reward they will ever get. But when you give to someone in need, **don't let your left hand know what your right hand is doing.** Give your gifts in private, and your Father, who sees everything, will reward you.* Matthew 6:1–5

The teachings of Jesus emboldened above are practically identical to a famous hadith (saying of Muhammad). In reference to certain deeds that will earn God's special mercy and protection on the Day of Judgment, Muhammad declared: "A person who practices charity so secretly that his left hand does not know what his right hand has given."[4]

And (God does not love) those who spend their possessions on others (only) to be seen and praised by men, the while they believe neither in God nor in the Last Day. 4:38 (Asad)

In the following sermon, Jesus emphasized the private, not-for-show acts of worship—not just charitable giving but also prayers and fasting:

When you pray, don't be like the hypocrites who love to pray publicly on street corners and in the synagogues where everyone can see them. I tell you the truth, that is all the reward they will ever get. But when you pray, go away by yourself, shut the door behind you, and pray to your Father in private. Matthew 6:5–6
And when you fast, don't make it obvious, as the hypocrites do, for they try to look miserable and disheveled so people will admire them

for their fasting. I tell you the truth that is the only reward they will ever get. But when you fast, comb your hair and wash your face. Then no one will notice that you are fasting, except your Father, who knows what you do in private. And your Father, who sees everything, will reward you. Matthew 6:16–17

JEWISH PRAYERS AND POSITIONS

In a book titled *To Pray as a Jew: A Guide to the Prayer Book and the Synagogue Service,* Rabbi Hayim H. Donin discusses the prayers of the ancient Jews and shows illustrations of various positions during the regular prayers that included bowing and prostration. The images of the various positions during the prayers have striking resemblance to those of the Muslim daily prayers.

He goes on to comment, "In most contemporary congregations very few people keep to the tradition of falling prostrate. Sometimes it is only the prayer leader and the rabbi who does so. In more traditional congregations, however, some worshipers, men and women, will join the prayer leader and rabbi in the act of prostrating themselves. In Israeli synagogues, the practice is more widespread than in synagogues elsewhere."[5]

Discussion Points for Dialogue and Healing

- The five pillars of Islamic faith are *shahada* (testimony to One God and Muhammad as His prophet), *salat* (prayers), *zakat* (charity), *sawm* (fasting), and *hajj* (pilgrimage to Mecca).
- The Bible makes many references to fasting, regular prayers (and some of its rituals), charity, and the Oneness of God, though not in the exact manner as the Qur'an does. The Qur'an insists that *salat* (regular prayers), *sawm* (fasting), and *zakat* (charity) were also ordained on prior prophets and communities.
- The Ten Commandments start with referencing the first part of Muslim *shahada* (i.e., believing in God and making no partners with Him and that there is no deity besides Him). Except for observing the Sabbath, every other commandment is also commanded by Islam (and Christianity).
- Some of the ancient Jewish traditions of prayer resemble Muslim prayers, though they are not often practiced currently.

- Charitable giving is highly emphasized in the Bible and the Qur'an. Giving in private is much better than giving in public. This forms the basis for taking care of the needy in the community and an important part of striving for social justice and equality. In fact, helping the needy is a great way to put interfaith dialogue into action by working together to establish food banks, homeless shelters and orphanages, just to name a few.
- Feel free to ponder on the points noted below and add your own.

Time to Ponder

- Is there one universal way to worship God? Are rituals more important than the spiritual connection one needs to make with God during prayers and various other forms of worship? Does God accept or prefer one form of worship over others? If so, is that belief supported by the scripture?

CHAPTER 15
Jihad (To Strive)

*Far from being the father of jihad, Mohammad
was a peacemaker, who risked his life and nearly lost the
loyalty of his closest companions because he was determined
to effect a reconciliation with Mecca.*
Karen Armstrong

Jihad is the most misunderstood and misused article of Islamic faith. Used at times for political purposes by Muslims and non-Muslims alike, it has become a subject of great intrigue recently, though many still don't seem to have a clear understanding of it. Jihad has been used interchangeably with *terrorism* committed by Muslim radicals such as ISIS and Al Qaeda, despite numerous condemnations of these acts by the majority of Muslims. The bombings of restuarants, shops, airports, and hotels have unfortunately become relatively frequent news. Most of these acts of terror are committed overseas though there has been a recent increase in terrorism involving radicalized Muslims in the United States, including the Boston marathon bombing in April 2013; the shooting in San Bernardino, California in December 2015; the mass killings at a gay nightclub in Orlando, Florida in June 2016. However, there have been numerous other acts of terrorism such as the the Columbine high school shooting in Colorado in 1999; the mass killing in a theater shooting in Aurora, Colorado in July 2012; the shooting involving the Sandy Hook elementary school in Newport Connecticut in December 2012; the killing at a Planned Parenthood clinic in Colorado Springs, Colorado in November 2015; a shooting at a historic black church in Charleston, South Carolina in June 2015, to mention a few. Many news outlets are reluctant to call these acts *terrorism* unless the acts are committed by Muslims, choosing to use the term "violence" or generic statements such as "gunmen opened fire" instead. Similarly "jihadist" has been used to describe the Muslim terrorists, once again despite objections from a large majority of Muslims, pointing out that these violent actions are acts of terrorism and have nothing to do with the Islamic concept of jihad. It is interesting to note that jihadist means *mujahideen,* or "those fighting a jihad." As we may all recall, we in the United States were actively supporting and arming the *mujahideen* in Afghanistan fighting the Russians back in the 1980s. From the ashes of this war, when the United States simply left the arena, arose groups such as the Taliban, and later Al-Qaeda. In more recent times, an environment has been created whereby one thinks of terrorism automatically when the words such as Islam, Muslims or jihad are brought up and vice versa. In fact during my speeches and presentations, jihad and terrorism are by far the most common questions and topics that are brought up by the audience. This is a good opportunity to separate the facts from fiction.

TERRORISM DEFINED

Though one may believe that acts of violence committed by Muslims defines terrorism, the World Health Organization's definition of terrorism is "The intentional use of physical force or *power,* threatened or actual, against oneself, another person, or against a group or community, which either results in or has a high likelihood of resulting in injury, death, psychological harm, maldevelopment, or deprivation."[1]

A War Between Islam and the West

According to an article published in the *New York Times,* Charles Kurzman and David Schanzer reported that, based on their survey conducted with Police Executive Research Forum involving 382 law enforcement agencies, the right-wing terrorists, at least in the United States, pose a bigger terrorist threat than Muslim extremsits.[2] Moreover, the "Islamic" terrorists have killed, by far, many more Muslims worldwide, than Christians, Jews, and people of other faiths (and people of no faith). There is a clear portrayal of the terror campaign by these radicals as a war between Islam and the west. A terrorist attack on July 5, 2016 in Medina, considered the second holiest city in Islam, during the month of Ramadan is a stark reminder that these terrorists, despite their claims, do not represent Islam or its values. As outlined earlier in the introduction, these terrorist organizations' mission is based more on geopolitical, social, and economical forces rather than a theological basis. Many of the perpetrators of suicidal bombings are known to have been engaged in activities, just prior to their acts of terrorism, that are considered un-Islamic, such as attending night clubs and drinking alcohol. Retired Lt. General Michael Flynn of the U.S. Army, former head of the Defense Intelligence Agency, and now White House chief of staff in the Trump administration, in July 2016 stated that 80 percent of the laptops captured from the ISIS fighters contained pornography, far from the image of the pious messages they may try to convey to others. This was reported widely on mainstream media, including CNN, ABC and the *Washington Times*.[3]

Many Muslims, including myself, have often been asked where all the "moderate Muslims" are to condemn these attacks. Many organizations in the United States such as Islamic Network Group (ING), Council of American Islamic Relations (CAIR) and numerous Islamic centers around the country have condemned these attacks, numerous times, not just in the United States but around the world. The fact of the matter is that they actually do, it's just that they don't get the press. American Muslims have told me they are twice as upset as the rest of America, because these terrorists attack our country *and* attack our religion. Muslim Americans feel that the terror groups have done more harm to Islam and Muslims that the Islamophobia industry has. It is of note that many of the victims of terrorist attacks in America, France, and Britain, are Muslims. The victims of the Boston marathon attacks, for example, included hijabist marathon runners. Conversely when the victims were taken to the nearby hospitals, some of the doctors tending to the wounded were Muslim. The Charlie Hebdo attacks in Paris in January 2015 included a French Muslim police officer, Ahmed Merabet.

FATWAS AGAINST TERRORISM

Muslims frown at the slightest suggestion that terrorist acts are labeled as jihad by the western mainstream media, as well as by the perperators themselves. Muslims feel they are actually the victims of terrorism. Many Muslim organizations have issued fatwa, or "religious edicts" against terrorism in general, and against specific organizations such as Al-Qaeda and ISIL. Many of them go unreported in mainstream media, though as we will note below, some outlets have reported them. In 2005, the Fiqh Council of North America issued a fatwa aginst terrorism, as reported by National Public Radio.[4] The representatives on the council inluded the Muslim Public Affairs Council and Muslim American Society. Islamic Supreme Council of Canada issued a fatwa on March 11, 2015 against ISIL or joining ISIL.[5] Sheikh Abdullah Bin Bayyah of Mauritania and a lecturer at Aziz University in Jeddah, Saudi Arabia, a prominent and widely respected scholar, also issued a fatwa against ISIS in September 2014.[6]

Jihad as Defined in the Qur'an

As we have noted, jihad means "to strive" or "to struggle." The struggle must be in the path of God (struggling to get a date for prom, for example, would not be considered jihad). There are two basic forms of jihad: the nonmilitary form and the military form (*qital* in the Qur'an). The military struggle is in self-defense and not an act of aggression. The "greater jihad" refers to personal struggles with one's self. The "lesser jihad" refers to group struggle and includes armed conflicts. Jihad and its derivatives are mentioned by name six times in the Qur'an. The word *qital*, the military form of jihad, appears eight times. Jihad is often wrongly translated as "holy war."

THE NONMILITARY FORM OF JIHAD

Nonmilitary is the more common form of jihad referenced in the Qur'an. Ironically, it is the less emphasized form of jihad by both Muslims and non-Muslims. This form includes personal struggles to find the right path (an internal struggle within one's self and against desires), as well as a group struggle. This may be in the form of standing up for justice and against tyranny, oppression, and evil. Jihad can be accomplished by the tongue and by pen (speaking up and writing against injustice, for example). The struggles must be in the path of God, not just for political or personal reasons. In this regard, striving against intoxicants and indecent acts like pornography and prostitution would be considered jihad. Striving to "enjoin what is good and forbidding evil" is also a form of jihad.

> *The believers are those who believe in God and His Messenger, who do not change their belief into doubt and who **strive hard** for the cause of God with their property and persons. They are the truthful ones.* 49:15 (Sarwar)
>
> *Have faith in God and His messenger and **strive hard** for His cause with your wealth and in persons. This is better for you if only you knew it.* 61:11 (Sarwar)

The emboldened words are the translations of jihad or its derivative—translated as "striving."

The greater jihad is the personal struggle against evil. This is warfare, but within the individual and not on the battlefield. The struggling, once again, is in the path of God. The personal struggles against desires and temptations are forms of greater jihad.

Verse 25:52 instructs believers to make jihad with the Qur'an. The words used for the phrase in bold below are **jihad al-kabira**. This "mighty striving with it" instructs believers to use the Qur'an, its wisdom, blessings, and teachings when doing jihad; this refers to the nonmilitary form.

> *And strive against them a **mighty striving** with it [the Qur'an].* (Translated by Shakir)
>
> *Hence, do not defer to those who deny the truth, but strive hard against them, by means of this (divine writ), with **utmost striving**.* (Translated by Asad)

QITAL (MILITARY FORM OF JIHAD/LESSER JIHAD)
The Qur'an permits armed resistance in self-defense, when believers are under attack and when the way of God is in jeopardy. These verses spell out various situations and reasons for such struggle:

And fight in God's cause against those who wage war against you, **but do not commit aggression—for, verily, God does not love aggressors.** 2:190 (Asad)

Permission (to fight) is given to those upon whom war is made because they are oppressed, and most surely God is well able to assist them. 22:39 (Shakir)

Therefore let those fight in the **way of God,** *who sell this world's life for the hereafter; and whoever fights in the way of God, then be he slain or be he victorious, We shall grant him a mighty reward. And what reason do you have not to fight in the cause of God,* **to rescue the helpless oppressed old men, women, and children who are crying:** *'Our Lord! Deliver us from this town whose people are oppressors; send us a protector by Your grace and send us a helper from Your presence?' Those who are believers fight in the cause of God, and those who are unbelievers fight in the cause of Taghut [evil]: so fight against the helpers of Taghut; surely, Satan's crafty schemes are very weak.* 4:74–76 (Shakir)

When faced with defiance, the Qur'an instructs believers to defend with utmost resistance. Some who criticize the Qur'an for "preaching violence" often cite this verse, but an examination of the context will shed light on its perspective:

And kill them wherever you find them, and drive them out from where they drove you out, and persecution is severer than slaughter, and do not fight with them at the Sacred Mosque until they fight with you in it, but if they do fight you, then slay them; such is the recompense of the unbelievers. 2:191 (Shakir)

Verse 2:191 is put in context by the previous verse (2:190 quoted above): "And fight in God's cause against those who wage war against you." This refers to the pagans of Mecca, who persecuted early Muslim converts, tortured them, drove them out of Mecca, and continued to wage war when they settled in Medina. Their purpose was to wipe out this early, small community of believers. It was critical to use force to defend that budding community.

And even so, the Qur'an commanded not to start the aggression (verse 2:190) highlighted by the emphasis—*do not commit aggression,* and *verily, God does not love aggressors.* Moreover, if the enemy initiated the hostilities, the instructions were to stop fighting when they do and to deal with them with fairness and kindness.

> *But if they cease (their hostilities), Allah is oft-forgiving, Most Merciful. And fight them on until there is no more tumult or oppression, and there prevail justice and faith in Allah; but if they cease, let there be no hostility except to those who practice oppression.* 2:192–193

NO COMPULSION

War *cannot* be used to propagate Islam. The following verse is true for the armed struggle, as well as in the matters of everyday observance of the faith. Coming close to God must be at one's own free will:

> *There is no compulsion in religion.* 2:256 (Shakir)

There are other places where invitation to God's way is encouraged but without force, as is implied in the following verses. The second verse quoted below is from a short chapter in reference to the idolaters, essentially saying, "you go your way. I will go mine."

> *And say: The truth is from your Lord, so let him who please believe, and let him who please disbelieve.* 18:29
> *To you your way (religion). To me my way (religion.)* 109-6

WHEN YOU DO FIGHT, DO SO JUSTLY: CODE OF CONDUCT

Military jihad is allowed in self-defense and to help the oppressed in the cause of God, but even then, the code of conduct as ordained by God must be followed. It must not be done out of simple hatred for people or personal reasons.

O you who believe! Be upright for Allah, bearers of witness with justice, and let not hatred of a people (toward you) incite you not to act equitably; Act equitably, that is nearer to piety, and be careful of (your duty to) Allah; surely Allah is Aware of what you do. 5:8 (Shakir)

Ali, son-in-law of Muhammad and his trusted commander, was once involved in a one-on-one combat during a battle between the Muslims of Medina and the pagans of Mecca. The enemy fell and lay helplessly, and as Ali was about to kill him, he spat on Ali's face out of desperation and hatred. Ali instantly stood up and started to walk away. Startled, the enemy asked Ali why he spared his life, Ali responded by saying that the battle was in the cause of God, and the spitting had made him angry; he didn't want to kill him for a personal insult.

Verse 4:90 indicates military jihad is not allowed against noncombatants. This is in conformity with verse 2:190, prohibiting aggression. Islam forbids the destruction of trees, crops, and livestock during military struggles.

Fight to Protect Mosques, Churches, and Synagogues

In the following verses, the Qur'an explains why fighting in the cause of God is allowed. If it weren't for the armed struggle, the unbelieving forces would have demolished places of worship and the name of God and His message. In fact, places of worship like mosques, churches, and synagogues must be protected, as they are places for remembrance of God. Military jihad is allowed to *protect* mosques, churches, and synagogues against those who were bent on destroying them. It seems the terror groups destroying churches, mosques and synagogues in many predominantly Muslim countries never got this memo.

Permission to fight back is hereby granted to the believers against whom war is waged and because they are oppressed. Certainly Allah has power to grant them victory—those who have been unjustly expelled from their homes only because they said, "Our Lord is Allah." Had Allah not repelled some people by the might of others, the monasteries, churches, synagogues, and mosques in which Allah's praise is daily celebrated, would have been utterly demolished. Allah will certainly help those who help His cause; most surely Allah is Mighty, Powerful. These are the people who, if We establish them in the land, will establish Salah and pay Zakah, enjoin justice and forbid evil; the final decision of all affairs is in the hands of Allah. 22:39–41 (Malik)

Here is a compendium of armed struggle (*Qital*/Lesser Jihad):

- Purpose. Defend life and the way of God (2:190–193) and defend human rights for the oppressed and to protect the freedom to worship (22:39–41).
- One cannot be the aggressor. It is in self-defense, when war is waged upon you (2:190, 22:39).
- One must follow a code of conduct. If the enemy stops fighting you, you should cease hostilities (2:192–193). One must not harm noncombatants (4:90).

PROTECT LIFE

The Qur'an honors life, and killing is seen as a grave offense against humanity. Even though the following verse is in reference to the commands for the Israelites, in the Qur'anic style of drawing lessons by narrating the past stories and commandments, the command is equally applicable to the primary audience in the Qur'an—Muslims.

Because of this did We ordain unto the children of Israel that if anyone slays a human being-unless it be [in punishment] for murder or for spreading corruption on earth-it shall be as though he had slain all mankind; whereas, if anyone saves a life, it shall be as though he had saved the lives of all mankind. 5:32

WHAT ABOUT VERSE 9:5?

Another verse that has been flashed on TV screens in the past to point out how the Qur'an is "preaching violence" is quoted here:

So when the sacred months have passed away, then slay the idolaters wherever you find them, and take them captives and besiege them and lie in wait for them in every ambush, then if they repent and keep up prayer and pay the poor-rate, leave their way free to them; surely Allah is Forgiving, Merciful. 9:5 (Shakir)

This is another example where reading one verse out of context can be very misleading. The context of the verse is examined here by a review of the start of chapter 9 of the Qur'an.

Verse 9:1 announces the treaty between the pagans of Mecca and the Muslims of Medina under Muhammad, known as the Treaty of Hudaibiyya. It guaranteed peace for ten years between the two parties, unless one group broke the treaty by violating its clauses. The pagans of Mecca continued to harass and ambush some Muslim groups, eventually leading to the Muslims marching back into Mecca in a bloodless takeover of the city, where Muhammad gave a general amnesty.

(This is a declaration of) immunity by Allah and His Messenger toward those of the idolaters with whom you made an agreement. 9:1 (Shakir)

Verse 9:4 then goes on to instruct that the pagans who still followed the treaty should be left alone:

Except those of the pagans with whom you made an agreement, then they have not failed you in anything and have not backed up anyone against you, so fulfill their agreement to the end of their term; surely Allah loves those who are careful (of their duty). 9:4 (Shakir)

This was then followed by verse 9:5, which instructs believers to kill that particular brand of pagans who kept breaking the treaty and continued their hostilities and attacking ordinary Muslims. However, believers were not to fight the pagans who kept the treaty; the next verse instructs the believers to show mercy and give asylum to the pagan enemies seeking refuge:

If one amongst the pagans ask you for asylum, grant it to him, so that he may hear the word of Allah; and then escort him to where he can be secure. That is because they are men without knowledge. 9:6

Reviewing verse 9.5 with proper context seems to be a far cry from a picture painted by some critics, whereby Muslims are seen as following the teachings of the Qur'an and "bent on just killing all infidels," when verse 9:5 is discussed in isolation.

Jihad Ordained for the Pre-Muhammad Prophets

The military form of jihad (*qital*), according to the Qur'an, was not limited to Muhammad's time. The Qur'an refers to the battles of other biblical prophets as jihad against the unbelievers, whom are also referred to as *kafir*, the same term used for the nonbelievers fighting against Muhammad.

How many of the prophets fought (in Allah's way), and with them (fought) large bands of devoted men? But they never lost heart if they met with disaster in Allah's way, nor did they weaken (in will) nor give in. And Allah loves those who are firm and steadfast. 3:146

When Saul and David fought against the unbelievers in Goliath's army, the Qur'an states:

When they advanced to meet Goliath and his forces, they [the army of Saul and David] prayed: "Our Lord! Pour out constancy on us and make our steps firm: Help us against the unbelieving people." 2:250 (Shakir).

*So they put them to flight by Allah's permission. And David **slew** Goliath, and Allah gave him kingdom and wisdom, and taught him of what He pleased. 2:251*

The word emboldened above is a derivative of *qital*, the word for the military form of jihad used in the Qur'an.

There is a purpose to such struggles between good and evil as shown here:

And were it not for Allah's repelling some men with others, the earth would certainly be in a state of disorder; but Allah is Gracious to the creatures. 2:251 (Shakir)

Jihad/Qital—Armed Struggle for the Sake of God in the Torah

Just like some Muslim groups have used religion to commit horrific acts of violence, Christian and Jewish groups have also been engaged in terror attacks, though many of them are not categorized that way by mainstream media. Whether intentional or unintentional, this seems to result from, and perhaps fuels the popular perception, that an act of terrorism cannot be considered terrorism unless a Muslim commits it, otherwise it is just "violence." As we will see in the following section, these acts are also far from the teachings of the scriptures. Earlier in this chapter I mentioned the reports citing that right-wing terror groups are a bigger threat to America. A *Newsweek* article by Kurt Eichenwald titled "Right Wing Extremists Groups are a Bigger Threat to America than ISIS," states that "'Law enforcement agencies in the United States consider anti-government violent extremists, not radicalized Muslims, to be the most severe threat of political violence that they face,' the Triangle Center on Terrorism and Homeland Security reported this past June, based on surveys of 382 law enforcement groups."[7]

These are a few of those organizations considered "anti-government violent extremists": Though not labeled as terrorist group, the Southern Poverty Law Center views the Westboro Baptist Churh as an extreme right wing hate group; The Army of God being the group responsible for the well-known abortion clinic bombings; The Ku Klux Klan (KKK) is widely known as an anti-Semetic, anti-Catholic, racist terror organization; The Lord's Resistance Army (LRA) does not get the same attention as Boko Haram, but Human Rights Watch has reported thousands of brutal murders and rapes committed by them in Uganda, Congo, and Sudan. Warren Blumenfeld, a Huffington Post blogger, makes the point that Hitler was a Christian terrorist, quoting Hitler's *Mein Kampf:* 'Today I believe that I am acting in accordance with the will of the Almighty Creator: by defending myself against the Jew, I am fighting for the work of the Lord.'"[8]

RULES OF WAR FOR MOSES AND THE CHILDREN OF ISRAEL
Deuteronomy chapter 20 goes on to describe the regulations concerning
war for the Israelites. It starts by word of encouragement to the Israelites,
so they are not intimidated by the large size of the enemy army:

> *When you go out to fight your enemies and you face horses and
> chariots and an army greater than your own, do not be afraid. The
> Lord your God, who brought you out of the land of Egypt, is with you!*
> Deuteronomy 20:1

The Israelites were instructed to offer peace first:

> *As you approach a town to attack it, you must first offer its people
> terms for peace. If they accept your terms and open the gates to you,
> then all the people inside will serve you in forced labor. But if they
> refuse to make peace and prepare to fight, you must attack the town.
> When the Lord your God hands the town over to you, use your swords
> to kill every man in the town. But you may keep for yourselves all
> the women, children, livestock, and other plunder. You may enjoy the
> plunder from your enemies that the Lord your God has given you.*
> Deuteronomy 20:10–14

For the rest of the towns, the destruction was to be total, not sparing
anyone, even livestock. The purpose of such destruction, it goes on to
explain, was to prevent future generations from imitating (replicating)
the perversions of the destroyed nations.

> *But these instructions apply only to distant towns, not to the towns
> of the nations in the land you will enter. In those towns that the
> Lord your God is giving you as a special possession, destroy every
> living thing. You must completely destroy the Hittites, Amorites,
> Canaanites, Perizzites, Hivites, and Jebusites; just as the Lord your
> God has commanded you. This will prevent the people of the land
> from teaching you to imitate their detestable customs in the worship of
> their gods, which would cause you to sin deeply against the Lord your
> God.* Deuteronomy 20:15–18

After Moses passed away, the children of Israel were led by Joshua and eventually entered the Promised Land (Canaan) and took Jericho. The battle and its regulations, similar to the ones mentioned above, are described in detail in Joshua chapter 6.

Discussion Points for Dialogue and Healing

- Jihad means "to strive" or "to struggle." The struggle must be in the path of God.
- Though often translated as such, jihad is not equal to "holy war." Jihad does not mean, "kill all the infidels." Jihad does not necessarily mean "armed struggle" and jihad certainly does not equate acts of terrorism.
- In fact Muslims frown upon the word *jihadist,* used often to describe the acts of terrorism committed by some Muslim groups, as this is seen as misguiding, derogatory, and simply inaccurate. A very large majority of Muslims not only condemns the terrorist attacks, they are more often the victims of the terrorist attacks.
- There are two forms of jihad; the nonmilitary as well as the military form. The military struggle is in self-defense and not an act of aggression. The Qur'an warns Muslims not to commit acts of aggression. Thus, using the word jihad to only mean the military form is erroneous. In fact, the "greater jihad" refers to personal struggles with desires, temptations, and striving for social justice. The "lesser jihad" refers to group struggle against oppression and tyranny and military form.
- The Qur'an enforces a strict code of conduct and behavior during armed struggles.
- The military form of jihad is not unique to Muslims or Muhammad. The Qur'an used a derivative of *qital* (military jihad) to describe David's war against Goliath. The Bible describes many battles between the Israelites and nonbelievers in search of the Promised Land.
- Feel free to ponder on the points noted below and add your own.

Time to Ponder

- The Qur'an and the Bible consider killing a grave sin. However, the scriptures do allow it during military struggles and, in fact, make it mandatory as long as certain conditions are met. What are the defining criteria separating a grave sin from an obligation? Is there only a fine line between the two, subject to an individual's interpretation?

- Muslim terrorist groups may call their actions jihad but a very large majority of Muslim scholars and organizations have consistently condemned the terrorist attacks as un-Islamic, and claim that the extremists have hijacked their religion. Why does the media still insist on calling the terrorists jihadists?

- There are reports clearly showing that Muslim terrorist groups have killed Muslims many times more than non-Muslims or Westerners. Moreover there are thousands of Muslims reported being killed, raped or misplaced by other groups such as by Buddhists in Myanmar. Why then, are Muslims solely labeled as the perpetrators rather than the victims? Why are these attacks perceived as a war between Islam and the west?

- When violence is committed by non-Muslims, such as in theaters, schools and work places, they are often reported as "gunmen opened fire, killing…," whereas if the attackers are identified as Muslims, the incident is often labeled as a "terrorist attack." Do we now define *terrorism* as "violent attacks committed by Muslims" only? Can we talk about Islam without mentioning terrorism and vice versa? If not, how did we come to this narrative? How do we overcome the stereotyping?

- Why do the "Islamic" terror groups such as Al-Qaeda and ISIS happen to arise from the lands we have had military interventions? If these groups are waging "Islamic war" against the west, why have other western countries such as Canada and Switzerland, not been the focus of their war?

CHAPTER 16
Women

*Being a woman is a terribly difficult task, since it
consists principally in dealing with men.*
Joseph Conrad

The Abrahamic scriptures' views on women in society and gender equality have long been a focus of attention and many debates. The Old and New Testament have been criticized for rendering women as second-class citizens. In my presentations, women's issues as they are presented in the Qur'an, are usually among the most commonly asked questions. Muslim women, especially the ones wearing a hijab (a veil covering the head and chest), are viewed as oppressed. The issue of the women not being allowed to drive, or go out without their husband or other relatives in Saudi Arabia is brought up frequently. Whereas the latter is indeed true, we tend to forget that the Saudi example is an exception and that women play an active role in most other Muslim majority countries around the world in the fields of education, business, banking, sports, politics, media, and film. Most people in the west may not realize that many Muslim countries have women's international sports teams such as the Pakistani cricket and hockey teams. In many countries, women play a significant role in politics. In fact according to the data compiled by the inter-parliamentary union as of June 1, 2016, in terms of the percentage of women representatives in the lower house and parliaments, the United States of America was number 96 out of 193 countries listed. Many Muslim countries ranked higher such as Iraq, Afghanistan, Pakistan, United Arab Emirates, and Tunisia. Other western European countries did not fare as one might have guessed such as the United Kingdom (number 48) and France (number 60). Moreover it is also of note that Muslims have elected women as leaders of their country before America: Benazir Bhutto in Pakistan—twice; Indonesian President Megawati Sukarnoputri (elected 2001); former Turkish Prime Minister Tansu Ciller (served 1993-1995); former Senegalese President Mame Madior Boye (elected 2001); Bangladeshi prime ministers Begum Khaleda Zia (served 1991-96 and 2001-06) and Sheikh Hasina Wajed (elected 1996); former Iranian Vice President Masoumeh Ebtekar (served from 1997 to 2005); Malian President Cissé Mariam Kaïdama Sidibé (elected 2011); current president of Kosovo Atifete Jahjaga (elected 2011); and current president of Mauritius Bibi Ameenah Firdaus Gurib-Fakim (elected 2015).

There are numerous other examples of how Muslim women are far from being oppressed. Khadija, first wife of Muhammad, was a business-woman who hired Muhammad! All historical accounts are in agreement that their relationship was based on mutual love, respect, and trust. Muhammad's youngest wife Aisha has been reported widely in Islamic history to openly argue with Muhammad (in a respectful way), without him getting upset, once again showing that despite his elevated status, his relationship with his wives was based on mutual love and respect rather than on a superior-inferior axis. Another example of the beautiful relationship between husband and wife is the Taj Mahal in India—a symbol of love, and a product of Mughal emperor Shah Jahan's effort to honor the memory of his wife, Mumtaz Mahal.

It is indeed true that women are not given due rights in some Muslim majority countries. Many reports of overt abuse and violence have been reported such as honor killing. However, upon closer review, it becomes clear that these practices represent more socio-cultural aspects rather than religious practices. As is true in other non-Muslim regional countries such as India, where despite the secular laws to abolish the practice, women are still sometimes burned to death following the death of their husbands (a practice called *satti*). Female genital mutilation has also been discussed on television shows as an Islamic practice in some African and Asian countries, despite clear data showing it is not an Islamic practice. According to an article published in the *Review in Obstetrics and*

Gynecology, female genital mutilation is an ancient Egyptian practice pre-dating Abrahamic religions, and not confined to any particular religion or culture.[1] Moreover, it is equally, or more, prevalent in Christian majority sub-Saharan countries than in Muslim majority countries. Unfortunately the issue of women's rights remains thorny even in the United States and other western countries, including issues of domestic violence (specifically directed towards women), unequal pay, and discrimination at work.

Before we delve into the teachings of the scriptures related to women, we should ask ourselves the question: how do we define gender equality? It may have a different meaning for different people, ranging from the right to vote, equal pay and promotion at work, and personal choices. For many, it means all of the above. It becomes clear that many of these issues are of modern times, and before we "judge" the scriptures, we must keep in mind that they were revealed in the ancient androcentric cultures. The male-dominant cultures were not confined to the Middle East at the time of the revelations of the Torah, Gospels, and the Quran, as revealed by a quick glance into other dominant communities of the time, such as the Babylonians, Greco-Roman Empire, and the Persian Empire. If we look at the scriptures through a twenty-first-century lens, we may not be able to truly appreciate the passages. Having said that, the scriptures do provide many basic guidelines that can be used to protect and establish women's rights.

The Qur'an puts great emphasis on forming a society that is based on sound moral values and justice, and it provides guidelines for doing so. It views individuals as building blocks, the family as a small unit of individuals, and the society as a multitude of many such units. Individuals are given their own set of *rights,* as well as *responsibilities* within the family and the society. The Qur'an delineates laws related to financial undertakings, property, inheritance, and a system of justice. In short, the Qur'an describes a way of life set forth by God. It is worth pointing out that though some of these laws or guidelines are described in detail, the Qur'an is not meant to be an instruction manual. It provides broad guidelines, and the *sunnah* (Muhammad's actions) describes them in more detail. However, that can be complex and is a source of diverging opinions. There are many schools of thought or jurisprudence that interpret the same rules somewhat differently, at least on certain issues. Shi'a Muslim theologians add Muhammad's family and Imams for interpretation of the guidelines set forth in the Qur'an. Other Muslim scholars, though not representing the majority view, believe that the Qur'an itself is detailed enough that no additional help (neither the sunnah of Muhammad nor his noble family) are needed for interpretation or further guidance, though they are to be respected. These varying opinions notwithstanding, there is clear unanimity among all Muslims that man has no right to change the divine laws; that the Qur'an is the basic source of all such rules and guidance; and that the verdict of the Qur'an being the literal word of God is final.

In much the same way, the Torah ordains its own set of laws. The word "Torah" itself is variously translated as "instructions," "teach," or simply, "law."

This chapter will focus on the rights and responsibilities of individuals within a family—husband, wife, parents, and children—with special emphasis on women, since this issue is often a source of intense debate.

The Qur'an and Women

Women are considered a crucial part of the family. Their roles as daughter, wife, and mother form the building blocks, and their role as mother is considered one of great significance and respect. Chapter 4 of the Qur'an is named *Al-Nisa,* meaning "The Women." However, the subject is not limited to this chapter only.

SPIRITUAL EQUALITY

It is worth reviewing the status of women, as it existed in pre-Islamic days, in Arabia as well as in India, China, Rome, and Greece. Women had few if any legal rights and were considered spiritually inferior. In Arabia, newborn girls brought shame to a family; they were often buried or abandoned. It is also reported that women were forced to strip naked and dance in public for the pleasure of onlooking men. It was considered a coup when the Qur'an protected the honor of women and gave equal rights to men and women. Men are not superior to women, and women are not superior to men. What separates them in the eyes of God from each other is the level of their piety, not their gender.

Whoever works righteousness, man or woman, and has Faith, verily, to him will We give a new Life, a life that is good and pure and We will bestow on such their reward according to the best of their actions. 16:97

For Muslim men and women—for believing men and women; for devout men and women; for truthful men and women; for men and women who are patient and constant; for men and women who humble themselves; for men and women who give in Charity; for men and women who fast; for men and women who guard their chastity; and for men and women who engage much in Allah's praise, for them has Allah prepared forgiveness and great reward. 33:35

This spiritual equality was an alien concept in the seventh century, until the Qur'an declared men and women equal in God's sight. The above verse clearly indicates that men are not inherently superior to women in their spirituality. The Qur'an goes on to state that God will not waste the work of anyone regardless of his or her gender, for He is an equal opportunity Lord.

So their Lord accepted their prayer: That I will not waste the work of a worker among you, whether male or female. 3:195 (Shakir)

THE QUR'AN AND MARRIAGE

The relationship between a husband and wife is established on a foundation of mutual respect, kindness, and love:

And one of His signs is that He created mates for you from yourselves that you may find rest [tranquility] in them, and He put between you love and compassion; most surely there are signs in this for a people who reflect. 30:21 (Shakir)

Moreover, the husband and wife are "cloth" or garments for each other. This is not interpreted in terms of its physical aspects but rather implies they cover and support each other during hard times and protect each other's faith.

Permitted to you, on the night of the fasts, is the approach to your wives. They are your garments and you are their garments. 2:187

NO MARRIAGE AGAINST A WOMAN'S WILL: EQUAL STATUS FOR HUSBAND AND WIFE

In pagan, pre-Islamic Arabia, widows were often divided amongst the heirs of a deceased as goods. The heir either married the widow himself against her will, or gave her to marry someone else and kept her dowry, or demanded a payment as settlement to give her away. In addition, the wives were at times imprisoned in their homes in order that they may ask for separation and thus relinquish their dowry or inheritance. The following verse abolished these practices:

O you who believe! You are forbidden to inherit women against their will. Nor should you treat them with harshness, that you may take away part of the dowry you have given them, except where they have been guilty of open lewdness. On the contrary live with them on a footing of kindness and equity. 4:19

POLYGAMY

The Qur'an allows multiple marriages for men (up to four) *with* certain conditions. However, it clearly made polygamy much less desirable than monogamy:

*And if you fear that you cannot act equitably toward orphans, then marry such women as seem good to you, two and three and four; but if you fear that you will not do justice (between them), then (marry) only one or what your right hands possess; **this is more proper**, that you may not deviate from the right course. 4:3 (Shakir)*

It must be pointed out that polygamy was practiced before the revelation of the Qur'an but was uncontrolled and without regulations. The Qur'an does not encourage or promote polygamy and, on the contrary, attempts to limit polygamy (to having four wives) and attaches conditions to it. The above verse and the idea of having multiple wives has been misunderstood and misused by non-Muslims and, perhaps more so, by Muslims. In some parts of the Muslim world, men are reported to have married women with the clear intention of divorcing them after a very short period (at times, after a day or two). This is done for obvious reasons of satisfying sexual desires and in clear violation of the concept and purpose of marriage: achieving a harmonious relationship built on love and companionship to fulfill both physical and spiritual needs.

The Qur'an acknowledges later in surah 4 that it is very difficult for men to be fair and do justice with multiple wives, thus again implying it is much preferred to marry one woman:

> *It is not possible for you to do justice between your wives even if you wish to do so; therefore, in order to comply with Divine Law, do not lean toward one wife to the extent that you leave the other hanging in air. If you work out a friendly understanding and fear Allah, Allah is Forgiving, Merciful.* 4:129 (Malik)

Many Muslim scholars believe that polygamy was allowed for a specific time and for a specific reason. They point out that the allowance in verse 4:3 was related to the mothers of orphans *only*, to provide them psychological, social, and economical support (see Yuksel's commentary on the verse). The other intended purpose was to prevent indecent, illicit sexual activities. In any event, marrying other women without the free will and consent of the first wife is not allowed; and one can draw the conclusion that this in itself should put a stop to polygamy in most cases. Some Muslim scholars do maintain that permission from the first wife is not *required*, though highly recommended. However, if one analyzes the verse 4:3 (*if you fear that you will not do justice between them*), marrying without the free consent of the first wife essentially makes marrying multiple wives nearly impossible.

POLYGAMY ACCORDING TO ISLAMIC PRINCIPLES IN THE UNITED STATES
It must be noted that polygamy is illegal in the Unites States as well as many other countries. Many Muslim scholars point out that putting U.S. law and the Qur'anic commandments together makes it illegal *and* against

the teachings of the Qur'an to have multiple wives. They argue that such practice, in addition to being a violation of the law of the land, would mean that the second wife will not have the same rights (for example, inheritance, property ownership, and health insurance) as the first wife under local laws, and thus one would be dealing with her unjustly, thereby *also* violating the teachings of the Qur'an.

WOMEN'S RIGHT FOR DIVORCE OR SEPARATION: COMPROMISE IS BETTER

Divorce, considered distasteful, is nonetheless allowed by the Qur'an, but only after all attempts at reconciliation fail. Even in this setting, God orders men to not take advantage of women.

> *If a wife fears cruelty or desertion on her husband's part, there is no blame on them if they arrange an amicable settlement [reconciliation] between themselves; and such settlement [reconciliation] is best; And peoples' souls are swayed by greed.* 4:128
>
> *O Prophet! When you divorce women, divorce them for their pre-scribed time, and calculate the number of the days prescribed, and be careful of (your duty to) Allah, your Lord. Do not drive them out of their houses, nor should they themselves go forth, unless they commit an open indecency.* 65:1 (Shakir)

This is the opening of the chapter called *Al-Talaq*, or "Divorce." This verse addresses Muhammad in the beginning, as is the norm on many occasions, but the message is clearly intended for the community. It refers to a period of time called 'iddat, which is a waiting period before a woman should remarry. In case of a divorce, it is three months. This allows for a cooling-off period among other reasons. It also protects women from being evicted from their house, as was often the custom at the time. It then goes on to instruct men to treat their wives (or ex-wives) kindly. The following verse gives two options at the end of this period. In either scenario, men are ordered to treat women with kindness:

*Then, when they have reached their term, **take them back in kindness or part from them in kindness.** 65:2 (Shakir)*

And the Qur'an sends a warning to those men who keep women as their wives as an excuse so they can abuse them:

When you divorce women, and they fulfill their prescribed term, either take them back on equitable terms or part ways on equitable terms; but do not take them back to injure them, (or) to take undue advantage; if anyone does that; He wrongs his own soul. Do not treat Allah's signs [meaning verses] as a jest [mockery]. 2:231

IS WIFE BEATING ALLOWED BY THE QUR'AN?

By examining the verses at the beginning of this chapter, it would seem hard to imagine that the Qur'an would sanction wife beating, though that's what some critics claim. And many Muslim scholars have translated the following verse as such:

*Men are the maintainers of women because Allah has made some of them to excel others and because they spend out of their property; the good women are therefore obedient, guarding the unseen as Allah has guarded; and (as to) those on whose part you fear desertion, admonish them, and leave them alone in the sleeping-places and **beat them**; then if they obey you, do not seek a way against them; surely Allah is High, Great. 4:34 (Shakir)*

The first part about "Men are the maintainers of women" has been variously translated as "Men shall take full care of women" (Asad), "Men are the protectors and maintainers of women" (Yousuf Ali), and "Men are to support women" (Yuksel). All translators agree it does not make men "superior" to women but actually refers to men's *responsibility* to earn and bring sustenance on account of his physical attributes. Moreover, Laleh Bakhtiar, the only woman translator of the Qur'an (*The Sublime Qur'an*), and someone who has made verse 4:34 a focal point of her translation, points out that the verse talks about "some of them" to excel others because of their status as breadwinners. It does not imply that a woman cannot work. If they did, this distinction would vanish. Therefore, even this "status" is not for *all* men over *all* women in *all* affairs as a blanket statement, and therefore for the men who work, this "higher status" is meant to be just that (i.e., they have a financial responsibility and does not extend to other affairs).

The words "beat them" in the verse are the source of controversy. Because of the mistranslation over centuries, perhaps based on cultural practices, the classical and even most modern commentators have gone on the defensive and scrambled to find an explanation. Some have translated the word as "beat lightly" and commented that men should "beat lightly as with a toothbrush" or with a handkerchief. The defensive posture seems to be for naught, as the Qur'an never allowed a man to beat his wife, under *any* circumstances.

In addition to Laleh Bakhtiar, the most appropriate translation and commentary seem to be from Yuksel and Emerick. Laleh Bakhtiar takes the position that the Quran explains itself, and that the formal equivalence alone would translate this verse accurately. As we may recall from the introduction, there are two forms of translations: the formal equivalence, meaning a translation as close to the literal meaning as the original, and dynamic equivalence, where the essential thought or idea of the original language is captured. She comments that the verb *daraba* appears fifty-eight times in the Qur'an. In numerous other situations it means something other than "to strike," such as in verses 2:73 and 43:5 it means "to turn something about," in 13:17 it means "to compare," just to name a few. Bakhtiar goes on to draw attention to the fact that Muhammad was the "living Qur'an" and he never even came close to hitting his wife. Similarly, in Yuksel's commentary of the verse 4:34, especially for the underlined words "beat them," he states: "The second key word that is commonly misunderstood is *idribuhunna*. In almost all translations, you will see it translated as 'scourge,' or 'beat.' The triliteral verb DaRaBa is a multiple-meaning word akin to the English 'strike' or 'get.' The Qur'an uses the same verb with various meanings such as to travel, to get out (3:156, 4:101, 38:44, 73:20, 2:273), to strike (2:60, 73; 7:160; 8:12, etc.), to beat (8:50), to beat or regret (47:27), to set up (43:58, 57:13), to give (14:24, 16:75), to take away, to ignore (43:5). He goes on to say, "It is again interesting that the scholars pick the meaning BEAT, among the many other alternatives, when the relationship between men and women is involved, a relationship that is defined by the Qur'an with mutual love and care (30:21)."

Therefore, in the most logical translation, and the one most consistent with the Qur'an's overall message, the last part of verse 4:34 is translated as follows (Yuksel and Emerick):

*As for those women from whom you fear disloyalty, then you shall advise them, abandon them in bedchamber, and **separate (from) them**.*

In summary, the appropriate translation for this homonymous Arabic word, *daraba* seems to indicate that men should "separate" from their spouse, or get out of the relationship if other advice doesn't work out, but not beat them. This verse remains poorly understood and continues to generate debate with varying points of view, even among Muslims.

HIJAB/MODESTY

Yet another topic that has generated tremendous interest in recent times is the issue of Muslims wearing a hijab, or head covering. Hijab is widely viewed as a dress code for Muslim women. This viewpoint can be considered only partially accurate in all three categories: it is not *just* a dress code, it is not meant for Muslims *only*, and is not meant for women *only*. It must be emphasized at the outset that the essence of *hijab* in the Qur'an is more than a dress code; it revolves around modesty and piety, without public showing of one's physical beauty. It is interesting to note that the word hijab or its derivative appears in the Qur'an seven times, but never in connection with the hijab as we know it now. It is used to describe the barrier between hell and heaven (7:46), as well as a command for the believers to talk to the wives of Muhammad behind a curtain (33:53)

The interpretation of the extent of the covering varies between various Muslim scholars and countries. For example, *niqab*, as practiced in Saudi Arabia, is where the whole body is completely covered (including the face, hands, and feet). The traditional jurists feel that the *niqab* applied to the wives of Muhamamd only, who were ordered to maintain the highest form of chastity. Yet another interpretation is to cover the head, but leaves the face, hands and feet exposed. In the following verse, the command is not only for the wives of Muhammad, but also for other Muslim women:

> *O Prophet! Tell your wives and daughters, and the believing women, that they should cast their outer garments over their persons (when abroad): that is most convenient, that they should be known (as such) and not molested. And Allah is Oft-Forgiving, Most Merciful.* 33:56

The word used for "outer garments" is *jilabib*, plural for *jilbab*, and not hijab. Imam Feisal Abdul Rauf points out that this was the practice at the time in Arabia to distinguish between the Bedouin and the wives of the prophet and the believing women so they would be respected, and does not necessarily require that they wear hijab. He furthermore makes a point that the intent of this command was to be "recognized" and avoid being troubled, therefore in the current atmosphere in the west where wearing hijab may actually pose more risks, it can be counterproductive and against the intent of this verse.

The Qur'an considers sexuality sacred and sets rules for its expression. Sexuality is limited to a marital relationship and has no place in public, nor is there ever a reason for a public display, which may lead to sensual feelings and eventually immorality, which the Qur'an (and the Bible) detests. In this sense, hijab seems to be a preemptive effort to guard against eventual immorality. Chapter 24 verses 30 and 31 of the Qur'an address this issue:

> *Tell the believing men to lower their gaze and to be mindful of their chastity: this will be most conducive to their purity—(and) verily, God is aware of all that they do.* 24:30 (Asad)

Note that men are addressed first—a fact often lost upon many Muslim men, eager to enforce hijab on the women—and are also to dress modestly and "guard their private parts." The verse is then followed by instructions for women:

And tell the believing women to lower their gaze and to be mindful of their chastity, and not to display their charms (in public) beyond what may (decently) be apparent thereof; hence, let them draw their head-coverings over their bosoms [chest]. And let them not display (more of) their charms to any but their husbands, or their fathers, or their husbands' fathers, or their sons, or their husbands' sons, or their brothers, or their brothers' sons, or their sisters' sons, or their womenfolk, or those whom they rightfully possess, or such male attendants as are beyond all sexual desire, or children that are as yet unaware of private aspects of women; And let them not swing their legs [in walking] (or strike their feet) so as to draw attention to their hidden charms [or ornaments]. And O you believers—all of you—turn unto God in repentance, so that you might attain to a happy state! 24:31 (Asad)

According to these verses, men and women have equal responsibility for maintaining modesty. The headcovering referred to in 24:31 is *khumur,* plural for *khimar,* which was a traditional head covering in Arabia at the time of Muhammad. This verse calls for extending the head covering to cover the chest area. In addition to the physical dress code, the two verses start by instructing the believers to lower their gaze, as part of the modest behavior. It would not make sense for someone to be wearing a full hijab, but making provocative body gestures or eye contact. *Lowering the gaze* has been referred to as *hijab of the eyes* in order to protect from indecency. This concept is actually not too dissimilar to Jesus's teachings.

You have heard the commandment that says, 'You must not commit adultery.' But I say, anyone who even looks at a woman with lust has already committed adultery with her in his heart. Matthew 5:27-28

Women and the Old and New Testament

Women and their place in the family are mentioned frequently in the Bible.[2] Many are mentioned by name, including prophets' wives: Eve, Hagar, Sarah, and Rebekah among others. Mary is highly revered. So are Sarah, Rebekah, and the wives of Jacob and Joseph.

HUSBAND-WIFE RELATIONSHIP AND THEIR ROLES

The following is an attempt to summarize the teachings of the Bible, realizing it is an extensive subject:

The husband-wife relationship is built on love and respect. Wives are to submit to the authority of the husband, and husbands are considered head of the household and the bread-earners. Modesty for wives is emphasized. One of the greatest sins is adultery. Women should make themselves presentable to their husbands. The holy union and nearness to God is invoked in this relationship.

The concept of marriage in the Torah is one of companionship. Women and men are considered two halves of one whole. After creating Adam, God created Eve and made them husband and wife:

> *Then the LORD God said, 'It is not good for the man to be alone; I will make him a helper suitable for him.' Genesis 2:18*

WIVES

Wives are to remain modest, chaste, and obedient to their husbands. Their outward beauty is minimized, and their inner beauty and spirituality is what makes them dearer to God.

> *In the same way, you wives, be submissive to your own husbands so that even if any of them are disobedient to the word, they may be won without a word by the behavior of their wives, as they observe your chaste and respectful behavior. Your adornment must not be merely external—braiding the hair, and wearing gold jewelry, or putting on dresses; but let it be the hidden person of the heart, with the imperishable quality of a gentle and quiet spirit, which is precious in the sight of God. For in this way in former times the holy women also, who hoped in God, used to adorn themselves, being submissive to their own husbands; just as Sarah obeyed Abraham, calling him lord, and you have become her children if you do what is right without being frightened by any fear. 1 Peter 3:1–6*
>
> *Wives, be subject to your own husbands, as to the Lord. For the husband is the head of the wife, as Christ also is the head of the church,*

He Himself being the Savior of the body. But as the church is subject to Christ, so also the wives ought to be to their husbands in everything. Ephesians 5:22–24

RESPONSIBILITY OF HUSBANDS

The husband is responsible for the provision of food, clothing, and sexual intimacy:

> *If a man who has married a slave wife takes another wife for himself, he must not neglect the rights of the first wife to food, clothing, and sexual intimacy. If he fails in any of these three obligations, she may leave as a free woman without making any payment.* Exodus 21:10–11 (NLT)

Compare these verses to the Qur'anic verses relating to multiple wives and how men should approach the idea of multiple wives (verses 4:3, 4:19, 4:129).

According to the Torah, the husband should also take time off for a year to spend time with his wife, highlighting the importance of time needed to develop a healthy relationship between husband and wife. In the fast-paced world today, this seems like a luxury, but the Torah is clear on the requirement:

> *A newly married man must not be drafted into the army or be given any other official responsibilities. He must be free to spend one year at home, bringing happiness to the wife he has married.* Deuteronomy 24:5 (NLT)

And defaming the wife by false accusations of unchastity (before marriage when she was a virgin) is taken very seriously:

> *The elders must then take the man and punish him. They must also fine him 100 pieces of silver, which he must pay to the woman's father because he publicly accused a virgin of Israel of shameful conduct. The woman will then remain the man's wife, and he may never divorce her.* Deuteronomy 22:18–19 (NLT)

Compare that with Qur'anic verse quoted earlier (verse 24:4) for punishment of men for false accusation.

The wife, though submitting to the "authority of the husband," is an equal partner in this relationship. Compare these verses to the Qur'anic verses 30:21 and 65:2 (calling for kindness even if separating):

> *In the same way, you husbands must give honor to your wives. Treat your wife with understanding as you live together. She may be weaker than you are, but she is your equal partner in God's gift of new life. Treat her as you should, so your prayers will not be hindered.* 1 Peter 3:7 (NLT)

POLYGAMY

Most churches and Jewish traditions disallow polygamy. However, polygamy is mentioned throughout the Old Testament, and many prophets are known to have had multiple wives, including the patriarchs: Abraham, Isaac, and Jacob. The first mention of polygamy in the Old Testament starts with Lamech, seven generations removed from Cain:

> *Lamech took to himself two wives: the name of the one was Adah, and the name of the other, Zillah.* Genesis 4:19

The first prohibition is found in Deuteronomy, even though this was meant for kings, and not a general commandment:

> *He [the king to be chosen] shall not multiply wives for himself, or else his heart will turn away; nor shall he greatly increase silver and gold for himself.* Deuteronomy 17:17

However, there are other verses that seem to make polygamy legal but with certain conditions:

> *If he takes to himself another woman, he may not reduce her food, her clothing, or her conjugal rights.* Exodus 21:10

Many scholars acknowledge that the New Testament did not specifically prohibit polygamy. However, when asked about it, Jesus responds in Matthew 19:5 and Mark 10:8, making references to God's creation of Adam and Eve as man and wife and uniting them as one. This and other passages are generally taken as indications that Jesus promoted monogamy. Perhaps the strongest argument quoted by many is Matthew 19:8–9:

> He [Jesus] said to them, 'Because of your hardness of heart Moses permitted you to divorce your wives; but from the beginning it has not been this way. And I say to you, whoever divorces his wife, except for immorality, and marries another woman commits adultery.'

DIVORCE

Like the Qur'an, divorce is allowed but considered distasteful in the Bible:

> "For I hate divorce," says the LORD, the God of Israel, "and him who covers his garment with wrong," says the LORD of hosts. "So take heed to your spirit, that you do not deal treacherously." Malachi 2:16

However, divorcing a wife seems relatively easier than the procedures outlined in the Qur'an.

> When a man takes a wife and marries her, and it happens that she finds no favor in his eyes because he has found some indecency in her, and he writes her a certificate of divorce and puts it in her hand and sends her out from his house. Deuteronomy 24:1

And in one of his sermons, Jesus gives instructions regarding divorce, clearly disliking it and making one think twice before divorcing:

> You have heard the law that says, "A man can divorce his wife by merely giving her a written notice of divorce." But I say that a man who divorces his wife, unless she has been unfaithful, causes her to commit adultery. And anyone who marries a divorced woman also commits adultery. Matthew 5:31–32 (NLT)

Veil/Hijab in the Old and New Testament

As noted earlier, hijab is typically viewed as an Islamic dress code for women. Both accounts seem erroneous. Hijab is *not* merely a dress code, and it is not just for women; it also may not be an Islamic-only dress code. Though never viewed as wearing a hijab, it can be argued that the Christian nuns essentially do wear hijab with their head covered, as well as almost the entire body. Moreover, the nuns are supposed to act in modest ways, once again showing that hijab is more than just a dress code. Some may feel it is cultural, but the pictures of Virgin Mary in the churches around the world almost always show her with a head cover. Some biblical passages on the teachings of Paul and practices of highly acclaimed biblical women are quoted below:

> *Isaac went out to meditate in the field toward evening; and he lifted up his eyes and looked, and behold, camels were coming. Rebekah lifted up her eyes, and when she saw Isaac she dismounted from the camel. She said to the servant, "Who is that man walking in the field to meet us?" And the servant said, "He is my master." Then she took her veil and covered herself.* Genesis 24:63–65

In the following set of verses, Paul addresses Timothy in one of his letters, giving him many instructions:

> *And I want women to be modest in their appearance. They should wear decent and appropriate clothing and not draw attention to themselves by the way they fix their hair or by wearing gold or pearls or expensive clothes. For women who claim to be devoted to God should make themselves attractive by the good things they do.* 1 Timothy 2:9–10 (NLT)

In 1 Corinthians, chapter 11, Paul gives instructions for women to cover their head, at least when worshipping. The head covering is specifically meant for women only.

For this reason, and because the angels are watching, a woman should wear a covering on her head to show she is under authority. 1 Corinthians 11:10

Judge for yourselves: is it proper for a woman to pray to God with her head uncovered? 1 Corinthians 11:13

Discussion Points for Dialogue and Healing

- Women were subjected to abuse in pre-Islamic Arabia. The Qur'an gave women many rights they didn't have before and protected them from abusive practices. Women and men have their own set of rights and responsibilities and equal status in the Qur'an. What separates them in God's sight is their level of piety.

- The husband-wife relationship is built on mutual love and respect, though the Bible gives the husband authority over the wife and the Qur'an puts the husband "a degree above" the wife, in an apparent reference to their physical stature and role as bread-earner.

- Polygamy: The Qur'an allows polygamy but only under certain conditions; it clearly favors monogamy. The Old Testament makes references to many prophets with multiple wives without objection. The reference against polygamy relates to the kings. Most churches and scholars interpret many verses as an indication of the New Testament's prohibition of polygamy. As mentioned in the main body of the chapter, compliance with the prohibition of polygamy by local laws is in line with the teachings of the Qur'an.

- Divorce is allowed in the Qur'an and the Bible but is considered distasteful; every effort should be made to reconcile. When divorcing, one must do so with fairness and kindness.

- Hijab is more than just a dress code and is considered a sign of chastity and modesty; it applies to men and women. The Bible narrates passages of noble women covering their heads or faces when in front of strangers. Paul has instructions for women to cover their heads, at least during worship.

- The extent to which hijab covers the body of a woman is variable in the Muslim world, often a reflection of the cultural norms rather than religious teachings.

- Feel free to ponder on the points noted below and add your own.

Time to Ponder

- Is the notion of men's superiority (spiritual or otherwise) over women in accordance with the teachings of the scriptures? If so, is that more akin to a higher level of responsibility rather than absolute authority?

- Women in predominantly Muslim countries serve in the police, air force, work as teachers and scientists, and have been elected for Parliament and even as heads of state. Why are women often considered "oppressed" by many in the west?

- How do we avoid "othering" those who are not like us in appearance and other qualities?

- When a Christian nun wears their equivalent of a hijab, it is viewed as a sign of devotion to their faith. When a Muslim woman wears hijab, it is seen as a sign of oppression or "backwardness." What leads to these misconceptions? How do we overcome the stereotyping?

- Have you ever seen a picture or portrait of Virgin Mary without wearing a hijab? Given the recent trends in some Eouropean countries, would that be subject to a ban?

CHAPTER 17
Personal Behavior and Code of Conduct

Humility is not thinking less of yourself, it's thinking of yourself less.
C.S. Lewis

Be kind whenever possible. It is always possible.
Dalai Lama

Hans Küng, a Swiss catholic priest and theologian, has been an advocate for interfaith dialogue, realizing the importance of religion in peacemaking with the following convictions as part of the Declaration Towards a Global Ethic:

No peace among the nations without **peace** among the religions.

No peace among the religions without **dialogue** between the religions.

No dialogue between the religions without investigation of the foundations of the religions.

No survival of our globe without a global ethic, supported by both religious and non-religious people.[1]

The Declaration Toward a Global Ethic adopted at the Council of Parliament of the World's Religions in Chicago in 1993 emphasized this interconnection between religion and peace, and further offered principles of the Global Ethic necessary to make it all possible. They included:

- Every human must be treated humanely
- The Golden Rule: Do unto others what you wish for yourself
- Commitment to a culture of non-violence and respect for life
- Culture of tolerance: Life of honesty/truthfulness
- Culture of equal rights and partnership between men and women

The principles of the Global Ethic are derived from the religious teachings of various faith traditions. In this chapter, I will draw attention to the teachings of the three Abrahamic Testaments that speak to the moral values and ethics of daily life. These teachings can serve as guiding principles for interfaith dialogue to bring about harmony and peace. This is laid out in the form of the "Dos" and the "Do Nots" here; it is not meant to be an exhaustive list. In what follows, I will draw attention to the teachings of the three Abrahamic Testaments as they relate to the principles of the Declaratoin of a Global Ethic.

The Qur'an gives instructions on how an individual can attain a high level of spiritual and moral standards. The spiritual health and moral values of individuals and families would thus determine the health of a society. Muslims insist that though the concept seems idealistic, the structure provides a sound basis for a functional and just society. The Qur'an commands individuals to maintain purity of body and mind, the objective to form an altruistic society, calls for honesty in thoughts and actions, and commands individuals to fulfill social obligations in the form of assisting other people (the sick, poor, needy, widows, orphans, etc.).

The "Dos"
ENJOIN WHAT'S GOOD ('AMR BI'L MAR'UF)
As mentioned under "Pillars of Islam," followers are strongly encouraged to enjoin and promote what's good. The Qur'an often urges us to to do good and refrain from evil:

> And from among you there should be a party who invites to good and enjoin what is right and forbid the wrong, and these it is that shall be successful. 3:104 (Shakir)

Those who follow the Messenger, the unlettered prophet, whom they find written down with them in the Torah and the Gospel (who) enjoins them good and forbids them evil. 7:157 (Shakir)

HONESTY AND TRUTHFULNESS

Truthfulness implies more than being true with one's words or tongue. It means consistency between the inside and outside; actions and intentions; and conformity of speech with belief:

O you who believe! Be careful of (your duty to) Allah and be among the truthful. 9:119 (Shakir)

The Qur'an praises prophets and other noble persons for their truthfulness:

And mention Abraham in the Book; surely he was a truthful man, a prophet. 19:41 (Shakir)
The Messiah, son of Mary was but a messenger; messengers before him have indeed passed away; and his mother was a truthful woman. 5:75 (Shakir)

Similar passages are found testifying to the truthfulness of Ishmael (19:54) and Joseph (12:46).

The Qur'an warns those who are not honest in their businesses by not measuring items correctly (83:1–3). They are referred to as "defrauders."

FORGIVENESS/ANGER MANAGEMENT

The Qur'an instructs individuals on many life skills, and prominent among them is taking charge of one's temperament. Managing anger goes hand in hand with self-control, kindness, and forgiveness. The Qur'an gives numerous examples of prophets who, despite their nations' rebellion and hatred toward them, always asked for their forgiveness. The Qur'an mentions forgiveness and controlling anger together in the same verses on many occasions:

Those who avoid the greater crimes and shameful deeds, and, when they are angry even then forgive. 42:37

Those who spend (freely), whether in prosperity, or in adversity; who restrain anger, and pardon (all) men—for Allah loves those who do good. 3:134

Those who forgive can also expect God's forgiveness for their shortcomings. The verse 3:134 quoted above is immediately followed by such a promise. One of the many attributes of God in the Qur'an is *Al-Ghafur*, or "the Most forgiving."

If you do good openly or do it in secret or pardon an evil then surely Allah is Pardoning, Powerful. 4:149 (Shakir)

The recompense for an injury is an injury equal thereto (in degree): but if a person forgives and makes reconciliation, his reward is due from Allah: for (Allah) loves not those who do unjust [the tyrants]. 42:40

But indeed if any show patience and forgive, that would truly be an exercise of courageous will and resolution in the conduct of affairs. 42:43

KINDNESS AND MERCY

Forgiveness is an important ingredient for controlling anger, but kindness is essential for forgiveness, and as in the case of forgiveness, the Qur'an declares that God will show mercy to those who show mercy to others. In its fundamental form, all humans possess some portion of the divine attributes, kindness and mercy being two of the most important. The Qur'an asks believers to show kindness in many ways: in speech, in their treatment of others, and in actions. These include "random acts" of kindness, as well as more organized forms like charitable giving:

And serve Allah and do not associate any thing with Him and be kind to the parents and to the near of kin and the orphans and the needy and the neighbor of (your) kin and the neighbor who are strangers, and the companion in a journey and the wayfarer and those whom your right hands possess; surely Allah does not love him who is proud, boastful. 4:36 (Shakir)

Muhammad was a symbol of mercy and kindness to everyone around him, friends and foes alike. The Qur'an refers to that as a gift from God:

Thus it is due to mercy from Allah that you (O Muhammad) deal with them gently, and had you been rough, hard hearted, they would certainly have dispersed from around you; forgive them therefore and ask pardon for them. 3:159 (Shakir)

Many sayings of Muhammad instruct the importance of kindness and mercy to all—humans and nonhumans.

Those who are kind and considerate to Allah's creatures, Allah bestows His kindness and affection on them. Show kindness to the creatures on the earth so that Allah may be kind to you.[2]

The Qur'an ordains kindness to parents (6:151); to spouses, even during the course of a divorce (2:229); and toward people of other religion and captives, who are not waging wars against you (60:8). There are numerous other narrations for other groups, including orphans and the needy.

HUMILITY, SIMPLICITY, AND MODESTY

The very essence of Islam, or submission, is to humbly submit to God. The prostration, performed many times during each daily prayer, is the ultimate symbol of humility shown to God.

The Qur'an also instructs followers to be humble toward each other, of course, in ways other than the way to submit to God. The Qur'an makes it very clear that God does not like arrogance. Satan, in fact, was labeled a disbeliever when he showed arrogance and refused to prostrate to Adam when ordered by God to do so. He reasoned that Adam was made up from the clay (2:34 and 15:30–35).

And do not turn your face away from people in contempt, nor go about in the land exulting overmuch; surely Allah does not love any self-conceited boaster. 31:18 (Shakir)

REPEL EVIL WITH WHAT'S GOOD

Nor can goodness and evil be equal. Repel (evil) with what is better. 41:34

The following verse instructs believers to respond in kindness, even to the taunts of the enemy, a lesson perhaps even more relevant in today's world.

And the servants of Most Gracious (Allah) are those who walk on the earth in humility, and when the ignorant [pagans of Mecca] address them, they say, "Peace!" [Salaam]. 25:63

And be moderate [humble] in your pace, and lower your voice. 31:19

PROTECT LIFE

Preserving and honoring life is a basic human imperative, according to the Qur'an. The Qur'an instructs that killing one person is akin to killing all of humanity. The description of the murder of Abel by his older brother Cain (sons of Adam) is followed by this verse:

Whoever kills a person, except as a punishment for murder or mischief in the land, it will be written in his book of deeds as if he had killed all the human beings, and whoever will save a life shall be regarded as if he gave life to all the human beings. 5:32 (Malik)

The "Do Nots"

FORBID WHAT'S EVIL (NAHY 'AN AL-MUNKAR)

The opposite of "enjoin what's good" is "forbidding what's evil." In the following section, the focus is primarily on avoiding bad deeds in the context of personal behavior, rather in reference to "major" or "minor" sins.

SLANDER

The Qur'an sends clear warning to those who engage in backbiting and slandering. It is distasteful in the eyes of God:

O you who believe! Avoid suspicion as much (as possible): for suspicion in some cases is a sin: And spy not, neither backbite one another. Would any of you like to eat the flesh of his dead brother? No you would hate it. But fear Allah: For Allah is Oft-Returning [Accepter of repentance], Most Merciful. 49:12

And falsely accusing chaste women is a grave sin:

Those who slander chaste women, indiscreet but believing, are cursed in this life and in the Hereafter: for them is a grievous Penalty. 24:23

DON'T BE STINGY OR WASTEFUL (BE MODERATE)

The Qur'an repeatedly gives instructions for charity. Whereas there is plenty of praise for charitable work, being stingy, on the other hand, is considered distasteful:

And let not those who hoard up that which God has bestowed upon them of His bounty, think that it is better for them. No, it is worse for them. 3:180

Extravagant spending is also discouraged:

And He it is Who produces gardens (of vine), trellised and untrellised, and palms and seed-produce of which the fruits are of various sorts, and olives and pomegranates, like and unlike; eat of its fruit when it bears fruit, and pay the due of it on the day of its reaping, and do not act extravagantly; surely He does not love the extravagant [wasteful]. 6:141

The Qur'an asks for moderation where one does not go from being stingy to being wasteful. Elsewhere, in a series of verses describing the characteristics of the good servants of God, moderation in spending is emphasized:

Who, when they spend, are neither extravagant nor stingy, but keep the balance between those two extremes. 25:67

FORGIVING DEBTS

If the debtor is in a difficulty, grant him time till it is easy for him to repay. But if you remit it by way of charity [that is forgive the loan], that is best for you if you only knew. 2:280

TRANSGRESSION

According to *Merriam-Webster's Dictionary*, *transgression* means "infringement or violation of law, command, or duty." From the scripture's perspective, it means disobeying God and exceeding the limits and the laws set forth by Him. This can take many forms. Denying God is the worst form of transgression. Mistreating prisoners of war is a transgression in the battlefield, and tyranny is a violation of basic human rights, as ordained by God and one of the worst types of transgressions (the Pharaoh being a prime example in the Qur'an).

Successful indeed are the believers, who are humble in their prayers, And who keep aloof from what is vain, And who are givers of poor-rate [zakat], And who guard their private parts, except before their mates or those whom their right hands possess, for they surely are not blamable, But whoever seeks to go beyond that, these are they that exceed the limits [transgressors]. 23:1–7 (Shakir)

And do not eat up your property among yourselves for vanities, nor use it as bait for the judges, with intent that you may eat up wrongfully and knowingly a little of (other) people's property. 2:188

TYRANNY AND OPPRESSION

Tyranny is considered a form of severe transgression when a person (often a ruler), or a group, oppresses another group of people. The Qur'an is very harsh on oppressors and tyrants and warns them of a painful fate. Justice is the opposite of oppression. The story of the plight of the children of Israel at the hands of the Pharaoh is given as an example of tyranny:

And We made the children of Israel to pass through the sea, then Pharaoh and his hosts followed them for oppression and tyranny. 10:90 (Shakir)

ADULTERY

Adultery in its basic form is a sexual transgression. It is considered among the major sins in the Qur'an and is repeatedly condemned:

> *Nor come near to adultery: for it is a shameful (deed) and an evil, opening the road (to other evils).* 17:32

ALCOHOL

The Qur'an forbids alcohol, even for social purposes. One does not have to get drunk to disobey the divine ordinance. Drinking alcohol is considered a major offense in Islam:

> *They ask you about intoxicants and games of chance [gambling]. Say: In both of them there is a great sin [harm] and means of profit [benefit] for people, and their sin [harm] is greater than their profit [benefit]. And they ask you as to what they should spend. Say: What you can spare. Thus does Allah make clear to you the communications, that you may ponder.* 2:219 (Shakir)

In the verse above, "intoxicants" refer to alcoholic beverages, though the word *khamar* used is generic for all intoxicants. In fact some scholars have translated *khamar* as wine, such as AbdullahYusufali and Seyyed Hossein Nasr. Most commentators actually talk about wine, the predominant "intoxicant" at the time of the revelation, in their commentaries of this verse. Note the "harm" is not in the intoxication, but the intoxicants, thus the commandment to avoid the use of intoxicants, and not merely the state of intoxication. The verse acknowledges some benefits of alcohol but states that its benefits are far outweighed by the harmful effects (i.e., gastric ulcers, cirrhosis of the liver, dementia, pancreatitis, neuropathy, and cardiomyopathy, to name a few, as well as its negative effects on social life). Moreover, it is also well known now that a glass of grape juice can provide the same amount of protective antioxidant effects without any of the harmful effects of alcohol. This is referenced in the following verse.

And of the fruits of the palms and the grapes—you obtain from them intoxication [sakar], and goodly provision; most surely there is a sign in this for a people who ponder. 16:67 (Shakir)

Islamic Golden Rule

There is no comparable verse in the Qur'an but according to the hadith, Muhammad instructs his followers of what is considered the Islamic version of the golden rule, "Not one of you truly believes until you wish for your brother (others) what you wish for yourself."

Personal Behavior and Conduct in the Old and New Testament

The equivalent of *'amr bi'l ma'ruf* (enjoin what's good) in Hebrew might be *ma'asim tovim*, meaning "good works and actions." The Torah and the Gospel frequently give instructions to do good deeds. Similarly, there are commands to avoid certain acts and deeds. The Jewish Talmud describes 613 commandments, derived from the Torah, of which 248 are "positive commandments" (the Dos) and 365 are "negative commandments" (the Don'ts). These commandments are not limited to personal conduct but cover a full spectrum of personal and social life including worship, charity, marital laws, the treatment of servants, the judicial system, and war.

RIGHTEOUSNESS

Righteousness is defined broadly as fearing God and obeying the decrees and the commands of the Lord. This verse does not spell out the deeds like verse 2:177 in the Qur'an does, but it makes a reference to obeying "all the commands" to be counted as righteous:

And the Lord our God commanded us to obey all these decrees and to fear Him so He can continue to bless us and preserve our lives, as He has done to this day. For we will be counted as righteous when we obey all the commands the Lord our God has given us. Deuteronomy 6:24–25

And in Job, chapter 29, the prophet Job talks about his righteous deeds as being a father figure to the poor, assisting strangers, helping the blind, and rescuing victims from the godless.

HONESTY AND TRUTHFULNESS

Both the Old and the New Testaments frequently underscore the importance of truthfulness and honesty:

> *Who may climb the mountain of the Lord? Who may stand in His holy place? Only those whose hands and hearts are pure, who do not worship idols and never tell lies.* Psalm 24:3–4
>
> *Better to be poor and honest than to be dishonest and a fool.* Proverbs 19:1
>
> *Whoever can be trusted with very little can also be trusted with much, and whoever is dishonest with very little will also be dishonest with much.* Luke 16:10

And in the book of Proverbs, Solomon's advice to his son is described over many chapters. The set of instructions include avoiding lying:

> *There are six things the Lord hates—no, seven things he detests: haughty eyes, a lying tongue, hands that kill the innocent, a heart that plots evil, feet that race to do wrong, a false witness who pours out lies, a person who sows discord in a family. My son, obey your father's commands, and don't neglect your mother's instruction.* Proverbs 6:16–20

KINDNESS/MERCY/FORGIVENESS

These attributes are at the center of the teachings of Jesus Christ as well as a frequent subject of the teachings of the Torah. Many of the verses quoted are fairly self-explanatory even without a reference to their context:

> *Do not seek revenge or bear a grudge against a fellow Israelite, but love your neighbor as yourself. I am the Lord.* Leviticus 19:18

In the following verse, the Christians are asked to be kind to fellow Christians.

> *Get rid of all bitterness, rage, anger, harsh words, and slander, as well as all types of evil behavior. Instead, be kind to each other, tenderhearted,*

forgiving one another, just as God through Christ has forgiven you.
Ephesians 4:31–32

Make allowance for each other's faults, and forgive anyone who offends you. Remember, the Lord forgave you, so you must forgive others.
Colossians 3:13

Just like the Qur'anic commandments, the Gospel also instructs people to be merciful and to forgive others, so God can show mercy and forgiveness.

For if you forgive men their trespasses, your heavenly Father also will forgive you. Matthew 6:14

Judge not, and you will not be judged; condemn not, and you will not be condemned; forgive, and you will be forgiven. Luke 6:37

ANGER

Jesus teaches his followers to guard against anger as well as a host of other negative behavior including immorality, slander, lust, and dirty language. The book of Genesis indicates that Cain killed Abel out of anger (as well as jealousy):

'Why are you so angry?' the Lord asked Cain. 'Why do you look so dejected? You will be accepted if you do what is right. But if you refuse to do what is right, then watch out! Sin is crouching at the door, eager to control you. But you must subdue it and be its master.' Genesis 4:6–7

You have heard that our ancestors were told, 'You must not murder. If you commit murder, you are subject to judgment.' But I say, if you are even angry with someone, you are subject to judgment! If you call someone an idiot, you are in danger of being brought before the court. And if you curse someone, you are in danger of the fires of hell. Matthew 5:21–22

So put to death the sinful, earthly things lurking within you. Have nothing to do with sexual immorality, impurity, lust, and evil desires. Don't be greedy, for a greedy person is an idolater, worshipping the things of this world. Because of these sins, the anger of God is coming. You used to do these things when your life was still part of this world. But now is the time to get rid of anger, rage, malicious behavior, slander, and dirty language. Don't lie to each other, for you have stripped off your old sinful nature and all its wicked deeds. Colossians 3:5–9

Understand this, my dear brothers and sisters: You must all be quick to listen, slow to speak, and slow to get angry. Human anger does not produce the righteousness God desires. James 1:19–20

HUMILITY VERSUS ARROGANCE

Jesus Christ preached humility and is widely believed to have led by personal example. Throughout his life, Jesus spoke against arrogance and false pride:

But he gives us even more grace to stand against such evil desires. As the scriptures say, 'God opposes the proud but favors the humble.' So humble yourselves before God. Resist the devil, and he will flee from you. James 4:6–7

Humble yourselves before the Lord, and he will lift you up in honor. James 4:10

The following verse refers to the fate on the Day of Judgment:

But those who exalt themselves will be humbled, and those who humble themselves will be exalted. Matthew 23:12 (and Luke 14:11)

CHARITY

Teach those who are rich in this world not to be proud and not to trust in their money, which is so unreliable. Their trust should be in God, who richly gives us all we need for our enjoyment. Tell them to use their money to do good. They should be rich in good works and generous to those in need, always being ready to share with others. By doing this they will be storing up their treasure as a good foundation for the future so that they may experience true life. 1 Timothy 6:17–19

And don't forget to do good and to share with those in need. These are the sacrifices that please God. Hebrews 13:16

If anyone gives you even a cup of water because you belong to the Messiah, I tell you the truth, that person will surely be rewarded. Mark 9:41

There will always be some in the land who are poor. That is why I am commanding you to share freely with the poor and with other Israelites in need. Deuteronomy 15:11

Similar to the disdain shown by the Qur'an for those who like to show off, the Bible is equally harsh against such actions. Giving in secret is much preferred.

Watch out! Don't do your good deeds publicly, to be admired by others, for you will lose the reward from your Father in heaven. When you give to someone in need, don't do as the hypocrites do—blowing trumpets in the synagogues and streets to call attention to their acts of charity! I tell you the truth, they have received all the reward they will ever get. But when you give to someone in need, don't let your left hand know what your right hand is doing. Give your gifts in private, and your Father, who sees everything, will reward you. Matthew 6:1–4

ADULTERY

Adultery is repeatedly condemned in the Bible. Prohibited by one of the Ten Commandments, adultery is considered a great sin. Exodus 20:14 commands:

You must not commit adultery.

And in a verse that comes very close to the spirit of verse 17:32 of the Qur'an (that instructs "not to come near to adultery"), Jesus instructs his followers in the Gospel of Matthew:

You have heard the commandment that says, 'You must not commit adultery.' But I say, anyone who even looks at a woman with lust has already committed adultery with her in his heart. Matthew 5:27–28

And the punishment for adultery in the Torah was stoning of the guilty.

> *Jesus returned to the Mount of Olives, but early the next morning he*
> *was back again at the Temple. A crowd soon gathered, and he sat down*
> *and taught them. As he was speaking, the teachers of religious law*
> *and the Pharisees brought a woman who had been caught in the act*
> *of adultery. They put her in front of the crowd. 'Teacher,' they said to*
> *Jesus, 'this woman was caught in the act of adultery. The Law of Moses*
> *says to stone her. What do you say?' John 8:1–4*

The passage then goes on to describe Jesus' response that only those who have not sinned can stone the guilty, and since everyone else had sinned, the crowd filed out without stoning the woman.

ALCOHOL

Alcohol is often mentioned in the Old Testament as **shekar**, an intoxicating drink distilled from corn, honey, or dates. Compare that to **sakar**, the word used by the Qur'an in verse 16:67, quoted earlier in the chapter.

Wine and other alcoholic beverages are commonly consumed in Christianity and Judaism and are generally not considered sinful; only drunkenness is considered a sin, though some have divergent views. One can still find prohibition of alcohol for various people under certain situations.

> *You and your descendants must never drink wine or any other alcohol-*
> *ic drink before going into the Tabernacle. If you do, you will die. This*
> *is a permanent law for you, and it must be observed from generation*
> *to generation. Leviticus 10:9*

The following verses represent more generic prohibition rather than being directed at a specific person or a priest or for a specific place:

> *What sorrow for those who get up early in the morning looking for*
> *a drink of alcohol and spend long evenings drinking wine to make*
> *themselves flaming drunk. They furnish wine and lovely music at their*

grand parties—lyre and harp, tambourine and flute—but they never think about the Lord or notice what He is doing. Isaiah 5:11–13

Wine produces mockers; alcohol leads to brawls. Those led astray by drink cannot be wise. Proverb 20:1

Organizers at soccer matches and other sporting events probably would testify to the accuracy of the above verse.

DO GOOD AND FORBID EVIL

The Bible has numerous instructions on doing good and staying away from evil.

Keep your tongue from evil and your lips from telling lies. Turn from evil and do good; seek peace and pursue it. The eyes of the LORD are on the righteous, and his ears are attentive to their cry; but the face of the LORD is against those who do evil, to blot out their name from the earth. The righteous cry out, and the LORD hears them; he delivers them from all their troubles. Psalm 34:13–17

Do not be overcome by evil, but overcome evil with good. Romans 12:21

The Christian Golden Rule

What has come to be known as the golden rule of conduct was coined in Britain in the seventeenth century. However, many variations have been known in ancient Egypt, India, China and other civilizations as well.

Do to others what you want them to do to you. Luke 6:31

The Jewish Golden Rule

Many regard the passage in Leviticus as the Torah's version as the original version of the Hebrew golden rule.

Love your neighbor as yourself. I am the Lord. Leviticus 19:18

Hillel is considered one of the most prominent Jewish sages and a major contributor to the development of Talmud. Hillel's response to a gentile, who promised to convert to Judaism if he taught him the entire Torah while he stood on one foot, became another version of the Jewish golden rule, "What is hateful to you, do not do to your fellow: this is the whole Torah; the rest is the explanation; go and learn."

Discussion Points for Dialogue and Healing

- The Qur'an, the Old Testament, and the New Testament have striking similarities on personal codes of conduct. All of them repeatedly instruct followers on matters such as honesty, humility, kindness, charity, social justice, and truthfulness. How do we incorporate these as guiding principles in our daily life, as well as into an action plan as part of interfaith work?
- The adoption of the simple code of conduct as taught by scriptures can go a long way in healing the strained relationship between people of various faiths, especially among the Abrahamic traditions. Putting these guiding principles into action can serve as a strong antidote to the environment created by mistrust, prejudice, hate, fear and the "othering" effect that threatens to divide us.
- The three Abrahamic Testaments prohibit the opposite acts (the "Do Nots") such as cheating, boastful arrogance, rudeness, cruelty, lying, anger, stealing, and oppression.
- The Qur'an and the Bible forbid lewdness, adultery, and alcohol (or at least drunkenness). Most Christian scholars have interpreted the verses to mean that only drunkenness is prohibited and refer to passages where alcohol consumption is used in positive terms and consumed during feasts. Adultery and drinking alcohol are considered major offenses in Islam.
- Feel free to ponder on the points noted belowand add your own.

Time to Ponder

- The similarity of the code of personal conduct and behavior as commanded in the Qur'an and the Bible is striking. When differences do exist, are they a reflection of different interpretations of the same laws, or different sets of laws for different communities, to address their unique needs?

- Do the believers of the golden rule follow it in their daily lives, especially when they interact with people from different faiths? Does the golden rule call for kindness towards our own faith groups only? Does "love your neighbor" come with exceptions such as "love your neighbor except if they are Muslims (or belong to a faith tradition other than yours)"?

- In the current environment of hate, fear and violence, where does one find the justification in the scriptures? These questions have been posed before in this book but worth asking again at the end: What would Jesus do (or not do)? What would Moses do (or not do)? What would Muhammad do (or not do)?

In Closing ...

I have made a humble attempt to group various themes presented by the Qur'an and compared them with passages on similar themes in the Bible to highlight the often-unrealized commonality of these scriptures. This book was written for the common person with an open and investigative mind, with the objective of addressing the need to gain a basic understanding of the scriptures, and thus I have tried to use plain English to discuss passages from the Qur'an and the Bible. At times, I might have tried to oversimplify matters. This book should not be treated as an exegesis, because it is not one. I have made a conscious effort to provide candid answers to many of the questions people may have always wanted to ask but couldn't find in one, concise format. All of this is done with an overarching objective to start the healing process in order to bring all people, especially those of Abrahamic faiths, closer together. This work was undertaken with my strong belief that faith workers can be uniters, rather than dividers, if we all behaved in a manner instructed by our respective faith traditions.

This book barely scratches the surface of the various themes presented in the Qur'an and the Bible but hopefully it will serve as a stimulus to study the scriptures more closely, which in turn hopefully will prompt us to re-examine our built-in, or learned mistrust and fear of each other. My dream is to live in a world where we are all united by our shared values, such as striving for peace, faith in God, and to do good for "others." These "others" are variously described in the scriptures as *neighbors, brothers* and, yes, as *others.*

We must realize that the Qur'an and the Bible do not believe in being politically correct, hence we will find many passages in the scriptures that modern societies may not find to their liking. If one believes in the divine source of the scriptures and that the ultimate authority belongs to God, then it becomes easy to accept that the divine laws don't always correspond to man-made laws or opinions: they don't have to. It is not to imply, however, that one should ignore the law of the land. The scriptures do not encourage people to "take the law into their hands" if there is a discrepancy between the divine laws and the law of the land. A case in point might be the issue of polygamy. In most Western countries, it is illegal to have multiple wives. Even when allowed by the scripture, the law of the land must be followed. Conversely, at an individual level, even when the local laws allow certain actions, for example gambling and prostitution, the scriptures continue to prohibit their followers from engaging in such activities.

As I mentioned earlier, I have stayed focused on the similarities of the message in the scriptures, rather than the differences. It is up to the individual whether one wants to promote the similarities to find common ground or latch onto the differences that continue to widen the gulf between the followers of the world's most read scriptures. Even when we have reasons for disagreements, can we agree to disagree *respectfully and peacefully*? In doing so the followers of the Abrahamic faiths, I believe, will only be acting in accordance with the scripture they trust and respect.

One of the basic conditions for a fruitful interfaith dialogue is having an open mind. I often remind myself first and foremost that a mind is like a parachute: it works, only when it is open! By making a personal pledge to adopting these principles, which are derived from the religious teachings, I am confident we can start the healing process so desperately needed in this environment of mistrust, fear, hate and animosity. We must realize that the struggle is not between Jews, Christians, and Muslims, but rather between extremists of all faiths (and no faith traditions) on one side, and the descent silent majority of believers from all faiths (and no faith traditions) on the other. The key is for the silent majority to be silent no more. "Failure is not an option" has become a motivational phrase after actor Ed Harris uttered these words, playing the role of the flight director Gene Kranz in one of my all-time favorite movies, *Apollo 13*. This was based on a real story of the failed Apollo 13 mission whereby the goal of the flight control changed from landing on moon to bringing the three astronauts back to earth safely. *Failure is not an option* later became the title of Gene Kranz autobiography. In the turbulent times of hate and fear threatening to divide us, I feel obligated to leave you with this parting call to action:

Silence is not an option.

Peace!
Ejaz Naqvi, MD

Notes

BEFORE WE START . . .

1. "How Americans Feel About Religious Groups," Pew Research Center, http://www.pewforum.org/2014/07/16/how-americans-feel-about-religious-groups (last modified July 16, 2014).
2. "American Attitudes Toward Arabs and Muslims: 2014," Arab American Institute, http://www.aaiusa.org/american-attitudes-toward-arabs-and-muslims-2014 (last modified July 29, 2014).
3. Matthew Taylor, "Breivik Sent 'Manifesto' to 250 UK Contacts Hours Before Norway Killings." *The Guardian*, July, 26 2011. https://www.theguardian.com/world/2011/jul/26/breivik-manifesto-email-uk-contacts (accessed October 4, 2016).
4. Charles Kurzman and David Schanzer, "The Growing Right Wing Terror Threat" *New York Times*, June 16, 2015, http://www.nytimes.com/2015/06/16/opinion/the-other-terror-threat.html?_r=2 (accessed October 3, 2015).
5. "UN: Rohingya May be Victims of Crimes Against Humanity," *Headline News*, http://www.headlines-news.com/2016/06/21/1389771/un-rohingya-may-be-victims-of-crimes-against-humanity (last modified December 6, 2016).
6. Reza Aslan, *Zealot: The Life and times of Jesus of Nazareth* (New York: Random House, 2014), 51-52.
7. "Chapter 6 - Terrorist Organizations," U.S. Department of State, http://www.state.gov/j/ct/rls/crt/2006/82738.htm (last modified April 30, 2007).
8. Mick Krever, "ISIS Captors Cared Little About Religion, Says Former Hostage," *CNN* video, 13:39, February 4, 2015, http://www.cnn.com/2015/02/03/intl_world/amanpour-didier-francois. Accessed October 4, 2015.
9. Hans Küng, *Islam, Past Present & Future* (Oxford: One World Publications, 2007), xxiii.
10. Karen Armstrong, *Fields of Blood: A History of Religion and Violence.* (New York: Knopf, 2015), 3-4.
11. Martin Luther King, Jr., *Strength to Love* (Minneapolis: Fortress Press, 1977), 53.
12. "Fear, Inc.: The Roots of the Islamophobia Network in America," Center for American Progress, https://www.americanprogress.org/issues/religion/report/2011/08/26/10165/fear-inc (last modified August 26, 2011). Council on

American-Islamic Relations (CAIR), *Confronting Fear: Islamophobia and its Impact in the United States,* (DC & Berkeley: CAIR and UC Berkeley Center for Race and Gender, 2016), http://crg.berkeley.edu/sites/default/files/Final%20Report-IRDP-CAIR-Report2016_0.pdf.

INTRODUCTION TO THE QUR'AN

1. On the authorship and development of the Gospels, see Robert J. Miller, ed., *The Complete Gospels.* 4th ed. (Salem, OR: Polebridge Press, 2010) and Raymond E. Brown, *An Introduction to the New Testament* (New York: Doubleday, 1997).

2. Wayne A. Meeks, ed., *The Harper Collins Study Bible: New Revised Standard Version* (New York: HarperCollins, 1993), xiv-xvi.

3. See Robert Miller, *The Complete Gospels,* 3-8 for a discussion of the various scriptures used by early Christians, including those left out of the canon.

4. Papias, "Explanation of the Sayings of the Lord," quoted in Eusebius, *History of the Church* 3:39, G.A. Williamson and Andrew Louth, trans. (London: Penguin, 1990). New Testament scholars are not at all certain if Papias's views on an original Aramaic Gospel of Matthew are accurate or just legend. But it does seem clear that the earliest source for the Gospels, the Q source, was made of Jesus sayings, and these likely were originally circulated, at least in part, in Aramaic. See Maurice Casey, *An Aramaic Approach to Q: Sources for the Gospels of Matthew and Luke* (Cambridge: Cambridge University Press, 2002).

5. Irenaeus of Lyons, *Against Heresies,* 3:1:1, Christian Classics Ethereal Library, http://www.ccel.org/ccel/schaff/anf01.ix.iv.ii.html (accessed November 23, 2016).

6. Bart Ehrman, *The Orthodox Corruption of Scripture: The Effect of Early Theological Controversies on the Text of the New Testament* (New York: Oxford University Press, 1993), 4.

7. Norman O. Brown, *The Challenge of Islam: The Prophetic Tradition* (Berkeley: New Pacific Press, 2009), 13-28.

8. Miller, *The Complete Gospels,* 258.

9. Vincent Taylor, *The Text of the New Testament: A Short Introduction* (New York: MacMillan, 1961), 15.

10. Jeffrey Geoghegan and Michael Horman, *The Bible for Dummies* (Hoboken, NJ: John Wiley & Sons, 2010), 15.

11. Ibn Hanbal, *Musnad,* vol. 3, p. 59, quoted in Moojan Momen, *An Introduction to Shi'i Islam* (New Haven: Yale University Press, 1985), 16.

12. *Sahih Bukhari* 6:60:201, 6:61:509, www.sahih-bukhari.com (accessed November 22, 2016); See also Sohaib Sultan, *Koran for Dummies,* (Indianapolis: Wiley Publishing, 2004), 27–29.

13. Maurice Bucaille, *The Bible, the Qur'an and Science* (Qum, Iran: Ansariyan Publications, 2007), 132.

14. *Sahih Bukhari* 6:61:510, www.sahih-bukhari.com (accessed November 22, 2016).

15. Joussef Mahmoud, "The Arabic Writing System and the Sociolinguistics of Orthographic Reform" (PhD diss., Georgetown University, 1979), 8.

16. Malcolm Clark, *Islam for Dummies* (Indianapolis: Wiley Publishing, 2003), 101.

17. Carole Hillenbrand, "Muhammad and the Rise of Islam," *The New Cambridge Medieval History*, vol. 1, Paul Fouracre, ed. (New York: Cambridge University Press, 2005), 330.

18. "Birmingham Qur'an manuscript dated among the oldest in the world," University of Birmingham, http://www.birmingham.ac.uk/news/latest/2015/07/quran-manuscript-22-07-15.aspx (last modified July 22, 2015).

CHAPTER ONE: GOD

1. Bernard Lewis, P. M. Holt, Peter R. Holt, and Ann Katherine Swynford Lambton, *The Cambridge History of Islam* (Cambridge: Cambridge University Press, 1977), 32.

2. Al-Ghazzali, *Al-Ghazali on the Ninety-nine Beautiful Names of God*, David Burrell and Nazih Daher, trans. (Cambridge: Islamic Texts Society, 1999).

CHAPTER TWO: THE NATURE OF GOD

1. All biblical translations in this chapter are from the New American Standard Bible by the Lockman Foundation.

CHAPTER THREE: GOD IS KIND AND LOVING

1. Michael Sells, *Approaching the Qur'an: The Early Revelations*, (Ashland, OR: White Cloud Press, 2007), 21.

2. Arthur Kurzweil, *The Torah for Dummies* (Hoboken, NJ: Wiley Publishing, 2008) 30.

CHAPTER SIX: ATTRIBUTES OF GOD

1. Jacob Neusner, Baruch Levine, Bruce Chilton and Vincent Cornell, *Do Jews, Christians and Muslims Worship the Same God?* (Nashville: Abingdon Press, 2012), 100.

CHAPTER EIGHT: ADAM AND NOAH

1. All biblical translations in this chapter are from the New American Standard Bible by the Lockman Foundation.

CHAPTER NINE: ABRAHAM

1. All biblical translations in this chapter are from the New American Standard Bible by the Lockman Foundation.

2. Aidan Dodson and Dyan Hilton, *The Complete Royal Families of Ancient Egypt* (London: Thames and Hudson. 2004).

CHAPTER TEN: MOSES

1. All biblical translations in this chapter are from the New American Standard Bible by the Lockman Foundation.

CHAPTER ELEVEN: JESUS AND MARY

1. Note that the Qur'an recognizes the historical fact that in Muhammad's day there were different Christian sects arguing over the nature of Jesus and his message. This verse reminds us that the Christology of the Qur'an is in alignment with the beliefs of Jewish Christian sects such as the Ebionites. See my discussion above, 13-14.
2. Tarif Khalidi, *The Muslim Jesus: Sayings and Stories in Islamic Literature* (Cambridge: Harvard University Press, 2001).
3. Ibid., 96.
4. Ibid., 160.
5. Ibid., 199.
6. Michael Lodahl, *Claiming Abraham: Reading the Bible and the Qur'an Side by Side* (Grand Rapids, MI: Brazos Press, 2010), 154.
7. Ibid., 155.
8. Ibid., 184.
9. Robert J. Miller, ed., " Sayings Gospels," *The Complete Gospels*, 257.
10. Ibid., 258.
11. Bart D. Ehrman, "Conclusion: Changing Scriptures," *Misquoting Jesus: The Story Behind Who Changed the Bible and Why* (New York: HarperCollins, 2005), 207.
12. Bart D. Ehrman, *How Jesus Became God: The Exaltation of a Jewish Preacher from Galilee* (New York: HarperCollins, 2014), 2.

CHAPTER TWELVE: MUHAMMAD

1. Karen Armstrong, *Muhammad, A Prophet For Our Time* (New York: Harper-Collins, 2007), 7.
2. Lesley Hazelton, *The First Muslim: The Story of Muhammad* (New York: Riverhead Books, 2013), 10-11.
3. Deepak Chopra, *Muhammad: A Story of the Last Prophet* (New York: Harper-One, 2010), xii.
4. Armstrong, *Muhammad*, 83.
5. Ibid., 84.
6. See John Andrew Morrow, *The Covenants of the Prophet Muhammad with the Christians of the World* (Kettering, OH: Angelico Press / Sophia Perennis, 2013).
7. See note 6 above.

CHAPTER THIRTEEN: SCRIPTURES AND PEOPLE OF THE BOOK

1. Pooya Yazdi, and S. V. Mir Ahmad Ali, trans., "aal-'Imraan (The Family of 'Imraan)," The Noble Quran, http://quran.al-islam.org (last Modified May 2010).

For a more in-depth discussion see Pooya Yazdi, and S. V. Mir Ahmad Ali. *The Holy Qur'an—The Final Testament* (Elmhurst, NY: Tahrike Tarsile Qur'an, 2009).

2. Chopra, *Muhammad*, 259.

3. Gerard Hall, "A Call to Interfaith Dialogue," *Australian eJournal of Theology 5* (2005), 6, http://aejt.com.au/__data/assets/pdf_file/0005/395510/AEJT_5.9_Hall.pdf (accessed October 3, 2016); See also Gioia (ed.), *Interreligious Dialogue: The Official Teaching of the Catholic Church*, (New York: Pauline Books and Media, 2006), pp. 566-579, 608-642.

CHAPTER FOURTEEN: PILLARS OF ISLAM

1. According to the interpretation by Shia Muslims, there are five roots of faith (*usul al-din*). These are the basic, mandatory beliefs:

    1. *Tawhid*, or Oneness of God
    2. *Adl*, or Justice of God
    3. *Nabuwwat*, or Prophethood
    4. *Imammat*, or Leadership, or Succession to Imams after Muhamma by Divine Instructions
    5. *Qiyamah*, or the Day of Resurrection

2. "Letter from Mecca," Malcolm-x, http://www.malcolm-x.org/docs/let_mecca.htm (accessed October 3, 2016).

3. David Clinginsmith, Asim Ijaz Khwaja. And Michaesl Kremer, "Estimating the Impact of the Hajj: Religion and Tolerance in Islam's Global Gathering," *HKS Working Paper RWP08-022* (April 2008). https://papers.ssrn.com/sol3/papers.cfm?abstract_id=1124213 (accessed November 22, 2016).

4. *Sahih Bukhari* 2:24:504, https://www.sahih-bukhari.com/PagesBukhari_2_24.php (accessed November 22, 2016).

5. Hayim H. Donin, *To Pray as a Jew: A Guide to the Prayer Book and the Synagogue Service* (Jerusalem: Morshet Publishing, 1980), 41.

CHAPTER FIFTEEN: JIHAD

1. Etienne Krug et al., "The World Report on Violence and Health," *The Lancet*, 360, no. 9339 (2002): 1083-1088. http://dx.doi.org/10.1016/S0140-6736(02)11133-0 (accessed October 4, 2015).

2. Kurzman and Schanzer, "The Growing Right Wing Terror Threat."

3. Douglas Ernst, "ISIS Computers Packed with Porn: Terrorist Sex Fiends Outed by ex-Defense Chief," *The Washington Times*, July 14, 2016, http://www.washingtontimes.com/news/2016/jul/14/isis-computers-packed-with-porn-retired-lt-gen-mic (accessed October 3, 2016).

4. Jason DeRose, "U.S. Muslim Scholars Issue Edict Against Terrorism," *NPR News* (Washington, D.C.: NPR, July 28, 2005), http://www.npr.org/templates/transcript/transcript.php?storyId=4775588 (accessed November 22, 2016).

5. "Historic Islamic Edict (Fatwa) on Joining ISIS/ISIL," Islamic Supreme Council of Canada press release, March 11, 2015, Islamic Supreme Council of Can-

ada website, , http://www.islamicsupremecouncil.com/historic-islamic-edict-fatwa-on-joining-isis-isil (accessed October 3, 2016).

6. Dina Temple-Raston, "Prominent Muslim Sheikh Issues Fatwa Against ISIS Violence," *Morning Edition* (Washington, D.C.: NPR, 2014), http://www.npr.org/2014/09/25/351277631/prominent-muslim-sheikh-issues-fatwa-against-isis-violence (accessed October 4, 2016).

7. Kurt Eichenwald, "Right-Wing Extremists are a Bigger Threat to America than ISIS," *Newsweek,* February 4, 2016, http://www.newsweek.com/2016/02/12/right-wing-extremists-militants-bigger-threat-america-isis-jihadists-422743.html (accessed October 3, 2016).

8. Warren J. Blumenfield, "Radical Christian Terrorists," *Huffington Post,* April 4, 2016, http://www.huffingtonpost.com/warren-j-blumenfeld/radical-christian-terrori_b_9601980.html (accessed October 4, 2016).

CHAPTER SIXTEEN: WOMEN AND THE FAMILY

1. Nawal Nour, "Female Genital Cutting: A Persisting Practice," *Reviews in Obstetrics & Gynecology* 1, vol. 3 (Summer 2008): 135–139, https://www.ncbi.nlm.nih.gov/pmc/articles/PMC2582648/pdf/RIOG001003_0135.pdf.

2. All biblical translations in this chapter are from the New American Standard Bible by the Lockman Foundation, unless specified otherwise.

CHAPTER SEVENTEEN: PERSONAL BEHAVIOR AND CODE OF CONDUCT

1. Küng, *Islam: Past, Present and Future,* xxiii.

2. Hadith from Abu Dawud, cited in Jon Mayled and Libby Ahluwalia, *Discovery: Philosophy & Ethics for OCR GCSE Religious Studies* (Cheltenham, England: Nelson Thornes Ltd, 2003), 153.

Bibliography

Al-Ghazzali. *Al-Ghazali on the Ninety-nine Beautiful Names of God.* Burrell, David and Nazih Daher, trans. Cambridge: Islamic Texts Society, 1999.

Ali, Abdullah Yusuf. *The Holy Qur'an.* Elmhurst, New York: Tahrike Tarsile Qur'an, 2001.

Ali, Maulana Muhammad. *The Holy Qur'an with English Translation.* Lahore, Pakistan: Ahamadya Press, 1951.

Arab American Institute. "American Attitudes Toward Arabs and Muslims: 2014." http://www.aaiusa.org/american-attitudes-toward-arabs-and-muslims-2014. Last modified July 29, 2014.

Armstrong, Karen. *Fields of Blood: Religion and the History of Violence.* New York: Anchor Books, 2015.

_____. *Muhammad, A Prophet for Our Time.* New York: Harper Collins, 2007.

Asad, Muhammad. *The Message of the Qur'an.* Gibraltar: Dar al-Andalus Ltd, 1980.

Aslan, Reza. *No god but God. The Origins, Evolution, and Future of Islam.* New York: Random House, 2011.

_____. *Zealot: The Life and times of Jesus of Nazareth.* New York: Random House, 2013.

Blumenfeld, Warren J. "Radical Christian Terrorists." *The Huffington Post,* April 4, 2016. http://www.huffingtonpost.com/warren-j-blumenfeld/radical-christian-terrori_b_9601980.html. Accessed October 4, 2015.

Brown, Raymond E. *An Introduction to the New Testament.* New York: Doubleday, 1997.

Bucaille, Maurice. *The Bible, the Qur'an, and Science.* Qum, Iran: Ansariyan Publications, 2007.

Casey, Maurice. *An Aramaic Approach to Q: Sources for the Gospels of Mathew and Luke.* Cambridge: Cambridge University Press, 2002.

Center for American Progress. "Fear, Inc.: The Roots of the Islamophobia Network in America." https://www.americanprogress.org/issues/religion/report/2011/08/26/10165/fear-inc. Last modified August 26, 2011.

Chopra, Deepak. *Muhammad: A Story of the Last Prophet.* New York: Harper-One, 2010.

Clark, Malcolm. *Islam for Dummies.* Indianapolis: Wiley Publishing, 2003.

Clinginsmith, David, Asim Ijaz Khwaja, and Michaesl Kremer. "Estimating the Impact of the Hajj: Religion and Tolerance in Islam's Global Gathering." *HKS Working Paper RWP08-022.* April 2008. https://papers.ssrn.com/sol3/papers.cfm?abstract_id=1124213. Accessed November 22, 2016.

Council on American-Islamic Relations (CAIR), *Confronting Fear: Islamophobia and its Impact in the United States,* (DC & Berkeley: CAIR and UC Berkeley Center for Race and Gender, 2016), http://crg.berkeley.edu/sites/default/files/Final%20Report-IRDP-CAIR-Report2016_0.pdf

DeRose, Jason. "U.S. Muslim Scholars Issue Edict Against Terrorism." *NPR News.* Washington, D.C.: NPR, July 28, 2005. http://www.npr.org/templates/transcript/transcript.php?storyId=4775588. Accessed November 22, 2016.

Dodson, Aidan, and Dyan Hilton. *The Complete Royal Families of Ancient Egypt.* London: Thames and Hudson, 2004.

Donin, Hayim H. *To Pray as a Jew: A Guide to the Prayer Book and the Synagogue Service.* Jerusalem: Moreshet Publishing, 1980.

Ehrman, Bart. *The Orthodox Corruption of Scripture: The Effect of Early Theological Controversies on the Text of the New Testament.* New York: Oxford University Press, 1993.

_____. *Misquoting Jesus: The Story Behind Who Changed the Bible and Why.* New York: HarperCollins, 2005.

_____. *How Jesus Became God: The Exaltation of a Jewish Preacher from Galilee.* New York: HarperCollins, 2014.

Eichenwald, Kurt. "Right-Wing Extremists are a Bigger Threat to America than ISIS." *Newsweek,* February 4, 2016. http://www.newsweek.

com/2016/02/12/right-wing-extremists-militants-bigger-threat-amer-ica-isis-jihadists-422743.html. Accessed October 4, 2015.

Emerick, Yahya. *The Meaning Of The Holy Qur'an in Today's English.* Charleston, SC: Extended Study Edition, 2000.

Ernst, Douglas. "ISIS Computers Packed with Porn: Terrorist Sex Fiends Outed by ex-Defense Chief." *The Washington Times,* July 14, 2016. http://www.washingtontimes.com/news/2016/jul/14/isis-computers-packed-with-porn-retired-lt-gen-mic. Accessed October 4, 2015.

Fakhri, Majid. *The Qur'an: A Modern English Version.* Ithaca, New York: Garnet Publishing, 1997.

Fazley, Rabbi A. K. M. *Topics from the Holy Qur'an.* Tallahassee, FL: Father and Son Publishing, 2005.

Geoghegan, Jeffrey, and Michael Homan. *The Bible for Dummies.* Hoboken, NJ: John Wiley & Sons, Inc., 2003.

Ghattas, Rauf and Carol B. Ghattas. *A Christian Guide to the Qur'an.* Grand Rapids, MI: Kregel Publications, 2009.

Gioia, ed. *Interreligious Dialogue: The Official Teaching of the Catholic Church.* New York: Pauline Books and Media, 2006.

"Hadith of Bukhari." www.sahih-bukhari.com. Accessed October 4, 2015.

Haleem, M. A. S. Abdel. *The Qur'an: A New Translation.* New York: Oxford University Press, 2005.

Hall, Gerard. "A Call to Interfaith Dialogue." *Australian Journal of Theology,* vol. 5, August 2005, 1-10.

Hillenbrand, Carole. "Muhammad and the Rise of Islam." Quoted in Paul Fouracre, ed. *The New Cambridge Medieval History,* vol. 1. New York: Cambridge University Press, 2005.

Holy Bible, New American Standard Bible. LaHabra, CA: Lockman Foundation, 2008.

Holy Bible, New Living Translation. Carol Stream, IL: Tyndale House Publishers, 2007.

Irenaeus of Lyons. *Against Heresies,* 3:1:1. Christian Classics Ethereal Library. http://www.ccel.org/ccel/schaff/anf01.ix.iv.ii.html. Accessed November 23, 2016.

Islamic Supreme Council of Canada. "Historic Islamic Edict (Fatwa) on Joining ISIS/ISIL." Islamic Supreme Council of Canada press release,

March 11, 2015. http://www.islamicsupremecouncil.com/historic-islamic-edict-fatwa-on-joining-isis-isil. Accessed October 4, 2015.

Khalidi, Tarif. *The Muslim Jesus: Sayings and Stories in Islamic Literature.* Cambridge: Harvard University Press, 2001.

Khan, Aftab Ahmad. *The Creator.*

King, Martin Luther Jr., *Strength to Love.* Minneapolis: Fortress Press, 1977.

Krever, Mick. "ISIS Captors Cared Little About Religion, Says Former Hostage." *CNN* video, 13:39. February 4, 2015. http://www.cnn.com/2015/02/03/intl_world/amanpour-didier-francois. Accessed October 4, 2015.

Krug, Etienne, et al. "World Report on Violence and Health." *The Lancet* 360, no. 9339. (2002): 1083-1088. http://dx.doi.org/10.1016/S0140-6736(02)11133-0. Accessed October 4, 2015.

Küng, Hans. *Islam: Past, Present and Future.* Oxford: OneWorld Publications, 2007.

Kurzman, Charles, and David Schanzer. "The Growing Right-Wing Terror Threat." *New York Times.* June 16, 2015.

Kurzweil, Arthur. *The Torah for Dummies.* Indianapolis: Wiley Publishing, 2008.

Lewis, Bernard, P.M. Holt, Peter R. Holt, and Ann Katherine Swynford Lambton. *The Cambridge History of Islam.* Cambridge: Cambridge University Press, 1977.

Liepert, David. *Muslim, Christian, and Jew.* Toronto: Faith and Life Publishing, 2010.

Lodahl, Michael. *Claiming Abraham.* Grand Rapids, MI: Brazos Press, 2010.

Malcolm-x. "Letter from Mecca." http://www.malcolm-x.org/docs/let_mecca.htm. Accessed October 4, 2015.

Malik, M. Farooq-i-Azam. *Al-Qur'an, Guidance for Mankind: The English translation of the meaning of Al Qur'an.* Houston: Institute of Islamic Knowledge, 1997.

Mario. "UN: Rohingya May be Victims of Crimes Against Humanity." *Headline News.* http://www.headlines-news.com/2016/06/21/1389771/un-rohingya-may-be-victims-of-crimes-against-humanity. Last modified December 6, 2016.

Mahmoud, Joussef. "The Arabic Writing System and the Sociolinguistics of Orthographic Reform." PhD diss., Georgetown University, 1979.

Meeks, Wayne A., ed. *The Harper Collins Study Bible: New Revised Standard Version.* New York: HarperCollins, 1993.

Miller, Robert J., ed. *The Complete Gospels.* 4th Ed. Salem, OR: Polebridge Press, 2010.

National Public Radio. "U.S. Muslim Scholars Issue Edict Against Terrorism."

Momen, Moojan. *An Introduction to Shi'i Islam.* New Haven: Yale University Press, 1985.

Morrow, John Andrew. *The Covenants of the Prophet Muhammad with the Christians of the World.* Kettering, OH: Angelico Press / Sophia Perennis, 2013.

Neusner, J., B. Levine, B. Chilton, and V. Cornell. *Do Jews, Christians and Muslims worship the same God?* Nashville: Abingdon Press, 2012.

Nour, Nawal. "Female Genital Cutting: A Persisting Practice." *Reviews in Obstetrics & Gynecology* 1, vol. 3 (Summer 2008): 135–139. https://www.ncbi.nlm.nih.gov/pmc/articles/PMC2582648/pdf/RIOG001003_0135.pdf.

Papias. "Explanation of the Sayings of the Lord." Quoted in Eusebius. *History of the Church* 3:39. Williamson, G.A., and Andrew Louth, trans. London: Penguin, 1990.

Pew Research Center. "How Americans Feel About Religious Groups." http://www.pewforum.org/2014/07/16/how-americans-feel-about-religious-groups. Last modified July 16, 2014.

Pickthall, Muhammad M. *The Glorious Qur'an,* Hyderabad, India: Government Central Press, 1938.

Sahih Bukhari 6:60:201, 6:61:509, 6:61:510. www.sahih-bukhari.com. Accessed November 22, 2016.

Sarwar, Shaykh Muhammad and Brandon Toropov. *The Complete Idiot's Guide to the Koran.* Indianapolis: Beach Brook Productions, 2003.

Sells, Michael. *Approaching the Qur'an: The Early Revelations,* 2nd Ed. Ashland, OR: White Cloud Press, 2007.

Shakir, M. H. *The Qur'an: Arabic Text and English Translation,* Elmhurst, NY: Tahrike Tarsile Qur'an, 1999.

Sultan, Sohaib. *The Koran for Dummies*. Hoboken, NJ: Wiley Publishing, Inc., 2004.

Taylor, Matthew. "Breivik Sent 'Manifesto' to 250 UK Contacts Hours Before Norway Killings." *The Guardian*. July 26, 2011. https://www.theguardian.com/world/2011/jul/26/breivik-manifesto-email-uk-contacts. Accessed October 4, 2016.

Temple-Raston, Dina. "Prominent Muslim Sheikh Issues Fatwa Against ISIS Violence." *Morning Edition*. Washington, D.C.: NPR, 2014. http://www.npr.org/2014/09/25/351277631/prominent-muslim-sheikh-issues-fatwa-against-isis-violence. Accessed October 4, 2016.

Ünal, Ali. *The Qur'an with Annotated Interpretation in Modern English*. Clifton, NJ: Tughra Books, 2010.

University of Birmingham "Birmingham Qur'an manuscript dated among the oldest in the world." http://www.birmingham.ac.uk/news/latest/2015/07/quran-manuscript-22-07-15.aspx. Last modified July 22, 2015.

U.S. Department of State. "Chapter 6 — Terrorist Organizations." http://www.state.gov/j/ct/rls/crt/2006/82738.htm. Last modified April 30, 2007.

Yazdi, Pooya, and S. V. Mir Ahmad Ali, trans. "aal-'Imraan (The Family of 'Imraan)." *The Noble Quran*. http://quran.al-islam.org. Last Modified May 2010.

Yuksel, Edip, L. S. Al-Shaiban and M. Schulte-Nafeh. *The Qur'an: A Reformist Translation*. Breinigsville, PA: Brainbow Press, 2007.

About the Author

 EJAZ NAQVI is the immediate past president of the Islamic center in the East Bay San Francisco area and has been actively involved in many other local Islamic centers in various capacities. He is actively engaged in interfaith dialogue and is a frequent speaker at interfaith events and a guest on national radio shows. He serves on the board of interfaith council of Contra Costa County in the bay area and also serves on the Board of Directors of Islamic Scholarship Fund, a non-profit organization that aims to promote engagement of American Muslims in mainstream through educational scholarships and mentorship programs. He is author of *The Quran: With or Against the Bible?* and was the host of *Frank Talk with Dr. Ejaz* in 2013 on Toginet internet radio. A practicing physician and a "born-again Muslim" after reading the Qur'anic translation for the first time in its entirety about two decades ago, he has since then pondered over the verses of the Qur'an and discovered that many of its teachings remain arcane. Eager and in search of finding the common grounds, his subsequent study of the Qur'an and the Bible has led him to finding significant similarities in the teachings of the scriptures.